Artificial Intelligence in Accounting and Auditing

VOLUME 2

RUTGERS
SERIES IN
**Accounting
Information**
SYSTEMS

ARTIFICIAL INTELLIGENCE IN ACCOUNTING AND AUDITING
Using Expert Systems

VOLUME 2

Miklos A. Vasarhelyi
Rutgers University

 Markus Wiener Publishers
Princeton

For information write to:
  Markus Wiener Publishers
  114 Jefferson Road, Princeton, NJ 08540

Library of Congress Cataloging-in-Publication Data

Artificial intelligence in accounting and auditing
        (V. 2-   : Rutgers series in accounting information systems)
        Vol. 2 has subtitle: Using expert systems.
        Includes bibliographical references.
        1. Accounting—Data Processing. 2. Auditing—Data Processing
3. Expert systems (Computer science)   I. Vasarhelyi, Miklos A.
II. Series: Rutgers series in accounting information systems
HF5679.A78   1989   657'.028'5633   87-40223
ISBN 1-910129-72-X (v. 1)
ISBN 1-55876-055-5 (v. 2)
ISBN 1-55876-078-4 (v. 3)

Printed in the United States of America on acid-free paper.

CONTENTS

III. AI/ES IN AUDIT PRACTICE

ACKNOWLEDGMENTS

The editor and the publisher gratefully acknowledge the following authors and publishers:

Anthony K. Wensley, "Audit Planning and Expert Systems Research," unpublished working paper, University of Toronto, March 1991. Reprinted with the permission of the author.

Mohammad Abdolmohammadi and Mohammad Bazaz, "Identification of Tasks For Expert Systems Development in Auditing," EXPERT SYSTEMS WITH APPLICATIONS, Vol. 3, pp. 99-107, 1991. Reprinted with the permission of the publisher Pergamon Press Ltd., Oxford, England.

Ching-Ding (Stephen) Hsu, "An Evolving Conceptual Organization Schema For Database Systems," unpublished working paper, University of Southern California. Reprinted with the permission of the author.

William E. McCarthy and Stephen R. Rockwell, "The Integrated Use of First Order Theories, Reconstructive Expertise, and Implementation of Heuristics in an Accounting Information System Design Tool," unpublished working paper, Michigan State University. Reprinted with the permission of the authors.

J. Efrim Boritz and Anthony K. Wensley, "Validating Expert Systems with Complex Outputs: The Case of Audit Planning," unpublished working paper, University of Waterloo and the University of Toronto, Canada, 1991. Reprinted with the permission of the authors.

Therese Grahn Massaad and Leslie Richeson Winkler, "A Basic Introduction To Neural Networks For Accountants," unpublished working paper, University of Texas at El Paso, 1992. Reprinted with the permission of the authors.

Carol E. Brown, "Expert Systems in Public Accounting: Current Practice and Future Directions," EXPERT SYSTEMS WITH APPLICATIONS, Vol. 3, pp. 3-18, 1991. Reprinted with the permission of the publisher Pergamon Press Ltd., Oxford, England.

Miklos A. Vasarhelyi and Fern B. Halper, "The Continuous Audit of Online Systems," AUDITING: A JOURNAL OF PRACTICE AND THEORY, Vol. 10, No. 1, pp. 110-125, Spring 1991. Reprinted with the permission of the publisher the American Accounting Association, Sarasota, Florida.

Miklos A. Vasarhelyi, Fern B. Halper and Kazuo J. Ezawa, "The Continuous Process Audit System: A UNIX-Based Auditing Tool," THE EDP AUDITOR JOURNAL, Vol. 3, pp. 85-91, 1991. Reprinted with the permission of the publisher the EDP Auditor Foundation, Carol Stream, Illinois.

William F. Messier and James V. Hansen, "Inducing Rules For Expert Systems Development: An Example Using Default and Bankruptcy Data," MANAGEMENT SCIENCE, pp. 1403-16, December 1988. Reprinted with the permission of the publisher the Institute of Management Science, 290 West Minister St., Providence, RI, 02903.

Nils A. Kandelin and Thomas W. Lin, "An Object-Oriented Programming Approach To Credit Decision Making," unpublished working paper, University of Maryland at College Park and University of Southern California, December 1991. Reprinted with the permission of the authors.

I

Introduction

AI & ES in Accounting and Auditing: Progress, Regression and New Paradigms

MIKLOS A. VASARHELYI

Two years have passed since the publication of **Artificial Intelligence in Accounting and Auditing, Volume 1.** In these two years, the technology and its implications have lost some of their novelty and myth. On the other hand, we are witnessing the emergence of a set of paradigms and an increased understanding of the strengths and weaknesses of particular approaches. Carol Brown[1], in her article entitled "Expert Systems in Public Accounting: Current Practices and Future Directions," explores the applications of the paradigms within the major audit firms. In her evaluation she states, "The use of expert systems is rapidly pervading the field of accounting. All of the *big six* international accounting firms are either using expert systems in their practices or have systems under development."

Introduction

This book is divided into three parts. In this first part, we position the field and describe the main articles in the book. This introductory note attempts to link a set of selected articles into a vision of the current state of the art in the field. First, it describes the frame of the ensuing articles to allow the reader to navigate through the readings. Then, it draws a few conclusions on the state of the art and proposes avenues for future research.

The second part focuses on **methodological issues.** Wensley's article positions the evolving research issues in audit planning. Drawing on their CAPEX[2] experience, he develops an agenda of research issues and approaches for such a complex domain as auditing. Abdol-mohammadi and Bazaz prepare a systematic method of identifying applicable decision aids for a comprehensive inventory of audit tasks. Forty-nine experienced auditors identified tasks as candidates for knowledge-based expert system development from a list of 332 major audit tasks. Hsu recognizes the need to evolve conceptual schemi into database systems. This evolving view of the world would facilitate the construction of knowledge-based systems and their intrinsic database. McCarthy and Rockwell examine reconstructive expertise and imple-mentation heuristics in a design tool. They base their considerations on the REACH system that was designed to aid in the process of database design in general and in the sub-processes of view modeling and view integration. Wensley and Boritz, still in an audit planning context, use their CAPEX[3] experience to review and examine valida-tion issues. The last article of this session (Winkler & Massaad) intro-duces the evolving neural network paradigm to accountants and explores its implications.

The third part presents AI/ES in Accounting and Audit Practice. Brown surveys the field with particular concern for practices in public accounting. Vasarhelyi and Halper, as well as Vasarhelyi, Halper and Ezawa, propose a new "online auditing" paradigm and examine the implementation of the CPAS technology performed at AT&T. Two additional articles are included in this section as illustrations of poten-tial application areas. Messier and Hansen deal with bankruptcy pre-diction. The paper reports on the results of an experiment designed to assess the effectiveness of an inductive algorithm for discovering predictive knowledge structures in financial data. Kandelin and Lin use object-oriented programming to help in the credit decision mak-ing process.

Volume 2 of this series opens the path for Volume 3, being pub-lished simultaneously, which includes sections on Knowledge Elicitation and Representation, Belief Nets and Bayesian Revisions, Accounting Applications and the Future in AI & ES.

ENDNOTES

1. Brown, C., "Expert Systems in Public Accounting: Current Practices and Future Directions," *Expert Systems with Applications*, Vol. 3, 1991, p.3.

2. Boritz, J.E. and Wensley, A.K.P., "CAPEX Technical Manual Version 1.0," Unpublished Manuscript, School of Accountancy, University of Waterloo, Ontario, N2L 3G1, Canada, 1989.

3. Boritz, J.E. and Wensley, A.K.P., "Structuring the Assessment of Audit Evidence: An Expert Systems Approach," *Auditing: A Journal of Practice and Theory*, 1990.

II

Methodology

Audit Planning and Expert Systems Research

ANTHONY K.P. WENSLEY

Introduction

The 1980s saw the development of a variety of different types of expert systems in many business domains. The initial expert system were primarily what might be called "existence proofs," that is, systems built using current expert systems techniques to show that such techniques could be applied productively to the field of business. As expert systems research has progressed so too have expert systems in business. There is now a variety of examples of second-generation expert systems. These systems have some, or all, of the following characteristics:

- Representation of "deep" versus "shallow" knowledge.

- Use of multiple approaches to knowledge representation.

- Relatively sophisticated user interfaces with explanation facilities.

In addition, a number of researchers are beginning to conduct research using business expert systems that is likely to shed light both on the nature and construction of these types of system and also on the nature of the domain knowledge itself. Thus, business expert systems potentially provide an additional research tool with which to investigate the knowledge domain.

One of the central issues of concern to researchers who are investigating business expert systems concerns the value of the research that they are conducting. This concern may be elaborated through considering the following questions concerning the research:

1. Does it contribute to knowledge of the domain?

2. Does it contribute to knowledge that is relevant to the building and implementing of expert systems?

3. Does it systemize knowledge of the domain in some way or other?

4. Does it provide an active medium for communicating knowledge of the domain?

These issues and others, will be discussed in the following section.

Development or Research?

Questions have been raised as to whether the construction of expert systems constitutes a valid research activity (see, for instance, O'Leary [1987b]). To the extent that an expert system either implements a particular theory about a particular domain or attempts to investigate the nature and structure of the problem-solving process used by a particular individual, or set of individuals, it may represent a valuable research contribution. In particular, the validity of a theory of the domain or individual problem solving may be subject to a variety of tests. Such tests may well lead to increased knowledge about either the domain or about problem solvers. In the past, first generation expert system builders did not tend to make the theories on which their systems were constructed explicit. This is generally not the case with many builders of second-generation expert systems.

The construction of expert systems can potentially address research questions such as:

• Is the present state of knowledge of the domain complete and consistent?

• Does this knowledge interact in expected ways? (This question is particularly interesting when a domain is particularly complex and multi-layered.)

• How does the behaviour of domain experts change when they have access to the expert systems?

As expert systems evolve in terms of the richness of the knowledge that they are able to represent they will provide the researcher with an increasingly powerful tool for investigating a particular domain. When used in this way expert systems can be viewed as models of a particular domain. This type of modeling can help to refine some knowledge items and/or rules for combining/operating on particular entities. For instance, it has been suggested that the construction of the knowledge base for the expert system DENDRAL identified a variety of different types of inconsistencies in experts' "knowledge" and subsequently led to the development of an algorithmic model to solve the problem for which the expert system was originally constructed to solve (for a discussion of this issue, refer to Dreyfus and Dreyfus [1986]).

The construction, refinement, and use of expert systems is a cooperative activity between expert systems builder(s), expert(s), and the expert system itself. In a sense, an expert system allows for the establishment of an extended dialogue to take place between the expert system developer(s) and the experts. This dialectical perspective will be examined in more detail later in this paper.

Machine-assisted knowledge simulation is also made possible as a result of conducting domain knowledge bases. This is a relatively new field of enquiry. Michie (1984) refers to such simulation as "knowledge refinement". Once the knowledge can be processed by a computer it is possible to investigate how different knowledge items interact. This may lead to the restructuring of the knowledge, the deletion or modification of certain items of "knowledge" or additional knowledge acquisition phases to obtain richer, more refined items of knowledge. One quite significant problem with this technique is that the use of expert systems for knowledge simulation is a technique which requires that relatively complete information be available about the domain being investigated. Another problem concerns the validity of the contents of a particular knowledge base. To what extent does the knowledge base actually contain knowledge? These issues are discussed in the section entitled "Validation" and, in more detail, in Stamper (1984) and Wensley (1991).

Relatively little research has been conducted concerning the impact of expert systems on either the nature of an individual's decision making process or the nature and quality of the outputs of that process.[1] Since the overall objective in constructing many expert systems is expert augmentation, this type of research would seem to be of critical importance. One of the reasons for the lack of research in this area is that experiments that provide sufficiently rich results would be extremely time-consuming (hence expensive) and exhausting for participants.

An additional reason for the concern that expert systems research does not constitute genuine research relates to the failure of many researchers to develop adequate specifications for their systems. This may be compared to the situation in management science where the central issue revolves around the construction of a model that will incorporate the relevant variables and exhibit appropriate behaviors. Even in this area, however, there is considerable dispute about the objectives of such model construction. Some researchers would argue that attempts should be made to model an individual decision maker's perception of a particular situation. To the extent that the decision maker accepts the model and acts upon it the model may be judged to be successful. In this context model building is a shared activity. Researcher and decision maker attempt to make sense of the situation through the construction of a shared reality—the model.

Another expressed concern is that either expert systems provide us with some knowledge about expert decision making or they are simply clever toys—simulators of behavior not models of behavior. This would seem to be too simplistic a view of either the present status of expert systems research or the future promise of such research. As we have noted above, and will discuss further in the case of CAPEX, a variety of expert systems, and in particular second-generation expert systems, have moved away from only modeling an expert's perception of a particular domain to developing models of the domain that are more rooted in domain concepts and theories. Compare, if you like, an expert system that could predict the motion of bodies using Aristotelian expertise to one based on Newtonian mechanics. The first tells you a great deal about the way human beings see and interpret the world. The second tells you very little. From the standpoint of scientific research it is clear which tells you more about mechanics.

As a final parting shot, some researchers, including the author himself in an earlier incarnation (see, Wensley [1984]), have used the notion of competitive advantage to argue that some forms of expert systems research are best left to others. Thus, even if expert systems research is valid research it is best left up to others to do. Interestingly, our notions of competitive advantage, when used in the context of research, seem to lose much of the richness they had when they were applied in the analysis of the competitive environments of businesses. It would seem to be the case that, if there are competitive advantages for academics they would seem to concern the nature of domain knowledge and the use of expert systems as tools to investigate such domain knowledge.

It also seems to be the case that much of the thinking of what research should be done is based on either an overoptimism about how much knowledge we possess in various domains or a somewhat distorted view of what constitutes an acceptable activity that will provide us with new knowledge. Many researchers have taken the work of Kuhn (1970) to heart and have argued that, in many business areas, sufficient consensus exists for "normal" science to progress. This seems to us to be overoptimistic. In many business areas we are far from having established stable knowledge structures or research programs. We would seem to be very much at the pragmatic stage of the development of any discipline. In this stage the research agenda is set by practical problems that are of importance to individuals in the "real" world. The nature of these problems shapes the research agenda in a very definite way.

Knowledge Acquisition

In the past ten years considerable progress has been made in the study of the characteristics of different techniques for acquiring knowledge. One of the central problems that dogs work in knowledge acquisition relates to one of the enduring myths that has grown up concerning knowledge acquisition. Early on in the development of the study of expert systems a number of rather overenthusiastic proponents of the field were responsible for giving birth to the myth that knowledge is like precious metals—it can be mined from the expert provided that the right tools are available. This myth fails to recognize that in many instances it is necessary to assist the knowledge providers in structuring the knowledge that they are providing. At a deeper level the myth may be more appropriate, however. Extracting precious metals requires an ability to identify correctly ore bearing rocks, then knowing how to process and refine large quantities of ore in order to obtain very small quantities of ore. In a similar fashion very large quantities of "knowledge" may need to be sifted and refined in order to yield a small amount of knowledge.

As noted previously knowledge acquisition is a dialectical process. At the very least the expert system builder(s) and the expert(s) attempt to construct a shared reality in the guise of an expert system. Thus, as Wensley (1989) notes, much so-called knowledge acquisition is, in fact, knowledge construction. The traditional metaphor of "mining knowledge" was probably never appropriate even for the simplest expert systems and is certainly not appropriate as a metaphor for describing the knowledge acquisition process involved in the development of complex expert systems. Once we enter into the world of knowledge construction the notion of encoding an expert's understanding of a domain becomes increasingly vague.

It is worth noting that the very action of conducting the dialectic may be of value in itself. It should also be borne in mind that the expert's understanding of the domain is likely to be modified by working with others to construct his/her knowledge of the domain. At the very least this may lead to questions concerning the ability of independent experts to validate the outputs generated either by the expert knowledge providers or the expert system.

CAPEX, as a knowledge-based system, was built using knowledge obtained from a variety of different sources. One source of knowledge was expert auditors. However, the knowledge that they provided was not considered to be necessarily superior to that obtained from other sources. CAPEX is, to put it simply, a tool for integrating and investigating the nature of audit knowledge.

Knowledge Representation

As in the case of approaches to knowledge acquisition there are a variety of disputes concerning the "best" approach to knowledge representation. In some cases these are versions of classic reductionist arguments that have raged in the natural sciences and mathematics for centuries. For instance, some particularly vocal proponents of logical representations of knowledge argue that such an approach is not only the "best" approach but it is the only approach. If knowledge cannot be expressed in this form then, so they say, it is not worthy of the appellation knowledge. A more worthwhile approach would seem to be to keep an open mind on the issue. To attempt to represent the knowledge of a domain in a variety of different ways and compare the performance of the different representations both against each other and, where possible, some external standard.

One fertile field for future enquiry would involve providing a knowledgeable person with a variety of different knowledge structuring tools. This would allow him or her to examine the efficacy, ease of use, robustness etc. of the various different approaches in solving different types of problems.

In the context of auditing a variety of knowledge structuring tools are available of different levels of complexity. Acquiring audit knowledge brings one face to face with two problems. First, it is necessary that all the knowledge that is obtained through the use of the various knowledge structuring tools be collected and integrated. Second, it is necessary to choose an appropriate approach to representing this knowledge in computable form.

CAPEX represents the limited "audit" world in terms of accounting objects, management assertions, and audit procedures. Accounting objects are financial statements and financial statement items such as accounts receivable. These accounting objects have a variety of characteristics including dollar value, variability, type of account, etc. Management assertions relate to each financial statement item, its completeness, and its valuation. Finally, audit procedures may involve substantial analysis or tests of details, provide information concerning the presence, or absence, of errors in a particular financial statement item, set of items, or the financial statements as a whole, and have a variety of other characteristics including cost, time taken to complete, reliability, and relevance.

One of the interesting problems that arose during the construction of CAPEX related to the characterization of such seemingly obvious objects as auditing procedures. In the end it became necessary to relate audit procedures directly to the evidential messages provided. An audit procedure is thus defined as an activity that yields a single evidential message. For example, the procedure that involves the positive confirmation of accounts receivable is actually at least two procedures—one that provides a message concerning the existence of accounts receivable and one concerning the dollar value of those accounts receivable. Though this issue may seem fairly trivial it demonstrates the degree to which building expert systems of the complexity of CAPEX forces attention to be paid to a number of very detailed questions the answers to which may be difficult, or in some cases impossible, to obtain.

Broadly speaking, the interpretation of the meaning of the evidential messages provided by audit evidence-gathering procedure relates to the notion of *relevance* of the message while concerns with respect to the confidence that may be placed in such interpretations relates to the *reliability* of the message. As noted above, work that is directed towards representing audit knowledge, and, in particular, knowledge concerning audit procedures, may well result in elaboration and refinement of that knowledge. This is particularly true when considering, the reliability of the evidence which is generated by audit procedures. Uncertainty that arises because evidence is not perfectly reliable is but one of a number of uncertainties faced by an external auditor. The representation of relevant uncertainties is discussed in the following sections.

Since the knowledge we have available to encode in a particular knowledge base is often incomplete, it is also important to consider how such concepts as ignorance, uncertainty, ambiguity, and vagueness are to be represented. Since the overall planning objectives for CAPEX were stated in terms of the specific audit risk targets it was vitally necessary to select an appropriate formalism with which to represent a variety of different types of uncertainty associated with an external audit.

There are a variety of possible approaches to representing and analyzing the types of uncertainty that arise in audit planning. Traditionally, risk has been explicitly analyzed at a fairly high level. For instance, risk has been defined as the uncertainty associated with an assertion of the form.

The set of financial statements do not contain any material errors.

It has often been the case that, rather than making reference to risk, the concept of assurance has been used. Thus an external auditor is concerned to achieve a certain level of assurance rather than a target level of risk. The choice of perspective is not trivial and may well lead to the types of framing problems that have been discussed by Tversky and Kahneman (1982). The impact of biases due to framing might alter assessment of the characteristics of audit evidence-gathering procedures and also potentially alter the way in which audit program plans are constructed.

Traditionally, uncertainties associated with audit planning have been modeled as classical probabilities. This has proved problematic for a number of reasons the most important of which is the fact that it is unlikely that such probabilities can be known and the classical approach provides no principal way of taking the revision of uncertainties following the receipt of new evidence. Bayesian approaches have gained some favor. The principal problems that face the users of this approach relate, on the one hand, to the semantics of Bayesian uncertainty measures and, on the other, to the problems of ensuring that somewhat stringent independence conditions obtain between different items of evidence. An additional problem with the Bayesian approach, which it shares with the classical approach, is that it is not possible to distinguish between uncertainty that arises from randomness and uncertainty that arises from lack of knowledge.

Recently, Shafer and Srivastava (1987) and Shafer, Shenoy, and Srivistava (1989) have proposed an approach to modeling uncertainties in audit planning using belief functions.[2] Belief function approaches address some of the problems identified above but bring with them a number of equally difficult problems not the least of which relate to the semantics of belief functions. This issue has been addressed by Tversky and Shafer (1985) but is still in need of considerable elaboration before an adequate specification can be provided in the context of the uncertainties inherent in audit planning. The topic of uncertainty modeling in auditing is discussed extensively in Boritz and Wensley (1991).

In its present incarnation CAPEX can represent and combine uncertainties as either classical probabilities, subjective Bayesian probabilities or Dempster-Shafer belief functions. Audit evidence-gathering procedures are considered to provide evidence that reduces the uncertainty associated with the truth of a variety of different types of assertions that are considered to be relevant to a variety of accounting objects.

The encoding of a variety of different approaches to uncertainty modeling in CAPEX will allow the researchers to investigate the impact of the selection of one particular approach on the nature of audit plans, the process by which such plans are constructed, and resources consumed.

CAPEX is an expert system designed to generate audit program plans. As such it provides a medium for investigating aspects of planning problems in general and audit planning in particular.

Planning and Simulation

Planning involves the construction of sequences of actions that are expected to lead to the achievement of predefined goals. In order to develop plans it is necessary to be able to represent:

1. The state of the world in sufficient detail to be able to represent the impact of actions.

2. The characteristics of actions in sufficient detail be able to identify unique actions to the user and be able to validate the system accordingly.

Audit program plans specify sets of information-gathering actions.

These actions will be considered in more detail in the following section.

Information-Gathering Actions

In the context of audit planning we may think of the actions that are being performed as a set of information-gathering actions. Such actions provide information concerning possible states of the system being investigated. Given perfectly reliable information-gathering procedures that can be carried out at zero cost it will always be possible to construct some set of information-gathering actions that taken together will provide a precise specification of the state of the system. However, procedures are neither perfectly reliable, nor costless. Thus we are plunged into a familiar world where heuristics are required to:

1. Determine the tradeoff between different characteristics say, accuracy and reliability.

2. Reduce the complexity of the problem solving domain.

One way of conceptualizing the construction of plans that consist of information gathering actions is a set of actions that constrain the possible states of the world that could possibly obtain. As more actions are performed the set of possible states of the world becomes smaller and hence the likelihood of one possible state obtaining becomes higher. This way of looking at the problem of information gathering is useful because it tends to focus our attention on a number of important features:

1. In a world of uncertainty it is never possible to know, unambiguously, that a particular state of affairs obtains.

2. Our attention is directed towards collecting both information that tends to support the existence of a particular set of states of affairs and also information that tends to rule out other states of affairs.

One central issue relates to the descriptions that are used to describe the possible states of the world. The choice of an appropriate description language is vital since the descriptions must encompass all the relevant characteristics of the world that we might be interested in. If they do not so characterize the world we will not be able to construct an appropriate plan.

Consider, for example, a murder investigation. One would expect that the initial state of affairs, at first, could be presented by a set of statements each of which express the guilt of one party or another. As information is collected it would bear differentially on different members, or groups of members, of this set of statements. This situation is particularly clear-cut in the sense that the states of the world which actually obtained are either represented by a unary set,[3] or, at least, a set with relatively few members, if we consider a different example drawn from audit planning.

With no information about a particular client it is conceivable that all possible types of error occur in the client's financial statements or that no errors are actually present. We assume that we are absolutely in the dark as to the accuracy of the financial statements. In order to provide suitable characterization of the state of affairs that obtains in this case it is necessary to describe the state of affairs in terms of statements referring to the presence of all the different types of errors that can logically occur in the client's financial statements. One way of doing this is presented by the assertion based approach to audit planning. This approach is based on standards promulgated by both the AICPA in the United States and the CICA in Canada. The general characteristics of accounting objects are considered to be:

Existence: The accounting object exists.

Completeness: All the transactions that impact the accounting objects have been recorded.

Valuation: The accounting object is appropriately valued.

Ownership: The accounting object belongs to or is the responsibility of the client.

Presentation: The characteristics of the accounting object are correctly presented.

In this case the set of statements that can potentially describe the state of the world before any information is obtained can be represented in a number of different ways:

- Statements of the form "There is an error of magnitude Mt with respect to assertion At." In this case the set of all possible worlds will be a set of possible values of Mt associated with some probability distribution.

- A somewhat more restricted representation of the world

> would consider statements of the form "There is an error of Mt (which is equal to, or greater than, materiality) in assertion At."

The above assertion-based approach is an exhaustive approach to developing an audit program plan. An alternative approach is the error-based approach. In this approach, rather than consider the set of all possible assertions which can be made concerning relevant accounting objects the auditor considers a set of possible errors that may occur which would lead to material errors arising in a client's financial statements. There are considerable differences between the two approaches some of the most important are:

- With error-based approaches it may be easier to obtain information from practicing auditors though this information may be more "contaminated" than information obtained from procedures in an assertion-based approach.

- Uncertainty representation and processing is generally more straightforward in an error-based approach than in an assertion based approach. This is because the inherent structure of errors is more intuitive than the structure of assertion and/or simpler.[4]

- Error-based approaches may very well be less complete than assertion-based approaches and lead to less exhaustive audit program plans.

One way of visualizing the difference between the assertion-based approach and the error-based approach is traditional AI planning terms is as follows:

> Error-based approaches are similar to robot planning approaches that attempt to avoid all possible predefined errors that may impede the achievement of a particular objective while assertion-based approaches are based on an analytic framework, usually of three dimensional space, within which the impact of actions is represented.

One of the advantages of developing an assertion-based approach to audit planning is that it provides a basis for investigating both the efficiency and effectiveness of error-based strategies.

Sequential and Simultaneous Planning

In a broad sense, audit program planning involves the sequential execution of information-gathering actions. At the gross level CAPEX and most external auditors appear to generate plans in a similar manner. However, CAPEX develops detailed audit program planning from the outset whereas there is some indication that auditors may initially develop general plans that they subsequently refine as information becomes increasingly available. Auditors also tend to distinguish between information that is gathered at an interim audit and information that is gathered at year-end.

There are many avenues for further research into approaches that may be used to generate efficient and effective audit program plans. These appear to be situations where auditors may develop and subsequently modify default plans, where they use least commitment planning, and so forth. Expert systems such as CAPEX provide flexible research instruments for investigating the impact of such approaches.

One of the central problems we faced was to provide CAPEX with a heuristic to enable the selection of audit evidence-gathering procedures to include a particular audit program plan. This problem is discussed in the following section.

Examples of Naive, and Not So Naive Planning Heuristic

One of the heuristics that guides CAPEX in its selection of information-gathering procedures is a heuristic that we refer to as the "evidential power" heuristic. This heuristic attempts to guide the system in selecting the most cost effective procedures considering that we are operating, in a world of limited resources. In the following section we investigate the nature of this heuristic and a variety of other heuristics that might be used to address some of the shortcomings of the evidential power heuristic.

EVIDENTIAL POWER

In traditional decision theory a means is provided of measuring the value of information. Basically, this value is based on the insight that information reduces uncertainty. Thus, the value of an item of information is the expected value of a particular node in a decision tree before the item of information is received less the expected value of the decision at the same node once information has been received. CAPEX is concerned with differentiating between a number of information-gathering procedures. One could conceive of a complex function being built to determine the expected cost associated with different types of failure to detect errors and then determining the reduction in the expected losses that would accrue as a result of receiving information from particular audit evidence-gathering procedure. Clearly this approach requires that a larger body of assessments be obtained from expert users. In the initial implementation of CAPEX we chose a somewhat less information-intensive approach by developing a heuristic based on evidential power.

This heuristic attempts to determine the cost effectiveness of audit evidence-gathering procedures. Essentially it attempts to assess the total quantity of evidence as provided by particular audit evidence-gathering procedure

Evidential Power = Sum of maximum derivable assurances/cost (1.1).

In this formulation the maximum derivable assurances measure the maximum extent to which the uncertainty associated with each relevant financial statement item assertion can be reduced. One of the drawbacks of the simplistic evidential power heuristic is that it does not take into account whether a particular procedure is providing evidential support that will actually be needed in future to achieve the predefined objectives associated with a particular audit. A modified form of evidential power heuristic would make this type of comparison.

Evidential Power = Sum of useable assurances/Cost (1.2)

There are obviously problems with refining the evidential power heuristic in this way. One of these problems is that the more sophisticated versions of the heuristic are computationally more demanding. They are, of course, less demanding than exhaustive search strategies but none-the-less given the complexity of the audit planning problem, they increase very considerably the time taken to construct an audit program plan.

It is unlikely that the present strategy of using a heuristic to essentially avoid search can be sustained. At present the computational overhead involved in even very restricted search is excessive. It is hoped that future versions of CAPEX will allow both the use of more sophisticated planning heuristics and greater search.

DEVELOPING PLANS—LOOKING AHEAD

Presently CAPEX has a relatively naive strategy for selecting procedures to include in audit program plans. Although, as indicated above, it does not simply involve a one period look ahead strategy it does not allow for continuous refinement or other types of planning strategies that may result in the discovery of more efficient and effective plans. In defense of CAPEX the fact that it provides for a rich environment for modeling information necessary for developing audit program plans allows it to be used as a test bed for the investigation of different approaches to developing audit program plans, different procedure selection heuristics, different approaches to modeling uncertainty, etc.

Verifying and Validating Expert Systems With Complex Outputs

From relatively humble beginnings research into the verification and validation of expert systems has burgeoned. There is often some confusion as to the precise meaning of the terms. As a first cut let us consider the following definitions:

Verification: Does the knowledge base meet the specifications that were developed for it and does it have relevant characteristics such as consistency, completeness, etc?

Validation: Does the system perform as required?

One of the key issues concerning the verification of an expert system relates to the extent that the behavior of the system has been specified. Typically, both user requirements and system specifications are either not stated or stated very vaguely. From a research standpoint a number of related issues need to be investigated:

- How should system specifications and user requirements be developed for expert systems?

- Given that system specifications and user requirements have been adequately developed what types of verification and validation tests are appropriate?

O'Leary (1986, 1987, 1988) was one the first researchers to recognize the importance of research that addressed the verification and validation of expert systems. Unfortunately, there is insufficient space available in this paper to investigate general theoretical and practical aspects of this important topic further. The interested reader is directed towards O'Leary's papers, Boritz and Wensley (1991), Wensley (1990a, 1990b, 1989). However, specific issues with respect to validating CAPEX will be discussed in the following paragraphs.

In many traditional planning systems that have been addressed in the artificial intelligence literature it has been relatively straightforward to determine whether a plan achieves a particular goal, or set of goals. Thus one approach to validation has been simply to carry out the sequence of actions that have been specified and see if the desired state is achieved.

In the case of CAPEX the planning situation is more complex since it is not possible to objectively determine whether the goal state has been achieved. If we add to this the fact that the set of all possible combinations of actions that can possibly result in the achievement of any desired state is very large, if not infinite, both the validation and verification stages become very difficult.

When developing validation tests for CAPEX it was necessary to have the performance of the system assessed by independent experts. In this context a number of related questions are relevant:

1. Does the experimental situation adequately distinguish between a variety of different levels of performance?

2. What types of instruments can be used to assess the plans generated by such systems?

3. How reliable are the assessments provided by experts using these instruments?

4. Are there ways of cross-validating the assessments made by human assessors?

With respect to the first question, considerable attention was directed towards developing case materials for validating CAPEX that elicited different behaviors from individuals with different levels of expertise. Since audit program plans and the objectives they are designed to achieve are complex it was necessary to develop and pretest an extensive assessment questionnaire. Finally, one of the interesting aspects of the validation tests that were performed on CAPEX was that its performance was assessed by independent experts both absolutely and relative to plans that had been developed by the writers of the validation case material.

Conclusion

Expert systems are suitable instruments for conducting a variety of different types of research project. In the first third of this paper general issues with respect to the value of using expert systems as research instruments have been investigated. In the remaining two thirds of the paper specific research contributions that could potentially be provided by a specific expert system, CAPEX, have been discussed.

ENDNOTES

1. Though see Lamberti, 1987, Lamberti and Wallace, 1990; Peterson, 1988; and Rathburn 1989.
2. For further details concerning the belief function see Shafer (1976), and Shafer (1981).
3. A unary set of statements contains a single statement. Thus, evidence either supports the statement or does not support the statement. All too often it seems that criminal investigators work to establish the guilt of particular individuals from the beginning rather than enlarging the set of suspects and seeking evidence to narrow down the set of suspects with no particular bias or end in view.
4. An important research question relates to whether these statements are true. Computer-based structuring and assessment tools of which CAPEX is one and Auditor's Assistant (Shafer, Shenoy, and Srivastava 1988) is another, provide vehicles for investigating such questions.

REFERENCES

Boritz, J.E., and A.K.P. Wensley (1991a), Validating Expert Systems With Complex Outputs: The Case of Audit Planning," unpublished manuscript, School of Accountancy. University of Waterloo, Waterloo, Ontario, Canada, N2L 3G1.

————, and ———— (1991b) "Structuring the Assessment of Audit Evidence," *Auditing; A Journal of Practice and Theory,* Supplement 1991.

Wensley, A.K.P., and Boritz, J.E., "An Expert Systems Approach to Substantive Audit Planning", *International Journal of Exert Systems Applications* (supplement), 1991.

Boritz, J.E., and A.K.P Wensley. (1990b) "Evidence, Uncertainty Modelling and Audit Risk," Unpublished manuscript. School of Accountancy, University of Waterloo, Waterloo, Ontario, Canada, N2L 3G1, 1989.

————, and ————, CAPEX Technical Manual 1.0 Unpublished manuscript, School of Accountancy, University of Waterloo, Waterloo, Ontario, Canada N2L 3GI, 1989.

Dreyfus, H., and S. Dreyfus, *Mind Over Machine: The Power of Human Intuition and Expertise in the Era of the Computer,* New York: Free Press, 1986.

Hendler, J., Tate, A., and M. Drummond, "AI Planning: Systems and Techniques", *AI Magazine,* Vol. 11, No. 2, pp. 61-77, Summer 1990.

J-M, Hoc, *Cognitive Psychology of Planning,* New York; Academic Press, 1988.

Kahneman, D., and A. Tversky (1982) "Judgment Under Uncertainty: Heuristics and Biases," in Judgement Under Uncertainty: *Heuristics and Biases,* Kahneman, D., Slovic, P., and A. Tversky (eds.), Cambridge: Cambridge University Press, 1982.

Kuhn, T. *The Structure of Scientific Revolutions,* Chicago, Illinois: University of Chicago Press, 1970.

Lamberti, D.M., "Impact of Abstract Versus Concrete Information Presentation in Expert Systems on the Expert-Novice User Performance," Doctoral Dissertation, Rensselaer Polytechnic Institute, May 1987.

————, and ————, "Intelligent Interface Design: An Empirical Assessment of Knowledge Presentation in Expert Systems," *MIS Quarterly,* Vol. 14, No. 3, pp. 271-311, September, 1990.

O'Leary, D., "Methods of Validating Expert Systems," *Interfaces,* 18, No. 6, November-December, 1988, pp. 72-79.

————, "Validation of Expert Systems," *Decision Sciences,* Vol. 18, No. 3, Summer 1987, pp. 468-486.

————, "Validation of Business Systems," *Symposium of Expert Systems and Audit Judgement,* School of Accountancy, University of Southern California, February 1986.

Peterson, T.O., "The Acquisition of Managerial Performance Feedback Skills Through the Use of a Knowledge-Based Expert System: An Empirical Evaluation," Doctoral Dissertation, Texas A & M University, Texas, 1988.

Rathburn, T.A.. and G.J. Weinroth, "EXSTATIC: The Merger Of Expert Systems and Microcomputers as a Training Paradigm,"

International Journal of Computer Applications in Technology, Vol. 2, No. 2, pp. 77-88, 1989.

Shafer, G., (1976), *A Mathematical Theory of Evidence,* Princeton, NJ. Princeton University Press, 1976.

————, (1981), "Constructive Probability," *Synthese,* 48, 1981, pp. 1-61.

————, and R. Srivastava (1987), "The Bayesian and Belief-Function Formalisms I, A General Perspective of Auditing," *Symposium on Research In Auditing,* School of Accountancy, University of Waterloo, November, 1987.

————, and A. Tversky (1985) "Languages and Designs for Probability Judgment," *Cognitive Science,* 9, 1985, pp. 309-339.

————, Shenoy, P.P., and R.P. Srivastava (1987) "Audit Risk: A Belief-Functional Approach," Working Paper, No 212, School of Business, University of Kansas, 1989.

Stamper, R., "Management Epistemology: Garbage In Garbage Out," IFIP Working Group Meeting 8.4, Durham, UK, 1984.

Tiles, J.E., McKee, G.T., and G.C. Deans (eds.), *Evolving Knowledge in Natural Science and Artificial Intelligence,* London, UK: Pullman, 1990.

Wensley, A.K.P. "Developing Specifications for Expert Systems - Implications for Validation and Verification," Faculty of Management, University of Toronto, Ontario, M5S, IV4, Canada, 1991a.

———— (1990a), "Expert Systems Validation: Some Issues," unpublished manuscript, Faculty of Management, University of Toronto, Ontario, Canada, M5S IV4.

———— (1990b), "Validating Complex Audit Planning Systems: Instruments Experiments and Results," unpublished manuscript, Faculty of Management, University of Toronto, Toronto, Ontario, Canada, M5S IV4.

————., "The Feasibility of Developing as Assertion Based Approach to Audit Planning Using Expert Systems Methodology," unpublished thesis, Department of Management Science, University of Waterloo, October 1989.

————, "Research Issues in Expert Systems," in Dukidis, G., Land, F., and G. Miller (eds.), Knowledge Based Management Support Systems, New York: Ellis Horwood, 1989.

————., "User Interface Design for Expert Systems: Some Issues," IFIP Working Group Meeting 8.4, Durham, U.K., 1984.

Identification of Tasks for Expert Systems Development in Auditing

MOHAMMAD J. ABDOLMOHAMMADI

MOHAMMAD S. BAZAZ

1. Introduction

The Accounting Profession has shown significant interest in research and development of Decision Support Systems (DSS) and Knowledge-based Expert Systems (KES) in recent years. Reviews of the literature (Abdolmohammadi, 1987; Messier & Hansen, 1987, 1984; O'Leary & Watkins, 1989) indicate that such efforts have centered around complex audit tasks such as analytical review procedures, statistical sampling, auditing electronic data processing centers, going concern judgments, and evaluation of pertinent controls. This is based on some research indicating that expert systems are best suited to tackle unstructured audit tasks (Abdolmohammadi, 1987).

Although much time and resources have been spent on efforts to develop expert systems in auditing, these efforts do not represent a systematic approach to identification of tasks for expert system development. Instead, these efforts have been based primarily on consideration of tasks one-at-a-time. This study uses a systematic model to identify viable audit tasks for KES development. The model represents a mechanism to identify audit tasks individually, and in relation with other tasks, within each of the main phases of the audit. The model has the following components: (1) compilation of a comprehensive inventory of audit tasks; (2) organization of audit tasks into audit phases, audit parts within each phase, and audit tasks within each part; and (3) Identification of viable tasks for KES development by

23

very experienced auditors (partners and managers) from international accounting firms that have been particularly active in decision aid development in recent years.

The strength of the approach used in this study is its ability to identify tasks that are not only individually applicable for KES development, but that are also identified within a model of interrelated phases and parts of the audit. This would provide long-term opportunities for development of a series of interrelated expert systems that eventually could tackle major related parts within each phase of the audit.

The paper is organized as follows: Section 2 discusses background literature and the general audit model. Special terms are also defined here. The method of research is presented in Section 3. The method and source of the inventory of audit tasks is presented first followed by a discussion of the participating accounting firms, subjects, and the questionnaire. The criteria used to identify tasks for KES development will be discussed in Section 4, followed by a detailed listing and a brief discussion of the tasks. The analysis of the effects of accounting firm affiliation and audit phase differences is also presented in this section. The final section provides a summary and some concluding remarks.

2. The Model

2.1. DEFINITIONS

Major key terms need to be defined to provide a common understanding of the material discussed.

2.1.1. *The Audit Model.* The model used for this research is based on Felix and Kinney's (1982) state-of-the-art paper, Cushing and Loebbecke's (1986) firm classification monograph, and KPMG Peat Marwick's (1987) audit manual. The model has six sequential (concurrent in some parts) phases: (1) Orientation. (2) Preliminary Evaluation of Internal Controls. (3) Compliance Tests of Pertinent Controls, (4) Substantive Tests of Transactions and Balances, (5) Forming an Opinion, and (6) Financial Statement Reporting. Details of definitions of these phases are provided in Appendix A. KPMG Peat Marwick's (1987) audit manual was used to check on the correspondence of this model to practice.

2.1.2. *Knowledge-Based Expert System (KES).* There is no universal definition of expert systems. However, Abdolmohammadi (1987) found the following definition as a popular one: a KES is an interactive computer-based software that assists decision-makers by using an expert's decision rules. The decision rules of the expert(s) must be elicited by a knowledge engineer and programmed into the KES in terms of a number of IF-THEN production rules. Standard software packages called "expert shells," which prespecify the inference mechanism (called inference engine), are used to facilitate KES programming.

O'Leary (1987) indicates that from a technical point of view, an auditing KES processes symbolic information such as "if . . . then" rules rather than just numeric information and it is often developed using either Artificial Intelligence or KES shells. Decisions made in an audit task may depend upon the result of other audit tasks because audit tasks are interrelated. Thus, audit KESs should provide flexibility to accommodate this characteristic of auditing.

2.2. BACKGROUND

Accounting firms have developed a few KESs by identifying tasks for in-house KES development through a project proposal and approval mechanism. For example, ExperTAX was developed in-house by Coopers and Lybrand through a project proposal and approval mechanism (Shpilberg & Graham, 1986; Shpilberg, Graham, & Schatz, 1986). ExperTAX is designed to assist users in the tax planning consulting area. According to the *Wall Street Journal* (November 13, 1986), ExperTAX cost more than 1 million dollars and over 7,000 man hours to develop.

Accounting firms are willing to incur such large costs for developing expert systems because they expect the benefits achieved to outweigh the costs. Elliott and Keilich (1985) state that decision aids in general and expert systems in particular would potentially present the following benefits: (1) teach inexperienced professionals what information is combined in reaching a decision; (2) when human expertise is either scarce or not available, decision aids could be used by less experienced decision makers within an organization; (3) decision aids could focus the attention of the auditor on factors considered to be relevant to the task domain, and (4) although the decision maker is ultimately responsible for making decisions, the decision aid would essentially appear as a "second opinion."

Data on actual benefits and costs of expert systems are scarce. However, the accounting firms continue to show a considerable amount of interest in developing expert systems. In addition to the in-house developmental efforts discussed above, accounting firms have also supported research and development efforts by academicians. The academic efforts, similar to the in-house efforts, have been on a one task at a time basis and are the result of formal proposals by academicians and financial support by accounting firms. For example, EDP Expert is an expert system developed by Hansen and Messier (1986) in the EDP auditing area under grants from the Peat Marwick Foundation's Research Opportunities in Auditing Program. The systems developed thus far have dealt with only a limited subset of the audit function.

In addition to the above methods, which have resulted in development of actual expert systems, there have been efforts by academics (e.g., Abdolmohammadi, 1987; Bedard, Gray, & Mock, 1984; Messier & Hansen, 1984) and practitioners (e.g., Elliott & Kielich, 1985; Kieth, 1985) to identify audit tasks for decision aid development. However, none of these methods has resulted in a systematic approach for the identification of a series of interrelated tasks for the development of large-scale decision aids.

Further, the literature on criteria to use for expert systems development in auditing is not conclusive. In an early study, Abdolmohammadi and Wright (1987) identified 14 potential criteria ranging from structure of the task (i.e., the more unstructured the task, the more applicable the KES) to cost of development of the KES. However, there is a shortage of empirical data on extent of relevance of such criteria in practice. Consequently, the discussion below relies primarily on general models to set the stage for the application-oriented purpose of this paper.

Knowledge-based expert systems (KES) are developed based on experts' extant knowledge of the task under consideration. KES is developed to "solve what we generally consider difficult problems requiring expertise in well defined domain" (Bailey, Hackenbrack, & Dillard, 1987, p. 38). This indicates that similar to developing any decision aid, development of KES requires an understanding of the processes involved in performing the task, together with a suitable perspective theory that can serve as a normative formulation for the problem (Pitz & Sachs, 1984).

The above discussion indicates that models of the audit process are needed. These models must be sensitive to the theories and practices of human information processing in auditing. Recent psychological studies indicate that domain knowledge is first broken down into related parts and then used in relation to a taxonomic organization of the knowledge (Tversky, 1989). "Parts, then, seem to be simultaneously natural units of perception and natural units of function" (Tversky, 1989, p. 983) where, "knowledge of function depends on rather specific prior experience" (Tversky, 1989, p. 984). Stefik, et al. (1982) and Chandrasekaran (1984) suggest classification and identification of generic tasks as a means of assessing the suitability of the domain. They both offer guidelines to assist in the choice of tasks within suitable domains. Classificatory tasks are favored, as are tasks where the data and knowledge is reliable and static, with a small solution space. Using Chandrasekaran's guidelines, a large proportion of the knowledge may be represented by a small number of rules. The above theory and guidelines are particularly relevant to the process used in practice of auditing where much training and experience in partitioning the audit process into various phases, parts, taxonomies, and detailed tasks exists.

To conduct the audit according to current practice, the auditor would first break the whole audit into phases, parts, and detailed tasks, and then use the logic of professional standards and personal judgment to form taxonomies of evidence relating to each task, part, and phase. The auditor's final action would be to aggregate all evidence to form an overall audit opinion (Felix & Kinney, 1982).

Consequently, it makes sense to use the taxonomic and partonomic models of knowledge to identify tasks for application of expert systems in auditing. This indicates that the whole body of audit tasks needs to be identified and classified into various phases of the audit broken into parts of interrelated tasks for the purpose of KES development. This study reports very experienced auditors' perceptions of the applicability of KES for various taxonomies of the audit process.

3. Method

A comprehensive inventory of audit tasks is needed before audit tasks for which KES development can take place can be identified. Many resources could be consulted to develop such a comprehensive inventory of audit tasks. These resources include auditing texts, professional standards, and audit manuals. Based on audit manuals from three accounting firms, an auditing text, personal experience, and a pilot study with six very experienced auditors, Abdolmohammadi (1990) compiled a list of 332 major audit tasks in six phases and 50 parts.

The list of audit tasks was presented to 49 partners and managers from three international accounting firms. The questionnaire included over two pages of definitions and instructions to provide a common understanding of the terms used. To enhance participation of the very experienced and high-ranking subjects needed for this research, the authors secured support of a high-ranking partner in each of seven offices of three international accounting firms in Boston, Chicago, and New York. These coordinating partners were then sent a packet containing 11 copies of the task instrument. They were instructed to keep one copy for their own perusal and distribute the remaining 10 copies among partners and managers in their offices or offices in the regions under their authority. They were also requested to collect the completed questionnaires and send them back to the authors.

Six offices of three firms cooperated. From a total of 61 questionnaires distributed, 49 were completed and returned (response rate of 80%). The mean subjects' experience level was 10.01 years with a standard deviation of 5.56. The respondent group included 14 partners, 33 managers, and one supervising senior (one subject did not provide demographic data). For data analysis purposes, the supervising senior and the subject who did not provide demographic data were classified as managers. All in all, there were seven subjects from firm one, 16 subjects from firm two, and 26 subjects from firm three.

The subjects were provided with the definitions of several decision aids including the KES. The subjects were then asked to choose, among other things, the audit tasks that they viewed as candidates for KES development as opposed to complete automation, decision support systems, and strict human processing. The results are presented in the next section.

4. Results

Forty five tasks were identified for KES development by the subject group. To be included in this list, the tasks that were selected by the subject group with a relatively high degree of consensus were selected. However, as is common in behavioral research (e.g., Ashton, 1983), a considerable level of variation was observed in the judgments of the auditors. Consequently, the following practical criteria were developed to include a task in the KES task group:

1. a significant number of subjects from the three accounting firms chose the task for KES development. The benchmark chosen for this purpose was 20% of responses, which indicates

that a minimum of 10 (49 subjects*20% = 9.8) responses in support of inclusion of the task must be present. At least one response from each accounting firm must be in support of inclusion of the task in the group,

OR

2. at least 50% of subjects from one accounting firm should be in support of the inclusion of the task.

The above criteria recognize that there is a possibility of a firm effect if two firms do not view the task as a candidate for KES development, while the third firm might view the task particularly applicable for KES development. Furthermore, while there is a general understanding that KESs may have varying degrees of applicability in different parts of the audit, the extent of such application is not known. These issues are studied in this section. To analyze the data, the tasks identified for KES development are presented first, followed by a summary table to study the firm effect. The final subsection will discuss the issue of differences in the number of tasks identified in various phases of the audit.

4.1. TASKS SELECTED FOR KES DEVELOPMENT

In this section, the tasks selected for KES development and the number (and proportion) of subjects from each firm choosing each task are provided. Table 1 presents the results. This detailed table is particularly important for the purpose of generating interest in KES development efforts in specific task areas.

The five phases of the audit and the parts within each of the phases for which specific tasks were identified for KES development are identified in Table 1. The number and percentage of responses in support of the KES task is provided for each firm followed by a total number and percentage of responses. The table is self explanatory and provides a rich information set on tasks that individually and in some logical combination (within each part) can be subjected to further research and development efforts. However, there are some interesting observations.

First, a glance at the tasks selected indicates that these tasks are very complex and difficult to perform. This is consistent with the theory and application developments efforts of KES in practice. As stated in the background section, the KESs developed so far have tackled complex audit tasks. It is in these tasks that the need for decision aids is

TABLE 1
Tasks Selected for Knowledge-based Expert Systems Development

	Accounting Firm			
	1	2	3	Total

Orientation
Understanding the Client's Business

	1	2	3	Total
1. The assessment of the effects of external variables (significant industry trends, primary competitors, etc.).	3 (43%)	4 (25%)	5 (19%)	12 (24%)
2. The evaluation of key financial management characteristics (general planning, budgets, financial statements, managerial & internal reports and documents).	2 (29%)	3 (19%)	6 (23%)	11 (22%)

Engagement Risk Assessment

3. The assessment of the degree of regulation of the entity.	2 (29%)	5 (31%)	4 (15%)	11 (22)
4. The identification of contentious accounting issues.	2 (29%)	3 (19%)	5 (19%)	10 (20%)

Inherent Risk Assessment

5. The determination of unusual accounting policies and practices (consult the number and significance of audit adjustments and waived audit differences in prior year's audit).	4 (57%)	2 (13%)	2 (8%)	8 (16%)
6. The evaluation of the complexity of underlying calculations or principles.	4 (57%)	1 (6%)	3 (12%)	8 (16%)
7. The assessment of the susceptibility of the asset under audit to material fraud or misappropriation.	4 (57%)	7 (44%)	4 (15%)	15 (31%)
8. The assessment of the experience and competence of accounting personnel responsible for the account.	4 (57%)	0 (0%)	3 (12%)	7 (14%)
9. The assessment of the volume and complexity of transactions flow and control over these flows.	3 (43%)	2 (13%)	5 (19%)	10 (20%)

General Considerations

10. The identification of critical audit areas (areas difficult to audit, judgmental areas, high inherent risk areas).	4 (57%)	6 (38%)	4 (15%)	14 (29%)

Preliminary Evaluation of Controls
General Considerations

11. The preliminary evaluation of internal controls (client accounting policies and procedures, general condition under which accounting data are produced, processed, reviewed, and accumulated within the organization) including EDP operations.	5 (71%)	5 (31%)	6 (23%)	16 (33%)
12. The preliminary conclusion regarding level of reliance on major control areas.	5 (71%)	0 (0%)	2 (8%)	7 (14%)

Accounting Systems and Internal Controls

13. The evaluation of the orderly and efficient conduct of business by client, including adherence to management policies.	4 (57%)	0 (0%)	2 (8%)	6 (12%)
14. The evaluation of policies and procedures to safeguard assets.	4 (57%)	8 (50%)	2 (8%)	14 (29%)
15. The evaluation of policies and procedures to prevent or detect errors and irregularities.	4 (57%)	8 (50%)	3 (12%)	15 (31%)
16. The evaluation of the policies and procedures to secure the accuracy and completenes of the accounting records.	3 (43%)	7 (44%)	2 (8%)	12 (24%)
17. The determination of the controls that could be relied upon should compliance tests indicate low error rates.	4 (57%)	4 (25%)	3 (12%)	11 (22%)
18. The documentation of the system only to the extent needed to gain an understanding and develop an audit program which concentrates on substantive testing.	4 (57%)	1 (6%)	3 (12%)	8 (16%)

Special Internal Control Factors

19. The determination of the existence and adequacy of safeguarding controls.	4 (57%)	3 (19%)	3 (12%)	10 (20%)

Preventive Controls

20. The evaluation of the division of dutiesa of client staff.	4 (57%)	5 (31%)	2 (8%)	11 (22%)

Protection of Records and Assets

21. The evaluation of the policies and procedures to safeguard records and assets (e.g., recovery procedures, and detection of unauthorized access to assets & records).	4 (57%)	7 (49%)	4 (15%)	15 (31%)

EDP Control Environment

22. The evaluation of segregation of duties between EDP department and related user department.	4 (57%)	4 (25%)	2 (18%)	10 (20%)

TABLE 1 (Continued)

	Accounting Firm			
	1	2	3	Total
23. The evaluation of sufficiency of policies and procedures pertaining to access to computer, terminals, magnetic storage media, and documentation.	4 (57%)	7 (44%)	3 (12%)	14 (29%)
24. The evaluation of development controls concerning the design and testing of new systems.	4 (57%)	6 (38%)	4 (15%)	14 (29%)
25. The evaluation of controls entirely dependent on manual procedures.	4 (57%)	5 (31%)	3 (12%)	12 (24%)
26. The evaluation of the controls dependent upon a combination of manual and computerized procedures.	4 (57%)	5 (31%)	6 (23%)	15 (31%)
27. The evaluation of the existence and adequacy of EDP application controls: input, processing, and output controls.	4 (57%)	6 (38%)	6 (23%)	16 (33%)
Compliance Tests of Pertinent Controls				
Nature, Timing, and Extent of the Tests of Accounting Control Procedures that Leave an Audit Trail				
28. The estimation of the degree to which a client segregates incompatible functions of its staff.	4 (57%)	5 (31%)	3 (12%)	12 (24%)
29. The determination of adequacy of segregation of incompatible functions within the data processing department.	4 (57%)	3 (19%)	5 (19%)	12 (24%)
30. The determination of the degree of segregation between data processing and user department personnel performing review procedures.	4 (57%)	2 (13%)	5 (19%)	11 (22%)
31. The determination of adequacy of control over access to data and computer programs.	4 (57%)	3 (19%)	4 (15%)	11 (22%)
32. The evaluation of the propriety of the performance of the procedures.	4 (57%)	0 (0%)	2 (8%)	6 (12%)
33. The evaluation of the results of the tests during the interim period.	4 (57%)	2 (13%)	4 (15%)	10 (20%)
Audit Sampling for Compliance Tests				
34. The definition of error or deviations in relation to the tests objectives.	4 (57%)	0 (0%)	3 (12%)	7 (14%)
35. The definition of the sampling item in relation to the control procedure to be tested.	4 (57%)	0 (0%)	3 (12%)	7 (14%)
36. The selection of the sampling method (random selection, stratified random sampling, sampling with probability proportional to size, systematic sampling to be used.	4 (57%)	1 (6%)	5 (19%)	10 (20%)
Evaluation of Compliance Test Results				
37. Based on the results of compliance procedures, the evaluation of the adequacy of internal controls, and determination of the degree of reliance which is appropriate.	4 (57%)	2 (13%)	6 (23%)	12 (24%)
38. If reliance on a particular internal control is not appropriate, the ascertaining as to whether there is another control which would satisfy the purpose.	4 (57%)	1 (6%)	3 (12%)	8 (16%)
Substantive Tests of Transactions and Balances				
General Procedures				
39. The assessment of the risk of material misstatement associated with a given specific account area and a given audit objective.	4 (57%)	1 (6%)	2 (8%)	7 (14%)
40. The determination of the quality of audit evidence required to limit the risk to an acceptable level.	4 (57%)	1 (6%)	5 (19%)	10 (20%)
41. The selection of substantive audit procedures appropriate in view of the risk assessment.	5 (71%)	3 (19%)	7 (27%)	15 (31%)
Substantive Test Procedures for Fixed Assets				
42. The review of relevant accounting principles for propriety and consistency.	4 (57%)	0 (0%)	2 (8%)	6 (12%)
Substantive Test Procedures for Payroll and Related Costs				
43. The review of relevant accounting principles for propriety and consistency.	4 (57%)	1 (6%)	1 (4%)	6 (12%)
44. The review of disclosure of pensions and other benefit plans.	4 (57%)	2 (13%)	1 (4%)	7 (14%)
Forming an Opinion				
General Considerations				
45. The assessment of the adequacy and appropriateness of the scope of the audit.	4 (57%)	0 (0%)	1 (4%)	5 (10%)

the greatest. However, beyond this observation, the data do not provide general characteristics common between these audit tasks. As discussed in the final section, this is an issue for future research.

Second, although the tasks chosen in most sections do not seem to present a clear pattern, the tasks selected consecutively in some parts present a striking pattern. For example, the risk assessment part in the Orientation phase indicates a pattern of consecutive tasks selected. Similarly, the accounting systems and internal controls and the EDP control environment parts in the Preliminary Evaluation of Controls present a recognizable pattern of consecutive tasks. The whole phase of Compliance Tests of Pertinent Controls is another example as is the general procedure part of the Substantive Tests of Transactions and Balances. The data suggest that large-scale KESs could be developed to tackle the tasks in a systematic and interrelated manner for these consecutive tasks.

Most other parts of the audit fail to indicate a clear pattern of consecutive tasks chosen for KES development. For example, from some 168 tasks in the substantive procedures parts of the substantive tests of transactions and balances phase, only three tasks were selected for KES development. Most tasks in the substantive test parts (e.g., "the confirmation of physical quantities held by third parties") are mostly subject to human processing. This indicates that, unlike the consecutive tasks identified in other parts for KES development, small scale KESs may be sufficient to tackle just a few tasks identified in substantive test phase of the audit.

4.2. ACCOUNTING FIRM EFFECTS

The data presented in Table 1 indicate that a larger proportion of subjects from accounting firm 1 voted for the KES tasks than the other two firms. To formally study this issue, the data in Table 1 are summarized by phases of the audit and by the participating accounting firms as presented in Table 2. Table 2 also provides the total number of tasks in each phase of the audit. The KES column indicates the number and the corresponding percentage of the tasks selected for KES development. The total number of responses and the corresponding percentage to total possible responses for each accounting firm is also presented for every phase of the audit. The column titled "Total" shows the total number of responses along with the proportion of all subjects supporting the tasks selected for KES development. The final column presents the chi-square values for tests of differences in

TABLE 2
Accounting Firm and Audit Phase Effects

Phases of the Audit	Tasks		Responses From Firm				
	Total	KES	1 n = 7	2 n = 16	3 n = 26	Total n = 49	Chi-square
Orientation	45	10 (22%)	32 (46%)	33 (21%)	41 (16%)	106 (21%)	29.31
Preliminary Evaluation of Controls	41	17 (41%)	67 (58%)	81 (30%)	56 (13%)	204 (27%)	76.25
Tests of Pertinent Controls	34	11 (32%)	44 (57%)	19 (11%)	43 (15%)	106 (21%)	81.10
Tests of Transactions and Balances	171	6 (4%)	25 (59%)	8 (8%)	18 (12%)	51 (19%)	61.22
Forming and Opinion	23	1 (4%)	4 (57%)	0 (0%)	1 (4%)	5 (11%)	19.80
Total	314	45 (14%)	172 (55%)	141 (20%)	159 (14%)	472 (21%)	

Chi-square [5, 3] = 28.599; degrees of freedom = 8; significance = <.001.

accounting firm responses.

Table 2 lists only the first five phases of the audit because no task in the last phase, financial statement reporting, qualified under the two criteria to identify a task for KES development. However, some tasks in the financial statement reporting phase received a few responses in support of KES development. The vast majority of the tasks in the final two phases of the audit were viewed as subject to strict human processing rather than subjects of decision aid development.

This resulted in consideration of the 314 tasks in the first five phases of the audit of which 45 tasks were identified as candidates for KES development as presented in Table 2. Some 55% of the subjects from firm 1 supported the choice of these tasks as opposed to only 20% of responses from firm 2 and 14% of responses from firm 3. The responses ranged from 43% to 60% in firm 1, 0% to 30% in firm 2, and 4% to 16% in firm 3. These responses were significantly different (at the .001 Level of significance) for every phase of the audit using the chi-square test of independence (Gibbons, 1976, pp. 325-330). Thus the data indicate a significant firm effect. The firm that consistently showed a significantly larger proportion of auditors selecting the KES tasks, is a semi-structured firm in Kinney's (1986) firm structure classification.[1] Firm two is an unstructured firm and firm three is a structured firm. Implications of this evidence will be discussed in the final section.

Overall 21 % of subjects chose 10 tasks for KES development in the Orientation phase. 25% of the subjects chose 17 tasks in the preliminary evaluation of control phase. 20% of the subjects chose 11 tasks in the compliance tests of pertinent control phase, 17% of subjects chose

6 tasks in the substantive tests of transactions and balances, and 10% of the subjects chose one task in the forming an opinion phase. The grand average was 21% of subjects choosing 45 tasks for KES development.

4.3. EFFECT OF AUDIT PHASES

As Table 2 shows, the proportion of tasks chosen for KES development in each phase was different from other phases. The range was from only 4% of the substantive tests of transactions and forming an opinion phases to 22% of the tasks in the orientation phase to 32% of the tasks in the compliance tests of pertinent controls to 41% of the task in the preliminary evaluation of controls phase. As reported earlier, no portion of the tasks in the financial statement reporting phase qualified under the selection criteria. The chi-square test of independence was used to formally analyze the data for the effect of audit phases. The results of this test are shown in the last line of Table 2. As expected, the KES choices for the five phases were significantly different at the .001 level (chi-square = 28.599).

5. Summary and Conclusions

This study provided a systematic method of identifying applicable decision aids for a comprehensive inventory of audit tasks. Forty nine very experienced auditors identified tasks as candidates for knowledge-based expert systems development from a list of 332 major audit tasks. Table 1 provides the resulting detailed list of candidates for KES development in need of further research and development. The study also provides summary information on effect of different factors such as accounting firm and phase of the audit on the results.

A significant firm effect was observed indicating that the subjects from the semi-structured firm (per Kinney, 1986, classification) consistently selected more tasks for KES development than the other subjects. This evidence indicates opportunities for further research studying the correlation between audit structure and KES research and development.

Another firm effect observation in the study is that the firm representing a significantly greater proportion of responses in support of KES for tasks selected may be promoting the use of decision aids in its audit process. However, the number of participants from this firm was only seven and the respondents were all from the executive office of the firm. The latter issue may indicate that auditors with more policy making authority may be more in support of KES development. This issue needs further study.

Another interesting observation was that further classification of the subjects and a detailed analysis of the data indicated that auditors who specialized in EDP and/or high technology audits chose a fewer number of tasks for KES development than other auditors. This preliminary observation poses some interesting questions worthy of future research. What does the evidence indicate? Is KES more appealing to fewer EDP and/or high technology auditors or is it that the EDP/High technology auditors are more aware of the complexity of KES development and as such are being more realistic about practicalities of KES development? Future studies are needed to provide answers to these questions.

Finally, detailed data also indicated that, partners may be more in support of KES than managers. Future study is needed to investigate this issue further, and provide explanation for the effect. Given the magnitude of this research, some unavoidable limitations were present that provide for further study. For example, the sample limitations in this study (49 subjects from three accounting firms) indicate that future research should expand the sample to include more subjects representing more accounting firms. To do this, a subset of tasks identified in this study should be subjected to detailed study to investigate the general characteristics of KES tasks.

APPENDIX A:
Definitions of Various Phases of the Audit

The following definitions relate to the five phases of the audit model presented in Felix and Kinney (1982).

I. ORIENTATION

Orientation may be broadly defined as the gathering of information about the client and the environment in which the client operates. As such, the orientation process can be regarded as a prerequisite to the development of a planning scheme at a strategic level. In the orientation step, the auditor gains knowledge of the geographic, economic, and industrial setting of the client organization, the nature of the client's operations the competence and ethics of managerial and financial personnel and the nature and characteristics of the accounting or financial reporting systems of the client (Felix & Kinney 1982).

II. PRELIMINARY EVALUATION OF INTERNAL ACCOUNTING CONTROLS

This evaluation is based on observation and inquiry involving a walkthrough of various types of individual transactions to establish that prescribed procedures are understood and applied. Basically, this is an assessment of the error-generation propensities of the various components of the client accounting system. Error-generation propensities are related to the auditor's assessment of the quality of the design of the internal accounting controls and the likely compliance of system operation with the design (Felix & Kinney, 1982).

III. COMPLIANCE TESTS OF PERTINENT CONTROLS

The purpose of compliance tests is to provide reasonable assurance that the accounting control procedures are being applied as prescribed. Such tests are necessary if the prescribed procedures are to be relied on in determining the nature, timing, or extent of substantive tests of particular classes of transactions or balances, but are not necessary if the procedures are not to be relied on for that purpose (AICPA, 1977, AU320.82). This was the definition provided to the subjects for this section. Although section 320 is now replaced by SAS 55 (AICPA, 1988), the essence of the definition still applies.

IV. SUBSTANTIVE TESTS OF TRANSACTIONS AND BALANCES

The purpose of substantive tests is to obtain evidence of the validity and propriety of the accounting treatment of transactions and balances or, conversely, of errors or irregularities therein. Substantive tests are applied when the auditor's purpose is to see whether the dollar amount of an account balance is materially misstated. Thus, substantive tests are used to obtain evidential matter.

V. FORMING AN OPINION

After reevaluation process is carried out for all components of the financial statements, the evidence from all of the components is, according to current practice, aggregated subjectively. As a result of this subjective aggregation process, the auditor is in a position to express an opinion in the auditor's report on the financial statements taken as a whole. An auditor report formally communicates the auditor's conclusion on the presentations of financial statements and concisely states the basis for that conclusion (Felix & Kinney, 1982).

VI. FINANCIAL STATEMENTS REPORTING

Although the auditor issues the audit report, management is responsible for the financial statements including related notes and supplementary data, whether contained in a document prepared by the client or submitted by the auditor. Even if the auditor drafts the financial statements and/or supplementary data, client management should either agree to accept the responsibility, or make such revisions as are considered appropriate (KPMG Peat Marwick, 1987).

** The authors gratefully acknowledge the constructive comments provided by an anonymous reviewer. This paper draws its data from a database developed under a generous grant from the Peat Marwick Foundation's Research Opportunities in Auditing Program to the first author. The views expressed are those of the authors and do not necessary represent the views of the KPMG Peat Marwick Foundation. Requests for reports should he sent to Mohammed J. Ahdolmohammadi, School of Accounting, Bentley College, Waltham, MA 02254.

ENDNOTE

1. Audit structure relates to the level of standardized audit methodology used by the firm; the more standardized the audit methodology, the higher the structure classification of the firm.

REFERENCES

Abdolmohammadi M.J., *A Taxonomy of Audit Task Complexity for decision aid development.* Unpublished working paper, Bentley College, Waltham, MA., 1990.

————, Decision support and expert systems system in auditing: A review and research directions. *Accounting and Business Research* **18,** 1987, pp. 173-185.

———— and A. Wright, *Criteria for developing decision aids in auditing.* Paper presented at the North East Regional Meeting of the American Accounting Association, Hartford, CT., 1987.

AICPA., *Codifcation of statements on auditing standards,* New York: American Institute of Certified Public Accountants, 1977.

————, *Statements of auditing standards, Number 55: Consideration of the Internal Control Structure in Financial Statement Audit.* New York: American Institute of Certified Public Accountants, 1988.

Ashton, R.H., *Research in audit decision making: Rationale, evidence, and implications* (Research Monograph No. 6). (Vancouver: Canadian Certified General Accountants Research Foundation, 1983.

———— and J.J. Willingham, Using and evaluating audit decision aids. In R.P. Srivastava & J.E. Rebele (Eds.), *Auditing Symposium IX Proceedings of the 1988 Touche Ross/University of Kansas Symposium on Auditing Problems* (pp. 1-25) Lawrence, KS: University of Kansas Printing Service, 1988.

Bailey, A.D. Jr. and K. Hackenbrack, P., De, and J. Dillard, Artificial intelligence, cognitive science, and computational modeling in auditing research: A research approach. *Journal of Information Systems,* **1**(2), 1987, pp. 20-40.

Bedard, J., G.L. Gray, and T.J. Mock, Decision support systems and auditing. *Advances in Accounting,* 1984, pp. 239-266.

Chandrasekaran, B., Expert systems: matching techniques to tasks. In W Reitman (ed.), *Artificial intelligence applications for business.* Ablex Publishing Co., 1984, pp.41-64.

Cushing, B.E., and J.K. Loebbecke, *Comparison of audit methodologies of large accounting firms* (Studies in Accounting Research No 26). Sarasota, FL: American Accounting Association, 1986.

Elliot, R.K., and J.A. Kielich, Expert Systems for Accountants. *Journal of Accountancy,* **160,** 1985, pp. 126-134.

Felix. W.L. Jr., and W.R. Kinney, Jr., Research in the auditor's opinion formulation process: State of the art. *The Accounting Review,* **LV11**(2), pp. 245-271.

Kinney, W.R., Jr., Audit technology and preference for auditing standards. *Journal of Accounting and Economics,* 1986, pp. 73-89.

Gibbons, J.D., *Nonparametric methods for quantitative analysis.* Holt, Rinehart and Winston, 1976.

Hansen, J.V., and W.F. Messier, Jr., A preliminary test of EDP expert. *Auditing: A Journal of Practice and Theory,* **6,** 1986, pp. 109-123.

Keith, J.R., *Expert systems in auditing: A practitioner's perspective.* Paper presented at the 1985 Price Waterhouse auditing symposium, Lake Tahoe, CA., 1985.

KPMG Peat, Marwick., *Audit Manual-US,* New York: KPMG Peat Marwick, 1987.

Messier, W.F. Jr., and J.V. Hansen, Expert systems in accounting and auditing: A framework and review. In S. Moriarity & E Joyce (Eds.), *Decision making and accounting: Current research,* Norman, OK: University of Oklahoma, 1984, pp. 182-202.

————— and ————, Expert systems in auditing The state of the art. *Auditing: A Journal of Practice and theory,* 1987, pp. 94-105.

O'Leary, D.E., Validation of expert systems with applications to auditing and accounting expert systems. *Decision Science,* **18,** 1987, pp. 468-486.

—————, and P.W. Watkins, Review of expert systems in auditing. *Expert Systems Review,* **2,** 1989, pp. 3-22.

Pitz, G.F. and N.J. Sachs, Judgment and decision: Theory and application. *Annual Review of Psychology,* **35,** 1984, pp. 139-163.

Shpilberg, D., and L. Graham, Developing ExperTAX: An expert system for corporate tax accrual and planning. *Auditing: A Journal of Practice and Theory,* **6,** 1986, pp. 75-94.

—————, ————— and H. Schatz, ExperTAX: An expert system for corporate tax planning. *Expert Systems,* **3,** 1986.

Stefik, M., J. Aikens, R. Bazler, J. Benoit, L. Birnbaum, F. Hayes-Roth, and E. Saceroti, The organization of expert systems, A tutorial. *Artificial Intelligence,* **18,** 1982, pp. 135-173.

Tversky, B., Parts, partonomies, and taxonomies. *Developmental Psychology,* **25,** 1989, pp. 983-995.

An Evolving Conceptual Organization Schema for Database Systems

CHING-DING HSU

Introduction

The development of conceptual organization schema of database systems should be directed toward meeting both users' needs and changes in organization needs by simply modifying or expanding the capacity of an existing system. An evolving organization schema enables management, with limited computer knowledge, to update users' conceptual schema of the database system by modifying the organization schema. A trend of designing applications for the evolving structure of conceptual organization schema in today's database systems is unavoidable. Alloway and Quillard (1983) surveyed managers' needs on computer-based information systems and found a big difference between supply of and demand for the inquiry systems.[1] The inquiry systems occupied only 12% of the installed computer application systems, but the survey showed that managers made the greatest demands on it in number of requests.

Most of today's database system research is focused on increasing the understandability and usability of the conceptual schema such as the integrity, availability, and shareability of data (see Davis & Olson, 1985) or the semantic relationship among the data (Afsarmanesh & McLeod, 1984). Few researchers have discussed the system's ability to adapt to changes in the system without requiring extensive modifications, i.e., robustness. In particular, the dynamic nature of users' needs, especially at the management level of the logical structure, has not been thoroughly identified. Although organization schema is more stable than user schema, environmental and operational directions of an organization change from time to time, causing the change in organizational needs. Once an organization changes its needs, it may find that the current capacity of its database system fails to match these changed needs. Moreover, it is not a simple task to modify the system.

A database system has an evolving conceptual organization schema if that schema can be changed in certain directions. The word "evolving" is used here as an associated interpretation of dynamic, changeable, modifiable, and improvable. An organization must have a database system in which its organization schema can be transformed from a lower or simpler structure to a higher or more complex state by management itself. The term "schema" is often used as a synonym for view, model, or diagram (Davis & Olson, 1985, p. 98). A conceptual schema is the out of a database design process that specifies the system's static and dynamic structures (King & McLeod, 1984). The conceptual organization schema serves as an intermediate stage between the user schema and real world events and then specifies the static and dynamic nature of the system that will fulfill organizational and management needs (Chen, 1977). In other words, the conceptual organization schema specifies the input and output of an organization's database system and describes the data elements and relationships to be included in data specifications for the whole organization.

Motivation for developing new concepts in designing the conceptual organization schema is twofold. First, either the current applied database systems are so general and flexible that users must possess a certain degree of computer programming knowledge to design the system structure or operate the system, or the systems are so specific that organizational needs and users' operation functions have been assumed in the packages and are very difficult to modify. Second, a big lag exists between the supply for and a demand of an evolving database system.

Organization Structures and Need

Although some users' needs, such as friendliness, natural language interface, output format specification, and ease-of-use, have been incorporated into the development of modern database systems, users' needs related to organization needs, i.e., management needs, have seldom been completely identified and integrated into these systems. Alloway and Quillard's (1983) survey of managers' needs from computer-based information systems revealed that not only do managers make strong demands on the inquiry systems, but that the invisible backlog for inquiry systems was 739% greater than the known backlog. This inability to integrate management's potential needs has been particularly significant given the dynamic structure of organizational needs and of the environment surrounding the organization.

Leifer (1988) categorizes several types of computer-based information system architectures, and links each type of organization structure with a system architecture that not only specifies the organizational needs but also enables the organization to be more effective and successful in using the system. He states that matching information system design to the organization design will determine the success of using that system inside the organization. Leifer also mentions that if a database system does not have the capacity to change its functions to match the organization's directions, the organization may need to change its structures to fulfill its needs. Under this circumstance, an organization's operations may be limited to its system's available capacity.

Certainly, the costs of changing an organization's structures are much higher than the costs of changing the system's functions. In particular, changing organizational structure to more adequately match the system architecture is neither easy nor quick. Matching the system structure to the organization is more cost-effective. Thus, it is wise for management to adopt a database system that can match organization's needs and the dynamic nature of its surroundings.

Changing organizational directions happens more often for the simply structured organization with stand alone database systems than for other types of organization. However, large organizations and their divisions will also face a need to change their directions sooner or later. For example, merging or adding new business functions may require modification of current database systems. Many organizations, such as divisionalized and professional bureaucracy, have very stable needs. These large organizations are more likely to use decentralized or distributed systems, with each division's needs identified and incorporated into the system. Such organizations seldom change their needs suddenly. In particular, these organizations should have system experts who can modify the database systems when organizational needs change. However, according to Delone's (1988) study, 98.2% of the organizations in the United States qualify as small business. Most of them are small, young, simply structured, and must be ready to change their directions to match changes in their surroundings if they want to survive.

DeLone (1988) also found that top management's knowledge of computers is the primary factor in an organization's successful use of its systems, but management's limited programming knowledge may be inadequate to solve problems and modify the system to meet user needs. Management may need to rely on database designers to modify the codings of system modules or of the entire system. In this case, the loss of information or its delay during transmission may reduce system efficiency. In particular, most organizations cannot afford to install new systems every time their structure changes.

Evolution of Database Systems

Historically, database systems have shifted from hierarchical (Haseman & Whinston, 1976) to network, and to relational database systems (Codd, 1970; and Everest & Weber, 1977). Recently, the concept of entity-relationships has been broadly applied to the design of accounting database systems (Chen, 1977; McCarthy, 1979; Mantha, 1988). In the early years of database research, system designers first tried to identify the needs of the users and of the organization. They would then build these needs hierarchically into the system structure because they thought that the organization structure was hierarchical. Soon, they discovered that integrating the system structure of the organizational needs with the relationships inside an organization is beyond the capacity of a hierarchical database model. The cross-relationships, parallel or hierarchical, of the organizational needs were captured and incorporated into the network database models. However, not until the early 70s did different users' needs begin to be identified. Hierarchical and network database systems had difficulty fulfilling the varieties of users' needs because both systems lack the flexibility to adapt to the changes in both the organization and the users' needs.

A relational database system is the most flexible database system and has the broadest applications in the current market. Data is stored in a large sharable table according to certain attributes (see Codd 1970). Users can construct the database systems according to their own needs for manipulating the data and interrelate the events after they have identified the interrelationships among the data and the events. Nonetheless, a problem in using relational database systems is that most users lack the programming knowledge to design the system. Because an organization may need to rely on system designers to develop its database system, users and system designers should consult with each other to ensure that user and organizational needs have been integrated into the system. The system designers may not be familiar with the management decision processes so they may, sometimes, rely on their own intuition or experience when designing an accounting database system.

Further, Chen (1977) introduced the concept of designing entity-relationship database systems to define the organization (or enterprise) schema and unify the organization needs. The user schema is usually not a direct representation of the real world. This makes the user schema difficult to understand and difficult to change. The organization schema serves as an intermediate stage in the database design process and can be translated into different types of user schemata to fulfill different users needs. Different users of a database system may have different views of the database, but an organization should have a unique and consistent view of the database system.

Chen assumed that an organization's needs are known, and that the relationships among the entities inside an organization could be interrelated and constructed in the database system. The data is organized into entity sets according to the homogeneous relationship of data in each entity set. Different types of relationships may exist among entity sets. A relationship set is a set of relationships of the same entity type that will integrate all entities and entity sets together to represent the dynamic and static environment structure of an organization. Recently, Mantha (1987) found that system designers can successfully specify the entities and attributes as well as their relationships to construct a database system using data structure concepts.

Dual-User Schema

Database systems users in organizations are either management or staff. Dual-user needs exist for developing an organization's database system because the tasks and responsibilities of management and staff are different. Generally, management is responsible for designing, planning, and controlling systems, while staffs are responsible for data entry and daily routine operations. Management users integrate organizational needs into the system with the help from the system (database) designers and may need to modify the data types and data relationships or the system structures as well as task functions when the organization's objectives change. End-user needs related to the changes must be known in advance and incorporated into the system so that the system's capacity can meet organizational needs in the future. On the other hand, data entry duty is tedious and mistakes are easy to make. Staffs need a regular pattern in routine work to reduce errors.

Accordingly, from users' viewpoint, two schemata should exist in the conceptual structure of a database system: the user schema and the organization schema (Chen, 1977). Both kinds of users—staff and management—can process data using the user schema. However, only authorized management users can access the organization schema (see Figure One). In current database systems, user schema have been well developed, but the dynamic needs and structure of organization schema are not similarly developed. User schema is usually designed to be efficient for a certain type of data processing operation. Whereas, organization schema is designed to optimize the data processing operations and serve organizational needs. The features of organization schema will be discussed in the next section.

Mainly, user schema is for staffs who need to perform data entry and routine everyday maintenance work. Independence may exist among each user schema. The structure of these user schemata should be easy to use, user friendly, able to detect human errors, and have a help function to assist the users when they need it. Moreover, it is not necessary for users to possess basic accounting knowledge such as the concepts of double-entry bookkeeping or end-of-month adjusting entries, but they should be able to follow certain routine procedures to perform the task. Changes in user schema should not necessarily affect the structure of organization schema. But the change in organization schema should certainly affect user schema because the output design processes of the system have been modified. A database system should be flexible enough to accommodate all the features and interrelationships of these two schemata.

However, most of the currently available database packages are either relational database models or general entity-relationship database models (see McCarthy 1979 and Weber 1986). Drawbacks exist when using these models. Management and system designers need to construct a database system together for the organization if using relational database packages. System designers could develop a system that meets the organizational needs and that can be updated, but most management do not have the programming expertise necessary to transmit changes of organizational needs into a machine. Thus, management may need to rely on system designers in constructing, developing, and updating the system.

In general entity-relationship accounting database packages that meet organizational and users' needs have been assumed and incorporated into the system. Usually, changing user schema in these packages requires changes in the system structure as well as in the relationships among the data and the data types in addition to data and events. Although modifying organization schema is much simpler than modifying user schema, the modification of organization schema will influence user schema. Thus, management must possess a certain degree of programming and database knowledge to modify these schemata. In this case, if an organization needs only to modify the system or recode the codings to fit its needs, it may incur higher costs for the company and cause timing problems in its daily operations.

The Evolving Conceptual Organization Schema

In addition to the end-users' viewpoint, from the system's functional viewpoint, a database system has two major structures: logical structure (or conceptual schema) and physical structure (Bonczek, Holsapple, & Whinston, 1978; and King & McLeod, 1984). The logical structure identifies the data type, the relationships among data and data type, the environment events, and the relationships among, as well as between, the events and the data. The physical structure is a collection of data values organized on the basis of the logical structure (Bonczek et al., 1978). Furthermore, from a system design viewpoint, a database should have two major structures: design schema and conceptual schema (King & McLeod, 1984). Design schema represents the environment as a set of process events using a high-level programming language. These events are interrelated according to organizational needs. Design schema will be mapped into a conceptual schema. Then the process events will become the application events in the conceptual schema. The conceptual schema describes the manner in which information is structured and manipulated in the application environment from the users' perspective. Conceptual schema can be further classified into conceptual user schema and conceptual organization schema according to end-users' needs. Users' needs are identified and integrated into either the conceptual user schema or the conceptual organization schema, whereas organizational needs and the interrelationships between the organization and its environment would be incorporated into the conceptual organization schema.

Figure One shows the interrelationships among a database system,

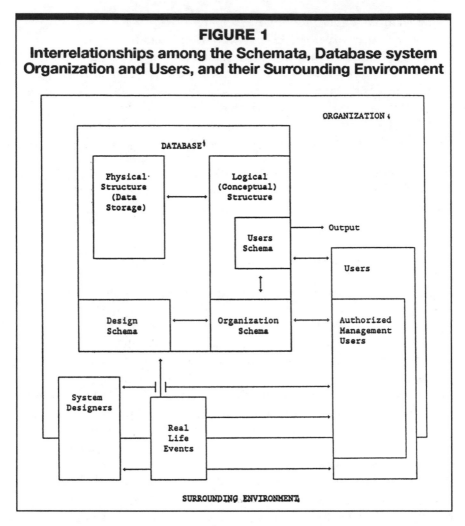

FIGURE 1

Interrelationships among the Schemata, Database system Organization and Users, and their Surrounding Environment

the organization and users, and their surrounding environment. The interrelationships among the physical structure, logical (conceptual) structure, users' schema, organization schema, and design schema inside the database system are also discussed. Users—staff and management—and system designers work inside an organization and also are exposed to the environment surrounding the organization. Users and system designers learn the real-life events both inside and outside the organization from its surrounding environment. Real-life events that interrelate with the organization are programmed into the design schema by system designers after the system designers consult with users to identify users' and organizational needs. The dynamic nature of future real-life events that related to the organization should also be incorporated into the organization schema to fulfill the changes of management needs in the future.

System designers interface with the design schema using a high-level programming language. These events, then, will be mapped into the conceptual organization schema. However, at the designing stage, only present real-life events need to be mapped into the user schema to improve system efficiency. Data, events, and interrelationships between data and events should be identified in the conceptual organization schema using data structure technique. The value of data will be stored in the physical structure of the system and organized according to the foundation designed in the conceptual schema. The output design process of the system is constructed after the present real-life events have been incorporated into the organization schema and transferred to the users' schema. Users interface with the conceptual schema to input the data and acquire the output information. Only authorized management users have the password to access the special functions in several specified modules inside the organization schema and to modify the system's output design process through the users' schema.

The organization schema should fulfill organizational needs at the present time and in the near future. Thus, organization schema must represent real-world events, including the dynamic structure of the environment—future events. This representation of real-world events may be independent from the data storage. Management can alter certain functions in the user schema by performing the predefined commands in the organization schema. Dramatic changes in the future organizational environment may require installation of a new system because of the limited system capacity. However, intermediate management needs should be achievable through the current system.

According to the above discussions, an evolving conceptual organization schema is an organization schema that has several event modules which enable authorized users to modify the output design process of the system in the user schema through defined functions in these modules. Such event modules are, for example, the output format specification of invoices, reports of accounts receivable, periodic financial statements, etc. Each events module represents a set of the interrelated real world events. The objects and the application events related to the organization are all defined in the conceptual organization schema according to users' requirements in terms of the information process and flow. If organization schema must be changed to reflect the changes of organizational environment, the changes should be easily performable by management. Moreover, management's needs related to an organization's future changes and interests should also be considered and mapped into events modules in the organization schema—such as adding or dropping a line, expanding from wholesalers to retailers, or expanding to other types of business—in the organization schema. In addition, management could alter the conceptual schemata with or without limited help from the system designers.

The change in conceptual organization schema should also update conceptual user schema so that user schema can be adapted to the environmental changes through the events modules in the organization schema. Changes in the organizational environment and operating events will require a change in the user schema. Authorized users should not have to understand programming languages to change the system's source codes. Rather, they will follow certain query procedures to modify the conceptual organization schema. The schema should be implemented with a high-level query capacity that allows the schema to be used by those who are unfamiliar with it or have limited programming knowledge. Management users should be able to follow instruction manuals with a specific class of queries to accomplish their needs regarding the output design of the system, such as the changes in report formats and the preparation of different periodic or continuous reports. Moreover, this change should not affect the configuration of data storage and operation efficiency of the system (Chen, 1977). Security protection is required so that only authorized management can access this schema and modify the system structure when changes in organizational needs have been identified.

The conceptual organization schema should also be flexible to meet the timing of management needs. With the help of computer technology, several traditional accounting bookkeeping procedures such as end-of-period adjustment requirements can be improved. For example, continuous reports can be generated at any time. Using manual accounting systems requires a company to close all accounts once a month so that the accounts will be ready for use in the next period. A computerized database system should not be limited to this constraint. The system should be capable of posting and closing the accounts when needed so that continuous or periodic reports for any time period can be presented to top management, without influencing the preparation of external reports. An organization should be able to have external or internal reports weekly, biweekly, bimonthly, or for any particular time period. Periodic reports can be acquired without disturbing normal system operations.

Conclusions

In database system designs, real-world events of an organization should be identified and modularized into the conceptual organization schema of the system. While most database system research has focused on understanding and using the conceptual schema of the system, the dynamic nature of organizational needs has been ignored. Because of rapid innovation and new technology, changes in organizational needs may reveal the inefficiency and insufficiency of current database systems.

Three viewpoints of system architecture—users, system design, and system functions—in designing a database system have been discussed. An evolving conceptual organization schema is needed for contemporary database systems. The conceptual organization schema should contain several events modules that would allow users to alter the output design of user schema through the designed functions in the conceptual organization schema when organizational needs have been changed. Because most of the users are not database specialists, the change in conceptual schemata should not affect the design schema of the system and should follow high-level query procedures so that management can manipulate the system without deep knowledge of programming languages. Security control of the use of organization schema and flexibility to meet the timing of management need should also be considered.

This paper discusses only changes in organizational needs and the concepts of designing an evolving conceptual organization schema. Detailed techniques for using advanced computer programming knowledge to design the system have not been mentioned. In addition, detailed knowledge of database specialties needed in integrating all management and organizational needs into the evolving system is also ignored.

ENDNOTE

1. Alloway and Quillard classified computer-based information systems into four different types—monitor, exception, inquiry, and analysis—according to the systems' functions. They defined the

inquiry system as a database with flexible inquiry capacity, enabling managers to design and change their own monitoring and exception reports.

REFERENCES

Afsarmanesh, H. and D. McLeod. "A Framework for Semantic Database Models," *Proceedings of NTU Symposium on New Directions for Database Systems,* May 1984.

Alloway, R.M. and J.A. Quillard. "User Managers' Systems Needs," *MIS Quarterly,* June 1983, pp. 27-41.

Bonczek, R.H., C.W. Holsapple, and A.B. Whinston. "Aiding Decision Makers with a Generalized Data Base Management System: An Application to Inventory Management," *Decision Science,* 1978, pp. 228-244.

Chen, P.P.S. "The Entity-Relationship Model: A Basic for The Enterprise View of Data," *Proceedings of AFIPS Conference,* 1977, National Computer Conference, June 1977.

Codd, E.F. "A Relational Model of Data for Large Shared Data Banks," *Communications of the ACM,* Vol. 13, June 1970, pp. 377-387.

Davis, G.B. and M.H. Olson. *Management Information Systems Conceptual Foundations, Structure. and Development,* 2nd Edition, McGraw-Hill, 1985.

DeLone, U.H. "Determinants of Success for Computer Usage in Small Business," *MIS Quarterly,* March 1988, pp. 51-61.

Everest, G.C. and R. Weber. "A Relational Approach to Accounting Models," *The Accounting Review,* April 1977, pp. 340-359.

Haseman, W.D. and A.B. Whinston. "Design of a Multidimensional Accounting System," *The Accounting Review,* Jan. 1976, pp. 65-79.

King, R. and D. McLeod. "A Unified Model and Methodology for Conceptual Database Design," M. Brodie, J. Mylopoulos, and J. Schmidt, (editors), *On Conceptual Modeling: Perspectives from Artificial Intelligence, Databases, and Programming Languages,* Springer-Verlag: 1984, pp. 313-331.

Leifer, R. "Matching Computer-Based Information Systems with Organizational Structures," *MIS Quarterly,* March 1988, pp. 63-73.

Mantha, R.W. "Data Flow and Data Structure Modeling for Database Requirements Determination: A Comparative Study," *MIS Quarterly,* December 1987, pp. 531-545.

McCarthy, W.E. "An Entity-Relationship View of Accounting Models," *The Accounting Review,* October 1979, pp. 667-686.

Weber, R. "Data Models Research in Accounting: An Evaluation of Wholesale Distribution Software," *The Accounting Review,* July 1986, pp. 498-518.

The Integrated Use of First-Order Theories, Reconstructive Expertise, and Implementation Heuristic in an Accounting Information System Design Tool

WILLIAM E. McCARTHY AND
STEPHEN R. ROCKWELL

I. Introduction

First-generation expert systems concentrated to a large degree on modeling of human cognitive processes. This means that the knowledge structures embedded in such systems were primarily restricted to those which directly emulated the heuristic methods by which a human decision maker would attempt to control the complexity involved in solving a given problem. By contrast, second generation systems attempt to incorporate knowledge structures of both the heuristic and non-heuristic type into their consultation sessions.

This paper describes the integrated use of different types of expertise in a second-generation tool which presently is being prototyped at Michigan State University in the Department of Accounting. This system is called REACH, and its detailed functioning is described by McCarthy and Rockwell [1988a]. REACH is designed to aid in the process of database design in general and in the subprocesses of view modeling and view integration in particular. To do this, REACH uses three kinds of *accounting domain* knowledge:

1. First-order theories of accounting derived from conceptual analysis of accounting practice and accounting theorists,

2. Reconstructive expertise of accounting system implementors largely derived from textbook descriptions of "typical" bookkeeping systems, and

3. Implementation heuristic for construction of events accounting systems derived from the experiences of the authors in such work.

For its entire consultation process, REACH must also avail itself of both methods knowledge (of data modeling, normalization, structured analysis, etc.) and target system knowledge (of possible hardware restrictions for example). However, such use is described elsewhere ([McCarthy and Rockwell, 1988b], [Loucopoulos and Harthoon, 1988], and [Ryan, 1988]), and we intend to concentrate here on the integrated use of the different types of domain knowledge in REACH.

The remainder of this paper is organized as follows. Section two describes the process of structured database design in an accounting context and the REACH approach to problem solving in this arena. Section three describes in more detail the different types of domain knowledge enumerated above. Although this system is still in its prototype construction phase, we give here some simple examples of problem solving for each type. Section four concludes with a summary and a discussion of future directions.

II. Design of Shared Environment Accounting Systems

Virtually all business enterprises have accounting information systems which track the inflow and outflow of economic resources (like inventory and cash) and which allow periodic compilations of company profitability. In their most primitive forms, such systems comprise account classifications and bookkeeping conventions which accommodate paper and pencil tracking of financial transactions. In their more modern forms, these systems consist of various computer files and programming modules such as general ledger systems, payroll systems, accounts-receivable systems, etc.

In a shared data environment in which non-accounting decision makers need common access to economic transaction information, most computerized accounting and bookkeeping systems are found wanting, and a need becomes apparent for a process which will redirect the design of these systems toward a database orientation. Such a design process is described in McCarthy et al. [1989], and the embedding of its knowledge structures in a CASE tool is the goal of the REACH implementation. A summary for the accounting systems design process involved here is illustrated in Figure 1 and explained below.

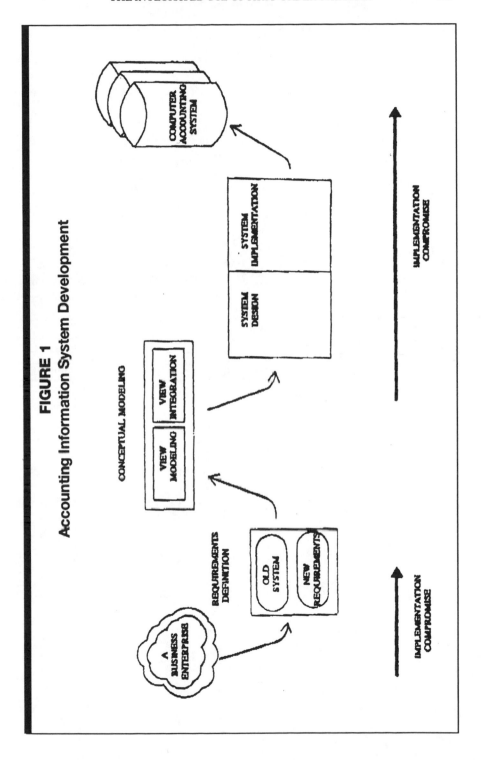

FIGURE 1
Accounting Information System Development

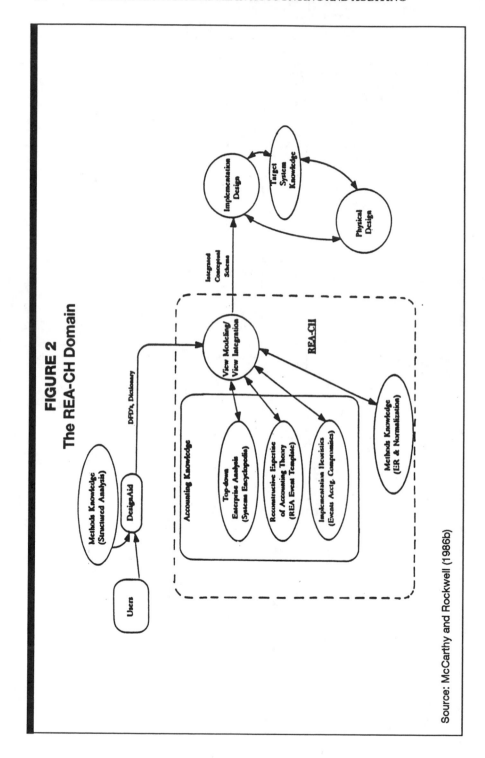

FIGURE 2
The REA-CH Domain

Source: McCarthy and Rockwell (1986b)

Accounting information system design begins with a desire to model the economic events, resources, and agents of a given business enterprise, and it ends with a specified and implemented computer system. Not all aspects of the business enterprise need to be captured in the formal information system, and most characteristics actually have little or no decision or accountability use (for example, the number of bricks in a company's headquarters building or the romantic interludes among its employees). The implementation and design process then is one of compromise (what to leave out) as it proceeds from start to finish.

In the REACH CASE tool, we are using a systems methodology adapted from structured analysis (DeMarco [1978]) and conceptual database design (Lum et al., [1979]). The requirements definition phase of this methodology begins the process of implementation compromise by extracting both old and new requirements from potential users and by documenting those requirements formally with the structured analysis tool **DesignAid** [NASTEC, 1988]. As illustrated in Figure 1, we then proceed into conceptual database modeling, a phase in which we attempt to temporarily suspend the process of implementation compromise through the use of first-order accounting theories and reconstructive enumerations of "typical" system elements. Beginning again with the later phases of view integration and proceeding to final implementation, implementation compromise resumes its central focus. Some of REACH's knowledge structures work here as well by dictating directions for leaving out certain types of conceptual components of events accounting systems.

The actual implementation domain of REACH is illustrated in Figure 2. Our tool works only in the second step of the four step database design process outlined by Lum et al. [1979]. We assume that requirements definitions are completely finished with a tool like DesignAid and handed to us in the form of data flow diagrams (DFD) and a data dictionary. REACH output consists of an integrated schema which is given to an implementation team for translation into a particular DBMS environment. Within REACH, three kinds of accounting knowledge structures are utilized, and it is this utilization that we turn to next.

III. Representation of Domain Knowledge

REACH aids the database design steps of (1) view modeling and (2) view integration [Teorey et al., 1986; Batini et al., 1986]:

1. **View modeling** takes a list of data elements (from a DFD data store or a potential user "wish list") and expresses them in the form of a conceptual Entity-Relationship (E-R) scheme [Chen, 1976]. A *view* consists of the actual data elements needed for a particular computer program to be run or for a particular decision to be made. Judgments involved in view modeling include the identification or reconstruction of entities, relationships, and attributes within the data set and correct specification of them in E-R form.

2. **View Integration** takes a series of modeled views and iteratively combines them into one integrated E-R scheme for the entire business enterprise. Judgments involved in this process include resolution of inconsistently-named data structures, identification of combination and/or integration bases for various views, and decisions either to omit some previously identified elements or to add some previously unidentified elements.

In a certain way, view modeling and view integration can be conceived as analogous to the process of combining certain chemicals (with known desirable properties) into a compound which will meet a variety of needs in an integrated fashion. The first step involves correct specification of the individual components, while the second step involves correct identification of inconsistent or superfluous elements and a process for seamless integration.

At the present time in our REACH implementation, we are using frame-based representation techniques (Fikes and Kehler [1985]) with **GoldWorks** [Gold Hill, 1988] to bring the three distinctly different types of accounting knowledge enumerated earlier to bear on the conceptual modeling process. In the subsections below, we summarize these various components.

a. First order theories of events accounting systems. Our conceptual starting point for the design of shared environment accounting systems is the REA model illustrated in Figure 3 (McCarthy [1982]). This "accounting event template" was derived both by semantic analysis of current practice and by appeal to the ideas of well known accounting theorists such as Ijiri [1975] and Mattesich [1964]. Its name is derived from the essential components of the transaction template which are its economic resources, events, and agents. The REA framework derives from fundamental accounting principles such as "accountabili-

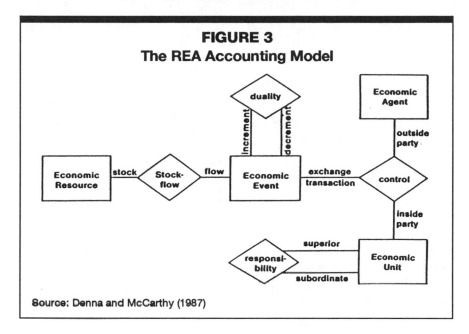

FIGURE 3
The REA Accounting Model

Source: Denna and McCarthy (1987)

ty" and "duality" which characterize the tracking of economic events in a business enterprise setting. REACH is a software system designed to augment CASE support for REA-Oriented accounting system design.

A view modeling consultation session in REACH is structured around a specific instance of an REA event type. Users are guided in their interpretation of view elements by this template, and they are also encouraged to use their own judgment in augmenting or reorienting a given set of data names. In a sense what they are asked to do (among other things) is to interpret the situation in front of them as a specific instance of a known constellation of entities and relationships. What these users will often find is that a given set of data elements is incomplete and misinterpreted in light of this theoretical framework because of unapparent implementation compromise.

During view integration, the REA template is used to guide model synthesis by identifying "intersection points" between views. For example:

- every increment event needs to be paired with a decrement event via a duality relationship and vice-versa; therefore, a view of sales order processing is linked to a view of remittance advice processing via a **cash receipt** *pays for* **sale** interpretation,

- every resource must have both inflow and outflow events;

therefore, sale order processing in a retail enterprise could be linked to purchase order processing via a **purchase** *is inflow* to **inventory** *has outflow of* **sale** interpretation,

- economic units are arranged in responsibility hierarchies; therefore, a view of sale order transaction processing could be linked to a regional sales report view via a **salesperson** *is assigned to* **sales region** interpretation.

The exact demarcation between knowledge supplied by the tool (REACH) and judgment supplied by the consulting user is a problem we have yet to fully explicate. We hope however, that the general principles of first-order theory use are apparent.

b. Reconstructive expertise of accounting system implementors. In the bookkeeping days of fifty years ago, part of an accountant's expertise would be the knowledge needed to design a chart of accounts (i.e., a declarative classification structure) and a set of bookkeeping procedures for a particular company. These accountants either carried in their head or had book access to "a journal and ledger template" for a particular type of business enterprise. Thus for instance, a good accountant would be able to identify an adequate chart of accounts for a particular store, for a particular funeral home, for a particular hospital, etc. before he or she even visited the actual establishment. Quite obviously, this framework would be tempered and altered by actual experience, but it would serve an invaluable role in summarizing the past experiences of knowledgeable experts in the field and in preventing sins of omission (as opposed to discouraging sins of commission) in accounting system design.

Reconstructive expertise of the type explained above is being built into REACH. For a given set of industry types, we are using Pescow's [1976] Encyclopedia of Accounting Systems which provides managerial advice, sample charts of account structures, and representative bookkeeping procedures by industry classification. We are transforming this advice into entity-based enterprise models and using them during view integration in lieu of the "management view" starting point often advocated by database theorists. This means that the industry entity template becomes the overall conceptual schema to start with and that view integration proceeds by adding individual modeled views onto it. There are certainly definite needs for this industry template in the view modeling process, but we are deferring that implementation to a later prototype stage.

c. Implementation heuristic for events accounting systems. A full events accounting system is a theoretical ideal which realistically would never be implemented. Nobody would keep full event histories perpetually unless storage technologies become absolutely costless and methods for abstracting from detail become absolutely painless. Event system implementation involves essential compromise (i.e., throwing both intensional and extensional database features away). Since this process is inevitable, we are attempting to provide in REACH heuristic guidance gleaned from our own considerable experience in events implementations. Some examples are explained below and illustrated in Figure 4.

1. **Temporal aggregation of event histories.** In cases where detailed transaction histories are not needed, the effect of flow events can be aggregated in attributes of economic resources or agents. Faced with the implementation of the data model in Figure 4(a) for example, an implementor could choose to not keep receipts and disbursements as separate entities and to only aggregate their effects in cash accounts. Such a decision would presume no decision usefulness to the event histories, a situation which might not be warranted in an enterprise using certain types of quantitative cash management models.

2. **Representation and use of a subset or superset.** In many decision cases, it makes more sense to maintain and use entities at either a more specific or a more general level than an REA interpretation might specify. Two examples of such use are portrayed in Figure 4(b). If sale orders become either filled or unfilled depending upon inventory circumstance, most of the decision usefulness accrues to the unfilled subset. Therefore, only that specific component would be declared and used. In a similar fashion, certain kinds of limited-credit companies might not need to view sales and cash receipts as different entities, only as revenue cycle transactions. In this second case, declaration only of the appropriate superset would be appropriate.

3. **Substantive non-implementation or procedural-declarative tradeoffs for entity sets.** The maintenance of certain REA components can be dismissed on a substantive basis if there is no decision need for their data. Certain firms might not need

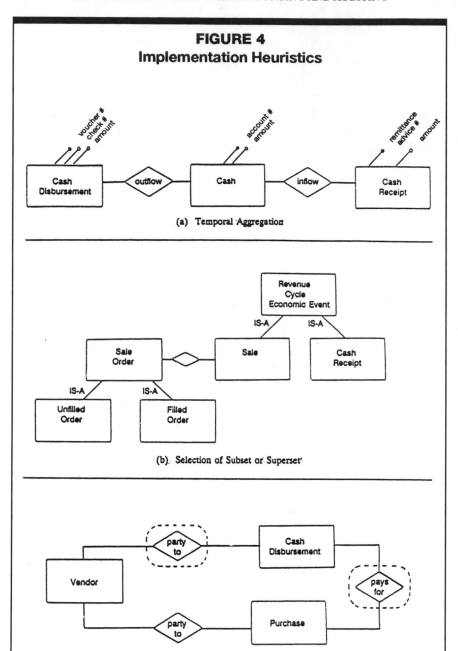

FIGURE 4
Implementation Heuristics

(a) Temporal Aggregation

(b) Selection of Subset or Superset

(c) Substantive Non-Implementation or Procedural Tradeoff

inside agents for example if they don't track financial responsibility for costs or revenues. Similarly, if the decision use for certain types of relationship connections is infrequent, it might make more sense to materialize those connections procedurally rather than maintaining them declaratively. In Figure 4(c), the "pays for" relationship might be dismissed substantively if the company tracks payables only by amount. Similarly, the "party to" relationship is one that could be materialized monthly from the rest of the structure if there was no more compelling use for its maintenance.

Within REACH, we are attempting to provide heuristic guidance of the type described above by having diagnostic questions posed to the user after view integration. The answers to these questions guide implementation suggestions. In a more advanced type of system which we hope to be working on in the future, knowledge of these heuristics would be embedded in the view modeling stage to guide the process of "reverse engineering" of present data files. Such guidance would attempt to identify instances where past system designers have made implementation compromises which might not be warranted in present circumstances.

IV. Summary and Future Directions

Second-generation expert systems avail themselves of a much wider array of knowledge structures than do first generation systems, and in that sense, they allow designers to be very ambitious with regard to final objectives. Our approach to the task for which REACH will provide consultation support—events accounting system design with a pervasive emphasis on suspension of implementation compromise—is one that no present human actually does. It would require detailed expertise in all three areas of domain knowledge described in this paper. In our present REACH prototype, we are attempting to implement a limited set of the structures described. For example,

- our first-order REA theory is being used during view modeling in only a forward engineering sense and we are concentrating initially on the most commonly occurring accounting transaction cycles;

- our reconstructive enterprise models are being used only during view integration and we are using just 4-5 industry types in our initial system;

- we are using just five types of implementation heuristics and delaying incorporation of others to later system versions; and

- we are delaying integration of methods knowledge (for both structured analysis and semantic database design) unless it is essential to prototype functioning.

In the future, we intend to remove many of the limitations described above. This is especially true with regard to the integrated use of the three domain knowledge types in a manner that spans all conceptual database modeling phases. In our present design, we integrate the different types in simple pairwise fashion either in view modeling or in view integration but not in both. We also plan to integrate our system seamlessly with a structured analysis CASE tool like DesignAid and to use parts of database design tools like DDW [Reiner et al., 1986] and MAST-ER [Batini and Ferrara, 1986] in support of our analysis and design consultations.

The REACH project is a very ambitious one. The design or reengineering of business accounting systems is one of the most common types of software engineering tasks, and there is a tendency to think that most of the problems in this arena have already been solved. This is decidedly not true, especially if one considers database environments where shared decision use of economic transaction data is a vastly undeveloped area. Most knowledge-based use of accounting data at present concentrates almost exclusively on account dollar analysis of the type illustrated in FSA [Mui and McCarthy, 1987]. We believe that we have a methodology, a theory, and a tool to design events accounting systems which will far surpass the limited capabilities of computerized "journal and ledger" implementation. The key to the automated support of such design is the integrated use of the knowledge types described in this paper.

REFERENCES

Batini, C., M. Lenzerini, and S.B. Navathe (1986), "A Comparative Analysis of Methodologies for Database Schema Integration," *ACM Computing Surveys*, December 1986, pp. 323-64.

———. and F.M. Ferrara (1988), "An Integrated Architecture for CASE Systems," *Proceedings of the Second International Workshop on Computer-Aided Software Engineering*, Cambridge, Mass., July 1988, pp. 1-7 to 1-12.

Chen, P. P. (1976), "The Entity-Relationship Model—Toward a Unified View of Data," *ACM Transactions on Database Systems,* July 1976, pp. 9-36.

DeMarco, Tom (1978), *Structured Analysis and Systems Specification,* Prentice Hall, 1978.

Denna, E. and W.E. McCarthy (1987), "An Events Accounting Foundation for DSS Implementation," in C.W. Holsapple and A.B. Whinston, *Decision Support Systems: Theories and Application,* Springer-Verlag, 1987, pp. 239-43.

Fikes, R. and T. Kehler (1985), "The Role of Frame-Based Representation in Reasoning," *Communications of the ACM,* October, 1985, pp. 904-20.

GOLD HILL (1988) *Goldworks Programmer Reference Manual,* GOLD HILL, Cambridge, MA., 1988.

Ijiri, Y. (1975), *Theory of Accounting Measurement,* American Accounting Association, 1975.

Loucopoulos, P. and C. Harthoorn (1988), "A Knowledge-Based Requirements Engineering Support Environment," *Proceedings of the Second International Workshop on Computer-Aided Software Engineering,* Cambridge, Mass., July 1988, pp. 13-10 to 13-14.

Lum, V. S., G. M. Schkolnick, D. Jefferson, S. Su, J. Fry, T. Teorey, and B. Yao (1979), "1978 New Orleans Data Base Design Workshop Report," Research Report RJ2554, San Jose, California: IBM Research Laboratories, 1979.

Mattessich, R. (1964), *Accounting and Analytical Methods,* Irwin, 1964.

McCarthy, W. E. (1982), "The REA Accounting Model: A Generalized Framework for Accounting Systems in a Shared Data Environment," *The Accounting Review,* July 1982, pp. 554-78.

———— and S. R. Rockwell (1988a), "On the Embedding of Domain Knowledge in Automated Software Engineering Tools: The Case of Accounting," *Proceedings of the Second International Workshop of Computer-Aided Software Engineering,* Cambridge, Mass., July 1988, pp. 2-15 to 2-18.

———— (1988b), "REACH: An Active CASE Tool Linking Accounting Domain Knowledge with View Modeling and Integration," Working Paper, Michigan State University, October, 1988.

———— and H. M. Armitage (1989), "A Structured Methodology for the Design of Accounting Transaction Systems in a Shared Data Environment," *Proceedings of the Fifth Structured Techniques Association Conference,* Chicago, IL., May, 1989.

Mui, C. and W. E. McCarthy (1987), "FSA: Applying AI Techniques to the Familiarization Phase of Financial Decision Making," *IEEE Expert*, Fall 1987, pp. 33-41.

NASTEC (1988), Design Aid User Guide, NASTEC, Southfield, Mi., 1988.

Pescow, J. K. (ed.),(1976), *The Encyclopedia of Accounting Systems*, Prentice Hall, 1976.

Reiner, D., G. Brown, M. Friedell, J. Lehman, A. McKee, P. Rheingans, and A. Rosenthal (1986), "A Database Designer's Workbench," *Proceedings of the Fifth International Conference on Entity Relationship Approach*, Dijon, France, November 1986, pp. 347-60.

Ryan, K. (1983), "An Experiment in Capturing and Classifying the Software Developer's Expertise," *Proceedings of the Second International Workshop on Computer-Aided Software Engineering*, Cambridge, Mass., July 1988, pp. 13-29 to 13-32.

Teorey, T. J., D. Yang, and J. P. Fry (1986), "A Logical Design Methodology for Relational Databases Using the Extended Entity-Relationship Model," *ACM Computing Surveys*, June 1986.

Validating Expert Systems with Complex Outputs: The Case of Audit Planning

J. EFRIM BORITZ AND
ANTHONY K.P. WENSLEY

Introduction

This paper describes a comprehensive validation approach for validating expert systems designed to produce outputs of the complexity of audit plans, which consist of numerous components, many interdependencies among those components, and many alternative solutions.[1] In addition, this paper describes the approach adopted to validating CAPEX, a knowledge-based system for audit program planning, and reports on the validation results. The development of appropriate validation methodologies is important for a number of reasons:

- From both a pragmatic and a research standpoint such a methodology can be a useful tool for validating processes which generate multivariate outputs such as audit program plans regardless of how they may be generated; i.e., whether by knowledge-based systems, conventional programs, or even manual systems based on forms and tables.

- Knowledge-based systems (KBSs) can be powerful research tools in their own right provided that they have been adequately verified and validated. For example, once validated, an audit planning KBS can be used to explore the impact of alternative heuristics for determining the reliability of audit evidence-gathering procedures. Another potential research application for such a system is to use it to investigate the

69

impact of using different approaches for combining the uncertainties associated with audit planning objectives.

- Many accounting firms are looking to use knowledge-based systems for supporting audit decision making. Clearly, an investment in validation of such systems will be required to warrant their use in practice.

In the past, validation tests of auditing expert systems have been primarily unidimensional. As O'Leary (1987, p. 475) points out, the number of correct responses obtained in a decision situation, often used to measure quality of human decisions, has also been the criterion used to validate expert systems. For instance, in the case of materiality, Steinbart [1985] was concerned to establish that the materiality values provided by his expert system were of an appropriate magnitude. Dungan [1983] was concerned that the provisions which had been made for bad debts were appropriate. These unidimensional approaches to validation are likely to be inappropriate when investigating the richness of outputs provided by an audit planning expert system.

It is well known that in any given audit situation there may be a large number of equally acceptable audit strategies. For example, placing more emphasis on one aspect of an audit (e.g., substantive testing) can compensate for less emphasis previously placed on another aspect of the audit (e.g., internal control testing). Even in the construction of a substantive audit plan, there are many alternative procedures and mixes of procedures that may be used. For example, doing more interim work (e.g., sales and cash transaction stream testing) can compensate for less year-end work (e.g., accounts receivable confirmations and alternate procedures for nonresponses).

Unlike some expert systems which are used to produce a single judgment, or a very small number of outputs (e.g., overall audit risk, materiality, etc.), a system that produces an entire audit plan results in a multivariate array of outputs. For example, CAPEX was designed to produce an audit plan consisting of a listing of suggested audit procedures, their timing and their extent. To adequately test the performance of CAPEX, it was necessary to identify appropriate performance variables and design instruments to elicit judgments from experts concerning these variables. This paper describes the approach used to validate the components of CAPEX and its suggested plans.

There is a considerable research literature which addresses validity and verification issues in the social sciences [Brinberg and McGrath,

1982, 1985], simulation [Shannon, 1975], and software engineering [Martin and McClure, 1985; Geissman and Schultz, 1988]. However, until relatively recently (see, for example, O'Leary, 1986, 1987, 1988; Klein and Mathlie, 1990) little of this work has been examined for its relevance to expert systems research.

O'Leary [1987] uses primarily the social sciences research tradition to develop an analysis of a variety of different types of validity and construct a validation "framework" which he subsequently uses to examine the extent to which previously developed expert systems in accounting and auditing have been validated. Although he considers many important aspects of expert systems validation O'Leary does not provide a detailed critique of previous expert systems validation methodologies or provide detailed guidance as to how a validation methodology should be developed for a particular expert system.

Hollnagel [1989] also provides a detailed analysis of the concept of validation. In addition he considers a variety of different validation techniques and investigates the appropriateness of each technique and ways in which the reliability and validity of the technique may be increased. Bonnet et al. [1988] provide a detailed description of a validation methodology using Turing-type tests paying particular attention to the manner in which the tests are administered.

The validation methodology developed in this paper only uses part of O'Leary's [1987] framework since we are concerned with a somewhat more restricted definition of validation. Since the instruments which have been developed for the validation tests involve a variety of different types of expert assessment, Hollnagel [1989] is a source of useful insights. In particular he suggests that experts should be called upon to compare the performance of expert systems to that of other experts and that explicit criteria should be established for performance assessment. For example, in a medical context, Yu et al. (1979) found that a group of expert evaluators who agreed with the diagnosis of an expert system 75% of the time were themselves rated at a 70-80% level by other experts. On the strength of these results, the investigators concluded that the expert system matched the performance of the "best" experts in the field.

Finally, we have taken account of the issues raised by Bonnet et al., most particularly those relating to the creation of the information sets which are used as the basis for any validation tests. They caution that any validation methodology must ensure that such information sets provide a sufficiently rich basis for eliciting expert behavior. In addition they propose methods which can be used to ensure that both the system and the experts are provided with the identical information.

While O'Leary [1987] discussed a number of previous approaches to validating expert systems in accounting and auditing, he did not explicitly consider the need to develop multidimensional approaches to validation, particularly in the domains of accounting and auditing. One reason for this omission may be that the validation work he reviewed related to expert systems whose performance could be measured using univariate approaches. When expert systems generate "rich" outputs whose essential nature can only be characterized multidimensionally, the validation process must itself become significantly more complex. In these cases, it becomes necessary to address the following questions:

1. What are the variables which appropriately characterize the outputs being generated by the system?

2. What instruments can be used to provide measurements of these variables?

3. How reliable are these instruments?

4. If it is not possible to measure the relevant variables directly are the variables which can be measured reliable and valid?

5. How competent are the assessors in making the types of judgments that they are required to make in order to provide the necessary assessments of the variables?

The first part of this paper discusses the concepts of verification and validation from a general perspective, including the deficiencies of the approaches used hitherto. The second part concentrates on the approach adopted to verify and validate CAPEX, using it as an illustrative case study/example of the comprehensive approach required to validate a complex knowledgebased system with multivariate outputs.

The Processes of Verification and Validation

The model of audit knowledge developed in this research is in the form of a computer program. Thus, it would seem appropriate to initially investigate the concepts of verification and validation from the standpoint of software engineering. Although O'Leary [1987] concluded that traditional software validation techniques were inappropriate for expert systems and proposed an alternative approach based on research design principles, we believe that it is necessary to review these techniques, particularly those derived from software engineering, for a number of reasons:

1. Systems engineering provides a basis for making a clear distinction between verification and validation. We believe that this distinction, often glossed over in expert systems research, is an important one to recognize if robust validation methodologies are to be developed for expert systems.

2. Software engineering stresses the need for clear and precise specifications to be established for any computer program. There are good reasons for its being difficult to provide such specifications for expert systems (see below). However, since the strength of any validation tests depends on the precision of the performance specifications there is a need to develop specifications which are as precise as possible.

3. As expert systems are increasingly based on "deep" knowledge of a domain it becomes both possible and increasingly necessary to develop formal specifications for these systems.

Formal methods developed by software engineers distinguish between verification and validation:[2]

- *Verification:* the correctness and completeness of the processes whereby software specifications are converted into software.

- *Validation:* the processes which determine whether the initial requirements correctly and completely specify the behaviors which the user(s) wanted the system to have.

One way of clarifying the differences between the two concepts is provided by Diagram 1.1. This diagram demonstrates that computer systems are constructed to satisfy some set of user requirements. In order to construct the system in the first place it is necessary to translate the user's requirements into a set of system specifications. Once these specifications have been established, the system can be developed. Generally speaking the greater the confidence we have in the processes which are used to map from system specifications to the completed code (labelled SYSTEM in Diagram 1.1) the less we need to be concerned with verification tests which check whether the system meets the specifications established for it. Similarly, the greater the confidence we have in the processes which are used to map from user requirements to system specifications the less we need to be con-

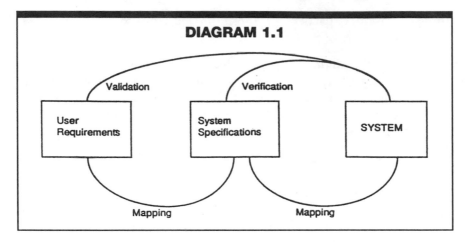

DIAGRAM 1.1

cerned with validation tests which seek to determine the extent to which the system satisfies user requirements.

Computer systems and programs have a particular internal structure. Some verification tests may involve investigating this structure **statically;** i.e, simple inspection or comparison with system specifications. However, it is often necessary to investigate the actual behavior of the system or program. That is, the internal structure can also be investigated **dynamically,** by investigating the types of behavior, in terms of intermediate results, processes invoked, and outputs which result from providing the system or program with a variety of different sets of input information. Verification of computer systems and programs generally requires both static and dynamic testing.

Developing extensive and reliable verification tests for expert systems may not be possible for a number of reasons:

1. A particular set of users is not explicitly identified for an expert system; hence, little, or no attempt is made to identify user requirements. Thus, it is very difficult to demonstrate that the mapping between user requirements and system specifications is accurate.

2. Even if a set of users has been identified, system specifications are often very vaguely defined. This causes problems with respect to verifying that higher level requirements are accurately translated into lower level requirements. It also creates significant problems with attempting to determine whether an expert system is meeting its specifications and thus reduces the strength of any validation tests which can be applied to the system.

3. Development methodologies for expert systems are relatively undeveloped and untested. Thus little confidence can be placed in their reliability.

In addition to verification tests, it is almost always necessary to also perform validation tests on a computer program. In some situations it may only be necessary to perform very limited validation tests. If it is possible to elicit, and refine, user requirements in a form which can be translated into system specifications in a straightforward manner, then it may be sufficient to show that the system which has been developed meets these specifications. Thus, the overall confidence that user requirements are satisfied will be high if:

1. The confidence level that user requirements have been accurately mapped to system specifications is high, and

2. The confidence level that the system actually developed meets system specifications is high.

Each of these confidence levels is a combination of the confidence levels associated with the relevant mapping process and the confidence level associated with the verification or validation tests which have been performed.

The importance of validation tests for expert systems is heightened because, even when some attempt is made to refine user requirements they are usually at a different logical level to system specifications. Usually, system specifications relate to the content of the expert systems knowledge base rather than the behavior which is expected of the system. It is tacitly assumed that behavior which will satisfy user requirements will be generated using a system which contains some representation of domain knowledge, either constructed in concert with experts or obtained from other sources.

In this type of situation it is possible to perform verification and validation tests defined in the following way:

1. Verification = Determining that the knowledge which is encoded in the knowledge-base corresponds to the knowledge which has been specified in the system specifications.

2. Validation = Determining whether the knowledge possessed by the knowledge sources corresponds to the knowledge specified in the system specifications.

However, if the overall user requirements are a system which exhibits certain behaviors which are typical of individuals possessing a particular level of expertise. Thus, it becomes critical to establish a robust validation methodology for investigating the behavior of the system. Since, in our opinion, this type of validation is critical to the overall confidence that we are able to invest in a particular expert system we have concentrated on its elucidation in this paper.

A variety of other problems arise with respect to developing validation tests for expert systems which typically do not arise in traditional validation situations. Usually, validation involves comparing the behavior of a system to the behavior of the actual system being modeled. However, in the case of many expert systems the comparison has to be made subjectively. Addressing this issue O'Leary [1987] advocates that the performance of expert systems should be compared to the performance of other models wherever possible. While this criticism may be appropriate in some limited circumstances, it fails to recognize that expert systems are most likely to be developed when there are no other practical alternatives. Therefore, in most domains in which it is sensible to develop an expert system in the first place, the ultimate arbiter of the quality of the solution provided by such a system is an expert or set of experts. It is unlikely that there would be other models of similar complexity to that embedded in the expert system in question.

In the current context, CAPEX encodes a variety of different types of knowledge about audit planning. Thus, in a broad sense, it encodes a theory of audit planning and specific data which can be used, along with the theory, to generate behavior. In this case the behavior of the system involves the construction of an audit program plan. At the present time we possess insufficient knowledge to be able to assess the validity and other properties of an audit program plan objectively. It is necessary to rely on experienced audit planners to provide these assessments.

Using experts to assess the performance of expert systems raises a number of important methodological questions which have rarely been addressed in the verification and validation literature.[3] For instance:

- What types of information do experts require to be able to assess the performance of either other experts or an expert system?

- How skilled are the experts selected at judging the behavior of others?

- What instruments should be used to elicit assessments?

- How reliable and/or valid are the assessments which are obtained using different instruments?

A variety of other characteristics of typical expert systems also create difficulties for designing and conducting validation tests. For example, if an expert system is built to satisfy the user requirements of the following form:

> Expert system **A** should exhibit behavior consistent with that exhibited by individuals with an expertise level **X** given a variety of different information sets.

What is meant by the term behavior? One important aspect of behavior relates to the output provided by the expert or the system. Thus, in the context of audit planning it is to be expected that the system generates certain types of audit program plans given certain types of input. However, this seems hardly sufficient to characterize the richness of the term behavior. There are also **process** dimensions. That is, experts do not generate audit program plans at random. They follow some generally accepted set of processes. These processes also are based on some generally accepted knowledge both of auditing and the general environment within which they are operating. Both of these types of behavioral specifications need to be explicated in much more detail.

Another aspect of the preceding type of specification is that the notion of expertise level needs considerable exploration. To what extent is it possible to identify a variety of different expertise levels? Do they overlap? Is it possible to identify, with any degree of accuracy, what expertise level a particular individual has achieved? At the very least some attempt must be made to specify expected expertise levels and develop ways of measuring the expertise level of the resulting system.

The expertise level exhibited by any expert system depends on a variety of factors, most importantly, (1) the content of the knowledge base and (2) the heuristics used in processing the knowledge in the knowledge base. Thus, to generate a system to meet the specifications it is necessary to construct a knowledge base and set of heuristics which have been provided by individuals whose expertise level is equal to, or greater than, the expertise level which has been specified in the initial specifications.

An additional problem arises if the solution itself does not indicate the level of expertise, but requires an explanation to, in some sense, validate the solution. In other words, the line of reasoning used in developing a given solution may be more important than the actual solution itself. Similarly, in some circumstances expertise may be evidenced not so much by the solution itself, but by the response of the individual to slight perturbations of the initial conditions which were used to develop the initial solution.

ESTABLISHING VALIDATION CRITERIA

It has generally been the case that relatively little about expert systems has been formally specified. This occurs primarily because the structure of the model which is implemented in an expert system is often insufficiently articulated. Some aspects of the model may, however, be amenable to precise specification and hence it is possible to perform verification tests to determine whether they have been correctly and completely implemented in the expert system's knowledge base. Generally speaking, such verification tests can only provide very limited confidence concerning the extent to which the system satisfies user requirements. Thus, it becomes critical to develop comprehensive and robust validation methodology as a basis for validating the system.[4]

One approach to elaborating expert system requirements and thereby establishing verification and validation criteria is to consider four different types of more detailed requirements/specifications: those relating to inputs, those relating to the knowledge encoded in the expert system's knowledge base, those relating to the process by which input data is transformed into output data, and, finally, the nature of the system's outputs.

Input Requirements

It is important to establish requirements with respect to the nature of the input information which an expert system is expected to process. Informally, this may be defined as all information which can be textually represented, or all information which may be provided by a variety of sensors, etc. Rarely are formal attempts made to establish detailed input requirements.

One of the problems with establishing input requirements for expert systems is that it is seldom known, with any degree of accuracy, what inputs experts use.[5] This type of restriction is particularly problematic when the desire is to construct an expert system which is designed to model the process by which experts solve a particular class of problems.

In the context of the current research the input requirements for the system can be stated informally as follows:

> Each information set $[I_i]$ used as a basis for investigating the behavior of an expert system should provide sufficient information to enable an experienced auditor to generate a competent audit program plan.

At the very minimum this type of requirement necessitates extensive pretesting of the information sets to ensure that they do provide sufficient information.

Knowledge Base Structure and Content Requirements

These types of requirements address issues which concern whether the structure and content of the knowledge provided by the knowledge sources has been preserved in the expert system. Typically, the knowledge base of an expert system contains facts and rules. At the very minimum it would seem to be necessary for the system requirements to establish what type of facts should be represented by the system and the rules which define relationships between one set of facts and another. In the context of CAPEX one set of facts establishes the reliability of different audit evidence-gathering procedures. With respect to the structuring of the knowledge base rules establish the relationships which exist between financial statement items and financial statement item assertions.

In some cases it may be possible for the knowledge sources to determine the correctness of the content of a knowledge base by inspection. In other cases it may be necessary to investigate the type of behavior which arises from the interaction of the knowledge encoded in the knowledge base, the information which is input into the expert system, and the heuristics and rules which process knowledge.

Process Requirements

From a process standpoint it is necessary to distinguish between a variety of generic types of process requirements:

> Expert system **A1** which is designed to exhibit behavior which is the same as the behavior exhibited by an individual with expertise level **X** by processing a variety of information sets *in the same way as* individuals with expertise level **X** process those information sets.

> Expert system **A2** which is designed to exhibit behavior which corresponds to the behavior exhibited by an individual with expertise level **X** by processing a variety of information sets *in a way which generates valid behavior.*[6]

CAPEX is an expert system of a type similar to **A2** above. The extent to which the system exhibits behavior which corresponds to the behavior of individuals with particular levels of expertise is assessed by domain experts as is the validity of the plans which are generated.

There has been considerable debate as to the value of constructing expert systems of type **A2**. It is our contention that expert systems of this type represent testable models of a particular domain. They thus have similarities to models which are developed and tested in management science.[7] Good examples of these types of system are medical expert systems such as MYCIN (Shortliffe, 1976) and ONCOCIN (Hickam *et al.*, 1985).

It may be possible to provide formal specifications for some aspects of an expert system's processing and hence be able to perform some limited verification tests. For instance, if a Bayesian updating scheme is to be used for revising uncertainty measures represented by the system it is necessary to exhaustively test the system to ensure that it is performing Bayesian revisions correctly. This does not require the intervention of an expert.

Output Requirements

The nature of the outputs which are to be generated by an expert system depend, to some extent, on the overall requirements which have been established for the system. We are concerned here both with the type of outputs and their evaluation.

In the context of the research reported here, CAPEX was required to generate output information which was equivalent to the information which would be generated by an experienced auditor.

Approach Used to Validate CAPEX

This section of the paper introduces the approaches adopted for validating CAPEX, organized under the elements discussed above: input/output, knowledge base, and process validation.

INPUT VALIDATION

The information provided to CAPEX was in the form of several cases such as the sample case provided in **Appendix A**. These cases were written by two experienced auditors and were designed to test the competence of audit managers with specific industry experience. Each case was comprised of a significant quantity of numerical information along with different types of more judgmental, qualitative information. As part of the validation tests of CAPEX, experienced auditors were required to generate their own solutions to the cases. The cases were extensively pretested both through interaction with the case writers and by other independent, experienced auditors.

Case Preparation

Cases were developed principally by two senior managers from a large accounting firm over a period of nine months. One of the managers had considerable experience with managing audits of merchandising and manufacturing clients, while the other had managed audits of a variety of financial institutions.

The case material was patterned, as much as possible, on the type and structure of information that would be available to an experienced auditor in the firm. Inevitably, however, the case material represented a significantly less rich information set than auditors would normally be presented with in constructing an audit program plan for a real client.[8]

For the cases to constitute a strong test of CAPEX it was necessary to ensure that they contained sufficient information to "engage" the expertise of the subjects. A case which engages the individual's expertise would be expected to have the following characteristics:

- It takes a reasonable time for the expert to generate a solution. In the pretesting stage of the development of the cases, subjects were taking about one and a half hours to complete each case using a wide variety of reference material.

- The reasoning process followed during the construction of the plan may involve considerable "thinking-through" and reference to prior experience.

- The plans generated by inexperienced auditors should be markedly different from those generated by the subjects.

As the case material was developed, it was structured to conform, as much as possible, to the relevant sections of the firm's audit planning worksheet.[9] The principal worksheet required the assessment of the following types of client information prior to the construction of an audit plan:

- Corporate structure and ownership;
- Capitalization and financing;
- Nature of manufacturing or processing operations;
- Accounting, budgeting, and reporting systems;
- Marketing philosophy and methods of distribution;
- Purchasing volume;
- Management structure; and
- Corporate employees.

Each case provided information in each of these categories where the case writer and pretesting indicated that it was appropriate for the construction of revenue cycle substantive audit program plans.

The firm's audit planning worksheet required that the auditor take into account factors external to the client which might affect the appropriateness of the audit conclusions or the emphasis of the audit work. These factors were provided in the form of descriptions of the client firm's environment and that of its customers.

After documenting and considering all the above information, the auditor typically conducts a "preliminary analytical review" to identify unusual relationships to be subsequently followed up. For the purposes of the cases, it was assumed that these analytic review tests would be included in any substantive audit program plan generated either by human auditors or CAPEX.

The next stage of the firm's audit program planning process is the creation of a summary audit program plan. This plan requires that the following characteristics be identified for each account balance, or assertion, associated with each account balance:

- Assessed inherent risk (high, medium, or low);

- Planned reliance on internal controls (high, medium, low, none);

- Whether the account is critical or significant;[10]

- The substantive procedures which are to be used to achieve the audit objective(s) identified for the account balance or assertion associated with the account balance.

Next the client's internal accounting controls are assessed to determine whether the planned reliance on internal controls can be sustained and a detailed audit program plan is then prepared. The detailed audit program plan consists of detailed subplans for each account balance. Each subplan specifies a set of audit evidence-gathering procedures and their extents. Thus, the process described above results in audit program plans which are very similar in structure to those generated by CAPEX and the case writers. That is, the audit program plans which are developed by the auditors in a standard audit consist of specifications of procedures and their extents.

To ensure that the cases provided sufficient information to engage the subjects' expertise, the cases were subjected to a number of pretesting stages. The manufacturing and retail cases were tested on three different sets of auditors, while the financial institution cases were pretested using two sets of auditors. The auditors who were used in the pretesting phases had no prior exposure to any aspect of the research.

The tests consisted of requiring each set of auditors to provide "solutions" to each case in terms of suggested substantive audit program plans for the revenue cycle. The participants were also asked to "think aloud" as they worked through the cases, and a debriefing was conducted at the end of each session. Participants were particularly directed to identify information they thought was lacking and the assumptions they felt they needed to make to compensate for the missing information. As a result of these pretests, and discussions with the case writers, the cases were revised in a number of areas.[11]

A limitation of the input validation test is that the information provided in the cases was somewhat structured in its presentation and limited in its scope; however, it was not artificial. To the extent that both human and system could produce acceptable outputs in response to the information contained in the case material, it is possible to conclude that the input validation was successful.

KNOWLEDGE BASE VALIDATION

CAPEX's knowledge base consists of a number of different modules which encode a variety of different types of knowledge of audit evidence-gathering procedures to knowledge of the structure of the accounting model.[12] It is important to distinguish between the structure and the contents of a knowledge base. Knowledge encoded in CAPEX knowledge base was structured primarily according to accounting theory and convention, and the assertion-based approach to audit planning. The approaches adopted to validating the structure and contents of the modules comprising CAPEX's knowledge base are discussed separately below.

Knowledge Base Structure Validation

The Expert Systems Research Approach (ESRA) as described by Bailey, *et al.* [1987] typically involves considerable interaction between the experimenter/researcher and the knowledge providing experts. This interaction normally ensures that both the knowledge base and the computational model are validated to a considerable extent during the construction of the expert system.

Developed through extensive interaction with a number of practicing auditors, this structure was not subjected to formal validation procedures. However, the knowledge base was subjected to intensive informal validation, throughout the system development process, by the subjects whose knowledge was being encoded. On many occasions, parts of the knowledge base were also discussed with other practicing auditors. Often these discussions resulted in some aspect of the knowledge base being revised and refined.[13] Once the overall structure of the knowledge had been satisfactorily validated, the next step involved the validation of the contents of the knowledge base.

Knowledge Base Content Validation

The knowledge base of CAPEX consists of four types of knowledge: knowledge about audit evidence-gathering procedures, procedural audit planning knowledge in the form of rules which may be used to generate substantive audit program plans given the factual knowledge, judgments concerning the relevance and reliability of the evidence provided by audit evidence-gathering procedures and the costs of performing them, and heuristic rules for assessing evidence, used to select sets of audit procedures and determine their evidential "value".

The knowledge concerning procedures and their characteristics was obtained from a number of experienced auditors over a considerable period of time. The interactive nature of the knowledge acquisition methods used for obtaining the procedural knowledge ensured that the knowledge was subjected to extensive, though informal, verification.

A number of different auditors from the same auditing firm participated in providing the knowledge which is represented in CAPEX's knowledge base. Some of the planning and evidential assessment heuristics used to generate audit program plans were obtained from the research literature or firm manuals, while others were provided by experienced auditors.

Once the content of the knowledge base and the structure of the computational model had been subjected to limited validation tests, a more extensive series of tests were performed which investigated the relationship between inputs provided to CAPEX and the outputs obtained from the system, as will be described later.

PROCESS VALIDATION

Part of the validation of the process by which CAPEX constructed audit program plans was conducted informally. There was general agreement expressed by the participating experts that the approach would result in valid audit program plans. However, the main validation of the process was conducted by having independent auditors evaluate the plans produced by CAPEX, after mixing the plans produced by the system with plans prepared by other auditors, using a single blinded procedure so that the auditors did not know which plans they were assessing, nor even that they were assessing any system produced plans. The auditors involved were completely independent of the auditors who had previously been involved in the development of the system and its knowledge base.

The principal objective in the development of CAPEX was "to construct a system to integrate auditing knowledge from a variety of sources sufficient to generate audit program plans." The system was not intended to model the process actually used by auditors in generating audit program plans. Thus, an "acceptable" plan was a plan which a domain expert considered to be appropriate, given the facts of the planning situation. It would not necessarily be identical to the plan he or she would have developed in that situation. This distinction is particularly important in the domain of audit planning since, as mentioned earlier, there may be a very large number of possible combinations of audit evidence gathering procedures which will achieve the overall objectives established by the auditor.

OUTPUT VALIDATION

The information provided by CAPEX was in the form of a list of procedures and their extents, organized by financial statement item assertion to which they were applicable. The principal test performed to assess the validity of the system output was to ask the knowledge-providers to assess the performance of CAPEX using a number of cases. The cases and the questionnaire which was used to assess the performance of CAPEX are identical to those used by the independent assessors to assess the external validity of the system.

Initially the overall validation objective for CAPEX was that audit plans generated by the system should be acceptable to domain experts at least 75% of the time. This is, admittedly, a modest objective compared with the traditional significance level of 95% which is used in statistical testing. One reason for setting the objective at this lower level is related to previous research into the degree of consensus among auditors (see, for example, Ashton, 1982). The second is that the large number, qualitative level, and complexity of the assessments which have to be made make a level of 95% too stringent.

As the instruments for evaluating the performance of CAPEX were developed, it became obvious that this objective was far too general for a number of reasons. First, it concentrated exclusively on the generation of acceptable audit program plans. Even if 75% of the plans generated were acceptable, it would be necessary to investigate in what way the remaining 25% were unacceptable. A system which generates 75% acceptable plans and 25% *totally* unacceptable plans should be evaluated in a very different way from one which generates 75% acceptable plans and 25% *marginally* unacceptable plans.[14]

Second, it may be that experienced auditors not only reject system generated plans but also audit program plans produced by other experienced auditors more than 25% of the time. More generally, where a weak consensus exists with respect to a "best", or at least a "most probable", solution, the degree of consensus between experts themselves must be investigated. If this is not done, the expert system may be expected to meet objectives which no human expert in the domain can actually meet. Thus, the independent assessors were asked to evaluate both the plans generated by CAPEX and those prepared by the case developers, who were also the principal knowledge providers.

Third, considering audit program plans as either acceptable or unacceptable does not provide very much information about *why* plans are unacceptable. It is likely that individuals interpret the notion of "acceptability" in a variety of different ways. In order to reduce the danger of this happening it is necessary to provide a more detailed definition of the term.

Fourth, a particular audit program plan may be acceptable to a particular auditor because it reduces the relevant risks to a sufficiently low level but may be unacceptable because it does so at an extremely high cost.

In light of the above issues it was decided that, rather than simply asking experts whether a particular CAPEX generated plan was acceptable, they would be asked to rate its acceptability, effectiveness, efficiency, and the level of experience/competence of the preparer. Experts were also asked to identify procedures which they considered should have been included in the plan but were not, and identify any procedures included in the plan which should not have been. This information would be particularly useful for indicating refinements which might improve the performance of the system.

Development of the Output Validation Instrument

As mentioned, the independent experts were asked to assess proposed solutions on three dimensions: effectiveness, efficiency, and acceptability. In addition, they were asked to assess the competence/experience of the preparer of each solution plan evaluated. Scales were developed to assist the experts in making these assessments (refer to Figures I, II and III).

FIGURE I
Effectiveness Rating Scale

1 = Target risks would not be achieved for any of the assertions concerning the financial statement item in question.

2 = Target risks would not be achieved for most critical assertions and most noncritical assertions concerning the financial statement item in question.

3 = Target risks would be achieved for most critical and some noncritical assertions concerning the financial statement item in question.

4 = Target risks would be achieved for all critical and most noncritical assertions concerning the financial statement item in question.

5 = Target risks would be achieved (or exceeded) for all assertions concerning the financial statement item in question.

Thus, a score of 5 with respect to a particular financial statement item indicates that the audit program plan being assessed is effective at achieving risk objectives with respect to all the assertions relevant to the financial statement item in question. In contrast, a score of 1 indicates that a particular plan fails to achieve risk objectives with respect to any of the assertions relevant to the financial statement item in question.

FIGURE II
Efficiency Rating Scale

1 = There are other sets of procedures which would result in the achievement of the same level of risks with respect to the assertions concerning the financial statement item in question as those achieved by the plan but at a significantly lower cost.

2 = There are other sets of procedures which would result in the achievement of the same level of risks with respect to the assertions concerning the financial statement item in question as those achieved by the plan but at a slightly lower cost.

3 = There are other sets of procedures which would result in the achievement of the same level of risks with respect to the assertions concerning the financial statement item in question as those achieved by the plan but at approximately the same cost.

4 = There are other sets of procedures which would result in the achievement of the same level of risks with respect to the assertions concerning the financial statement item in question as those achieved by the plan but at slightly greater cost.

5 = There are other sets of procedures which would result in the achievement of the same level of risks with respect to the assertions concerning the financial statement item in question as those achieved by the plan but at significantly greater cost.

Thus, an efficiency score of 5 represents an assessment that the plan is much more efficient than any alternative of which the assessor is aware. In contrast, an efficiency score of 1 represents an assessment that the plan is much less efficient than a variety of alternative plans.

FIGURE III
Acceptability Rating Scale

1= The plan is fundamentally unacceptable and even major revisions cannot change this conclusion.

2 = The plan is unacceptable and can only be made acceptable through major revisions.

3 = The plan is generally acceptable but some significant revisions are necessary.

4 = The plan is generally acceptable but some minor revisions are necessary.

5 = The plan is acceptable without any revisions being required.

The experts were asked to make overall assessments of the plans, assessments at the financial statement item level and assessments at the financial statement item assertion level. The complete questionnaire for evaluating audit program plans is presented in **Appendix B.** A number of difficulties might be encountered when a questionnaire of this complexity is administered:

- The interpretation of scale values and the related judgments may require a level of analysis that experienced auditors are unable to provide.

- There may be significant difficulties with respect to crosssectional comparisons of assessments, since different subjects may make significantly different assumptions to make up for missing information.

- Auditors rarely develop a substantive audit program plan "cold". An audit program plan is constructed sequentially and subject to fairly extensive revisions. The expertise of the auditor is often not evidenced in the initial audit program plan, but is often exercised through creative revisions of a relatively generic default plan as more information becomes available. This may result in there being relatively little difference between plans produced by individuals with significantly different levels of competence.

- To the extent that both CAPEX and the cases were developed to investigate structured approaches to constructing substantive audit program plans, subjects may exhibit bias either for or against them according to their attitudes to structuring audit planning in the first place.[15]

The questionnaire was pretested by four experienced auditors from the same firm as the case preparers, from a different office. They were asked to informally evaluate the questionnaire for understandability and appropriateness. They all stated that they found the questionnaire generally understandable, though one subject suggested a number of wording changes. In some cases they felt that the required evaluations were rather detailed; but, on the whole, they considered them to be appropriate.

Once the instruments had been developed, pretested, and revised, the case information, the CAPEX-produced plans, and the questionnaire were presented to the developers of six test cases to assess the solutions generated by CAPEX.

The major limitation of the output validation test stems from the fact that no explanations were provided for the system-produced outputs; i.e., the system's line of reasoning was not available to the auditors. Audit plans produced in practice typically contain a good deal of supporting documentation, partly in the responses to questionnaires, checklists, and forms, and partly in free-form narratives. As with the input test, to the extent that auditors could evaluate the system outputs in conjunction with the information contained in the case materials, it is possible to conclude that the output validation was successful.

Analysis and Discussion of Validation Results

In the following sections, the results of the validation tests are presented and discussed. These results are presented in tables summarizing the detailed assessments of efficiency and effectiveness of the various solution plans at the financial statement item level which are reported in **Appendix C**. The numerical values presented in each table refer to the effectiveness and efficiency ratings as set out in the plan evaluation questionnaire which all evaluators were required to fill out. The full text of this questionnaire is presented in **Appendix B**.

VALIDATION OF CAPEX BY THE CASE WRITERS

Assessments, by the case writers, of the effectiveness and efficiency of CAPEX's proposed audit program plans for the six test cases are presented in Table 1.1. For each case the writer was asked to assess the efficiency and effectiveness of the proposed audit program plan at achieving target risks with respect to each financial statement item.[16] In the table, scores above 2 indicate that portion of the plan is at least as efficient or effective as any other alternative of which the assessor was aware. In contrast, a score of 1 or 2 represents judgments by the assessor that the plan is less effective or efficient than any alternative plan.

TABLE 1.1
Frequency Distributions of Effectiveness and Efficiency Ratings by Case Writers

		Total Number of Judgments	Effectiveness Ratings					Efficiency Ratings				
			1	2	3	4	5	1	2	3	4	5
Case	1	13			5	4	4	2	11			
	2	8	7	1					8			
	3	15				2	13		15			
	4	15				3	12		15			
	5	37				2	35				23	14
	6	37					37		9	3		25
Totals		125	7	6		11	101	2	58		26	39
		100%	6	5		9	80	2	46		21	31

It will be noted that, with the exception of the plan developed for Case 2, the case writers judged that CAPEX generated audit program plans which were at least as effective as those they could develop. From the standpoint of efficiency the case writers provided a slightly less skewed set of judgments. This may be attributed, at least partially, to their concern that some of the audit plans would result in some of the financial statement items being overaudited. It will be noted that the effectiveness scale presented in **Figure 1** does not allow the assessors to explicitly recognize situations in which risks would be reduced significantly below target risks.

VALIDATION OF CAPEX BY INDEPENDENT EXPERTS

Stage 2 of the validation tests of CAPEX involved comparing the audit program plans generated, using the same set of input data, by CAPEX and by the auditors who had participated in the construction of CAPEX. It was decided that plans would be compared with respect to their effectiveness and relative efficiency. Since there are no objective standards which define the efficiency and effectiveness of audit program plans, these characteristics, among others, were assessed by a number of independent auditors.

Four senior audit managers from the U.S. practice of one "Big Six" accounting firm and one senior audit manager from the Canadian practice of a different "Big Six" accounting firm participated. None of the managers had any prior involvement with CAPEX, and they were all selected by the participating firms rather than the researchers. The researchers simply requested that they should have the appropriate levels of experience. Thus, two of the managers were required to have had experience managing audits of manufacturing clients, two were required to have had experience managing audits of financial institutions[17] and the last auditor was required to have had experience with audits of retail clients. The average industry specific audit experience of the managers was 6.75 years with a range from 4 years to 9 years. The average number of years experience of managing industry specific audits was 2.5 years with a range from 1 year to 4 years.

Each manager participating in the validation tests was presented with the following material:

- Two cases concerning the type of client with which he/she had most experience. Each case was presented in two different forms: one specifying target assurances for all the relevant financial statement item assertions and the other which left all target assurances unspecified. The version of the case with target assurances unspecified was always presented first. An example of the case material is included in **Appendix A**. Subjects were requested to provide detailed audit program plans using the types of worksheets they would use in normal practice.

- The subjects were first asked to construct a substantive audit program plan to achieve target assurances set by themselves for the first case. They were then requested to consider the second version of the case, a version with target assurances provided, and asked whether the additional information would lead them to revise their initial plan.

- After completing these two stages, the subjects were presented with two "solutions" to the case. One solution had been generated by CAPEX while the other was provided by the case writer who had also provided the relevant judgments encoded in the knowledge base.[18]

- Subjects were asked to fill out the same planning assessment questionnaire that the case writers had used to assess the plans generated by CAPEX during the verification phase. They were also asked to make an assessment as to the level of experience of the individual who had constructed each plan.

- Having completed the assessments of all the solution plans, subjects were asked to reinspect their own solution and decide whether they wanted to change it in any way. If they felt that any changes were necessary they were asked to indicate the precise nature of these changes. This process was repeated, in its entirety, for the second case.

Throughout all the activities described above, subjects were asked to "think aloud" into a tape recorder. They were directed to explain why they selected certain procedures over others, what assumptions they found they had to make if they felt that they had insufficient information, and any other comments that they had on the difficulties of solving the case or inconsistencies they perceived in the case material.

One problem related to the ordering of tasks for each of the subjects. It is possible that anchoring effects (Kahneman and Tversky, 1982) may bias the evaluation of plans presented after the initial solution has been generated, or presented. In this context, anchoring refers to using the first plan presented, or generated, as the reference plan against which to measure other plans for acceptability. This may lead the subjects to be biased in favor of plans which are modifications of the initial plan and biased against plans which represent radical departures from the initial plan.

One way of partially controlling for this effect would be to present the subjects with the plans which they are required to assess both before and after they have developed audit program plans themselves. This approach may partially control for anchoring; but, the initial assessments may differ from the later assessments because the subjects will have considered the case in greater detail as a result of having to construct their own audit program plans.

There is also the possibility that the subjects will anchor on the plans they are asked to assess. This type of anchoring is considered to be less likely, however, because of the source of the plans and the manner in which they are presented. The plans generated by the system and the case writers provide more detail than the assessors were typically used to.[19] There was also no indication as to the identity or prior experience and training of the preparers of the "solution" substantive audit program plans, which makes it less likely that the experienced auditors will anchor on them.[20]

We felt that each assessor should generate his/her own solution first, even though anchoring problems might result, to ensure that each assessor considered each case in detail before he/she evaluated the other case solutions. Since the potential bias of this experimental design is "against" the validation of the system, this type of experimental design was considered reasonable.

The detailed results obtained in the Stage 2 validation experiments are presented in **Table 1.2**.[21] In each cell the first figure relates to judgments made with respect to the human generated plan while the sec-

TABLE 1.2
Frequency Distributions of Effectiveness and Efficiency Ratings by Independent Experts

		Total Number of Judgments	Effectiveness Ratings					Efficiency Ratings				
			1	2	3	4	5	1	2	3	4	5
Case 1	#1	13				13,13			0,1	13,10	0,2	
	#2	13	0,2	8,3	5,8					13,13		
2	#1	08				8,6	0,2		4,7	4,1		
	#2	08		1,5	3,2	0,1	4,0	0,8		8,0		
3	#3	15	1,6	9,3	3,4		2,2	.		.		
4	#3	15	1,0	4,6	7,7	1,0	2,2	.		.		
5	#4	37		17,0	19,15	1,20	0,2		2,3	23,32	12,2	
6	#4	37		11,20	15,14	11,3			18,23	14,14	5,0	
Totals	Human	146	2	50	52	34	8	0	24	75	17	
	CAPEX	146	8	37	50	43	8	8	34	70	4	

ond figure relates to judgments concerning the CAPEX generated plan. Statistical analysis was precluded by the limited number of subjects and cases used. It should be noted that although a large number of assessments were made by each assessor with respect to each "solution" plan, these assessments are unlikely to be completely independent of each other.

It will be noted that there is considerable variation between the judgments made by the two auditors who assessed the CAPEX and human generated "solutions" for cases 1 and 2. Although the differences between the judgments are considerable both auditors seemed to make relatively little distinction between the human-generated plan and the CAPEX-generated plan.

With respect to the auditor assessing human and CAPEX-generated plans for cases 3 and 4, both types of plan were considered to be relatively ineffective. Indeed, the auditor in question was not prepared to make any assessments concerning the efficiency of the plans in question since she considered them to be so relatively ineffective.

It is important to note that assessors were asked to make large number of judgments even at the financial statement item achieved risk level. Thus each banking case required 37 judgments to be made.

An inspection of the overall totals at the bottom of **Table 1.2** indicates a fairly close match between the judgments concerning the efficiency and effectiveness of both human and CAPEX-generated plans.

Overall Plan Acceptability Ratings

The assessments made of the overall acceptability of both human-generated and CAPEX generated plans are presented in **Table 1.3**. The numerical values can be interpreted using **Figure III**.

All of the human-generated plans were deemed to be generally acceptable and nine of the thirteen CAPEX-generated plans for which assessments were made were judged to be generally acceptable. No plans were accepted by the assessors without reservation and most of the human-generated and CAPEX-generated plans were judged to require some significant revisions in order to be acceptable.

Competence Ratings

Although considerable care was taken in constructing the table which was used to make assessments of the competence of the solution plan preparers, some of the assessors did not provide useable responses. The responses provided by both the case writers and the independent assessors are presented in **Table 1.4**. (The full compe-

TABLE 1.3
Overall Plan Acceptability Ratings by Independent Experts

		HUMAN GENERATED	CAPEX GENERATED
Case 1	Case writer		4
	Auditor 1	4	4
	Auditor 2	3	3
Case 2	Case writer		3
	Auditor 1	4	2
	Auditor 2	3	1
Case 3	Case writer		4
	Auditor 3	3	2
Case 4	Case writer		4
	Auditor 3	3	3
Case 5	Case writer		4
	Auditor 4	n/r	n/r
Case 6	Case writer		2
	Auditor 4	3	3

TABLE 1.4
Competence Ratings of Plan Preparers by Independent Experts

		HUMAN-GENERATED	CAPEX-GENERATED
Case 1	Case writer		Staff with industry experience
	Auditor 1	Manager with industry experience	Manager with industry experience
	Auditor 2	No useable response	No useable response
Case 2	Case writer		Staff with industry experience
	Auditor 1	Manager with industry experience	Staff with industry experience
	Auditor 2		
Case 3	Case writer		Staff with no industry experience
	Auditor 3	Staff with no industry experience	Staff with no industry experience
Case 4	Case writer		Staff with no industry experience
	Auditor 3	Staff with no industry experience	Staff with no industry experience
Case 5	Case writer		Staff with industry experience
	Auditor 4	No useable response	No useable response
Case 6	Case writer		Staff with industry experience
	Auditor 4	No useable response	No useable response

tence matrix which was used to elicit competence assessments is presented in **Appendix B.**) The assessors assessed the competence of the preparer of human-generated plans to be equal, or superior to, the competence the preparer of the CAPEX-generated plans. The plans generated by CAPEX were generally assessed to have been generated at the staff level of competence.

There are a number of potential limitations related to these competence assessments:

- Staff level expertise may not be sufficiently high to qualify CAPEX as an "expert" system.

- When one individual provides a radically different solution to a problem other experts will often require that he/she explain and justify his/her solution. The prototype version of CAPEX was unable to provide such explanations and it was clearly inappropriate for the researcher to provide them in its place.

- Case writers may overestimate or underestimate CAPEX's competence because they knew its plans were constructed using knowledge which they had provided.

Missing Procedures

When the assessors were asked to identify missing procedures they typically provided more detailed descriptions of procedures already present in the plan(s). One way of interpreting this finding would be that it indicates that the level of description of the procedures in CAPEX may not be appropriate; i.e., the descriptions may be more detailed than the auditors are accustomed to thinking about them during the planning stage. This finding may also indicate that there is some variation in the descriptions of procedures, both between US and Canadian practices of the same firm, and between one firm and another.

Redundant Procedures

In response to the question requesting identification of redundant procedures, in almost all cases no redundant procedures were identified.

Ratings of Testing Extents

Finally, in some situations the assessors indicated that the planned extents for procedures were too small. A number of factors might cause the required sample size to be underestimated:

- CAPEX determines sample sizes using a Dollar Unit Sampling approach. In some cases, assessors did not consider this approach to be appropriate and thought that sample sizes should be larger.

- Some indirect supporting relationships may be too strong, both individually and/or in combination. This would lead to CAPEX taking more credit for indirect support than was considered appropriate by the assessors. Unfortunately, it was not possible to investigate, in details the auditors' assessments of the strength of relevant indirect supporting relationships. This represents a potentially valuable research project.

Concluding Remarks

The validation experiments reported here indicate that generally speaking, CAPEX's performance was acceptable to a variety of experienced auditors with respect to a variety of cases. However, there were a number of validation findings which merit further discussions.

First, there was considerable disagreement among assessors' views with respect to the same audit program plan. This result, although in broad agreement with behavioral research results (see, for example, Ashton, 1982), is a little surprising, considering that the writers of the cases, the generators of the case solutions, and all except one of the assessors of the case solutions were employees of the same accounting firm. The lack of consensus could be the result of a number of factors:

- The cases may have provided insufficient information to the assessors. This lack of information may result in each assessor having to draw on considerable personal experience and hence develop markedly different audit program plans.

- Although three of the participators in the validation experiments worked for the same firm, the case writers worked in Canada, while the solution assessors worked in the Unted States. Although there is considerable uniformity in the audit approaches adopted by the firm's offices in both countries, it is to be expected that there are significant differences in the interpretation and application of the audit approach.

- Although the audit approach exhibits considerable structure, it still allows considerable latitude for judgement. This, in turn, could lead to considerable variations in the procedures selected and the extents specified for each procedure.

Second, most assessors consider solution plans from both sources to be relatively inefficient. One explanation for this may be that, in assessing the cases, they were implicity considering the type of evidence they would typically obtain from other procedures directed towards financial statement items in other cycles. Another reason that CAPEX's audit program plans may have been perceived as being somewhat inefficient could stem from the fact that even procedures with very small sample sizes were included in the solution plan. Another explanation may be that most of them felt relatively uneasy with the definition of the numerical scale used to define the relatively efficiency of a particular plan. When the assessments were discussed with some of the assessors, there was an indication that they had interpreted the efficiency assessments as efficiency with respect to achieving the target risks. In this case, a plan which resulted in an achieved risk level significantly lower than the target risk level would inevitably be considered to be relatively inefficient at achieving target risks. Similarly, as noted earlier, a plan which was considered to be ineffective would automatically be considered to be inefficient too.

Third, some of the assessors indicated that it was difficult to assess the solution plans because they deviated from 'firm practice'. This indicates that some plans may have been assessed in terms of their correspondence or lack of correspondence with firm practice, indicating an apparent inflexibility on the parts of the auditors. This inflexibility may indicate that:

- contrary to our earlier statements, there really are not very many accaptable alternative ways of achieving a particular set of audit objectives.

- experienced auditors may find it very difficult to conduct this type of "thought experiment"

- the auditors were insufficiently experienced.

Developing methodologies for validating expert systems with complex multivariate outputs becomes an increasingly important topic for research as these systems provide more comprehensive models of auditing domains. In addition, such systems are also likely to be used to an increasing extent to support the decision making of practicing auditors. We do caution, however, that the validation approach descibed here is still a "laboratory approach". Comprehensive acceptance testing in the environment in which the system will ultimately be used is also required. For example, in a financial planning context, Sviokla (1986, cited in Benbasat and Nault, 1987) reports that even after validation testing the principals of the firm that developed the PlanPower expert system felt that it would take them 1-2 years to clearly assess the implications of using this expert system.

In the past attempts to provide methodologies for validating such systems have tended to concentrate on unidimensional measures of system performance. Artifacts as complex as audit program plans cannot be assessed unidimensionally. Hence, it is necessary to investigate the set of appropriate variables which should be used to characterize audit program plans and determine the nature of the instruments which can be used to obtain values for these variables for particular audit program plans whether they have been generated by human auditors or an expert system.

In this paper we have presented, in some detail, a validation methodology for an audit planning expert system. In addition to discussing the methodology, we have described the instruments which were used to elicit assessments of each audit program plan. Finally, a summary of these assessments has been presented and discussed. It is hoped that this paper will stimulate further research and discussion both with respect to validating expert systems similar to CAPEX in particular, and in issues relating to the characterization and validation of audit program plans in general.

APPENDIX A
A Sample Case Used as a Basis for Generating
Audit Program Plans

MANUFACTURING PROFILE -1

This is the first time your office has audited this company. Through audit procedures directed towards the opening numbers on the financial statements, others in your office have determined the figures are accurate, the previous auditors were competent, and they performed sufficient work for you to place reliance on the procedures they performed. The company has changed auditors as a result of the change of ownership of the parent company. The controlling shareholders of the parent company have always been clients of your company. Audited financial results have normally been released by the parent company to the press within 1 month of the year end.

Manufacturing 1 is a company with 7 offices centrally controlled through the company headquarters which is located at a manufacturing location. The company is controlled by Parent, which charges it a management fee and determines the level of dividends to be paid.

The company manufactures two types of heat exchangers which reduce the temperature of natural gas before it is transported via pipeline. Product A is an air-cooled exchanger which uses fins to dissipate heat to reduce the temperature of the natural gas. Product B is a water-cooled system. Product B is more difficult to build and maintain but it reduces the temperature of the gas more readily than Product A.

The two product lines use totally different engineering concepts although the materials are similar. All of the work completed by the individual locations for Product A is custom work which is bid locally. Product B is built under an agreement with Parent, which allows the use of their patent. Sales are referred by Parent, but are the responsibility of Manufacturing 1.

The overall economy in the natural gas industry has been fairly stable since the significant drop off in 1984. The company has managed to survive in a very competitive industry, where many firms have closed their doors or filed for bankruptcy, by providing excellent follow up service.

To control costs and revenues, there is a central administration system which controls the accounting, budgeting, and purchasing functions. Through stringent quality control guidelines the company has been able to gain a reputation for high quality work and as a result has been able to increase profit margins by two percent over the last year. To maintain this quality control a detailed set of records is maintained to monitor both quality and price of materials used in manufacturing. These records are reviewed on a contract by contract basis and reports of operations, for closed and in progress contracts, are completed monthly and annually.

Cash sales result from the sale of scrap which is readily usable by smaller manufacturers. Each location controls it own scrap sales.

From a review of the prior year's information it appears that the response rate for confirmations was approximately 90% for positive confirmations and 55% for negative confirmations.

Balances for:	OPENING	CLOSING	YEAR TO DATE
Accounts receivable-Product A	109,000,000	127,000,000	
Accounts receivable-Product B	153,000,000	205,000,000	
Total	262,000,000	332,000 000	
Cash Sales			6,500,000*
Sales on account-Product A			950,000,000
Sales on account-Product B			1,200,000,000
Total			2, 156,500,000
Cash receipts-cash sales			1,500,000
Cash receipts on account-Product A			932,000,000
Cash receipts on account-Product B			1,148,000,000
Total			2,081,500,000
Cash Balances-with bank	115,000,000	95,000,000	
Cash balances-on hand	100,000	110,000	
Total	115,100,000	95,110,000	
Doubtful accounts-Product A	2,500,000	2,200,000	
Doubtful accounts-Product B	5,000,000	5,500,000	
Total	7,500,000	7,700,000	
Writeoffs-Product A			2,000,000
Writeoffs-Product B			4,500,000
Total			6,500,000
Returns			5,000,000*

*Returns are included in cash sales numbers

Average balances for:	OPENING	CLOSING	YEAR TO DATE
Accounts receivable-Product A	872,000	1,104,348	
Accounts receivable-Product B	2,040,000	2,562,500	
Average of Total	1,310,000	1,702,564	
Cash sales			6,500
Sales on account-Product A			100,000
Sales on account-Product B			250,000
Average of total			140,948
Cash receipts-cash sales			1,500
Cash receipts on account-Product A			94,141
Cash receipts on account-Product B			273,333
Average of total			137,848
Cash balances-with bank	28,750,000	23,750,000	
Cash balances-on hand	10,000	11,000	
Average of total	8,221,429	6,743,571	
Doubtful accounts Product A	125,000	122,222	
Doubtful accounts Product B	200,000	239,130	
Average of total	166,667	187,805	
Writeoffs-Product A			117,647
Writeoffs-Product B			250,000
Average of total			185,714
Returns			6,667

Percentage of accounts comprising significant items:

	OPENING	CLOSING	YTD	REMAINDER $	AVERAGE $
Accounts receivable-Product A	30	35		30,000,000	401,388
Accounts receivable-Product B	50	50		20,000,000	500,000
Cash Sales			–	1,500,000	1,500
Sales on account-Product A			45	330,000,000	63,158
Sales on account-Product B			30	600,000,000	178,151
Cash receipts-cash sales			–	1,500,000	1,500
Cash receipts on account-Product A			38	400,000,000	65,168
Cash receipts on account-Product B			25	600,000,000	190,476
Cash balances-with bank	25	25		500,000	166,667
Cash balances-on hand	–	–		110,000	11,000
Doubtful accounts-Product A	–	–		2,200,000	122,222
Doubtful accounts-Product B	20	16		2,500,000	129,400
Writeoffs-Product A			5	1,500,000	92,879
Writeoffs-Product B			8	2,000,000	120,773
Returns			–	5,000,000	6,667

Principal Audit Document for Accounts Receivable: sub ledger
Client's method for estimating allowance for doubtful accounts: review of specific accounts
Experience and training level of staff performing analytic review: moderate

For each financial statement item, target risk and reliance on internal control accomplished through compliance testing of each financial statement item, prior to conducting the substantive phase of the audit are as follows:

	TARGET RISK	INTERNAL CONTROL
Accounts receivable-Product A	2%	max
Accounts receivable-Product B	2%	max
Cash Sales	25%	max
Sales on account-Product A	25%	max
Sales on account-Product B	25%	max
Cash receipts-cash sales	25%	max
Cash receipts on account-Product A	25%	max
Cash receipts on account-Product B	25%	max
Cash balances-with bank	2%	none
Cash balances-on hand	2%	none
Doubtful accounts-Product A	4%	none
Doubtful accounts-Product B	4%	none
Writeoffs-Product A	25%	none
Writeoffs-Product B	25%	none
Returns	25%	max

Number of items:	OPENING	CLOSING	YEAR TO DATE
Accounts receivable -Product A	125	115	
Accounts receivable -Product B	75	80	
Total	200	195	
Cash Sales			1,000
Sales on account-Product A			9,500
Sales on account-Product B			4,800
Total			15,300
Cash receipts-cash sales			1,000
Cash receipts on account-Product A			9,900
Cash receipts on account-Product B			4,200
Total			15,100

Cash balances-with bank	4	4	
Cash balances-on hand	10	10	
Total	14	14	
Doubtful accounts-Product A	20	18	
Doubtful accounts-Product B	25	23	
Total	45	41	
Writeoffs-Product A			17
Writeoffs- Product B			18
Total			35
Returns			750

Variability of non-significant item values:	OPENING	CLOSING	YEAR TO DATE
Accounts receivable -Product A	significant	significant	
Accounts receivable -Product B	significant	significant	
Cash sales			moderate
Sales on account-Product A			significant
Sales on account-Product B			significant
Cash receipts-cash sales			moderate
Cash receipts on account-Product A			significant
Cash receipts on account-Product B			significant
Cash balances-with bank	significant	significant	
Cash balance-on hand	significant	significant	
Doubtful accounts-Product A	significant	significant	
Doubtful accounts-Product B	significant	significant	
Writeoffs-Product A			significant
Writeoffs-Product B			significant
Returns			significant

significant-there is a variability in the account from 10% to 200% of average value, with no significant clusters.

moderate-the account values range from 50% to 150% of the average value.

low-the account values range from 75% to 125% of the average value.

Inherent risk associated with:

	OVER STATEMENT	UNDER STATEMENT
Accounts receivable -Product A	moderate	moderate
Accounts receivable -Product B	high	high
Cash Sales	low	moderate
Sales on account-Product A	low	low
Sales on account-Product B	low	low
Cash receipts-cash sales	low	moderate
Cash receipts on account-Product A	low	moderate
Cash receipts on account-Product B	low	moderate
Cash balances-with bank	low	low
Cash balances-on hand	low	low
Doubtful accounts-Product A	moderate	moderate
Doubtful accounts-Product B	high	high
Writeoffs-Product A	low	low
Writeoffs-Product B	low	low
Returns	low	moderate

Internal control review has been conducted on the sales/accounts receivable/cash receipts system. However no work has been performed on the cash balances doubtful accounts or the writeoffs systems.

APPENDIX B
The Plan Evaluation Questionnaire

PLAN EVALUATION QUESTIONNAIRE

PART 1

Please assess the effectiveness of the attached plan with respect to each financial statement item assertion on a scale of 1 to 5 by filling out the worksheet below. The interpretation of scale values is given below.

Note: When assessing the effectiveness of any procedure, or set of procedures please take into account the impact of evidence provided by all the other procedures which constitute the plan.

	Existence	Completeness	Accuracy	Valuation	Occurrence
Accounts receivable-Product A					
Accounts receivable-Product B					
Cash Sales					
Cash Receipts on Account-Product A					
Cash Receipts on Account-Product B					
Cash balances					
Sales on Account-Product A					
Sales on Account-Product B					
Allowance for Doubtful Accounts-Product A					
Allowance for Doubtful Accounts-Product B					
Writeoffs-Product A					
Writeoffs-Product B					
Returns					

Effectiveness scale at the financial statement item assertion level. Assume that the procedures constituting the solution plan are applied and that there are no indications of material error in the evidence they provide.

1 = The actual risk of a material error remaining undetected with respect to the financial statement item assertion in question is significantly greater than the target risk.

2 = The actual risk of a material error remaining undetected with respect to the financial statement item assertion in question is slightly greater than the target risk.

3 = The actual risk of a material error remaining undetected with respect to the financial statement item assertion in question is equal to the target risk.

4 = The actual risk of a material error remaining undetected with respect to the financial statement item assertion in question is slightly less than the target risk.

5 = The actual risk of a material error remaining undetected with respect to the financial statement item assertion in question is significantly less than the target risk.

PART 2

Please assess the effectiveness of the plan with respect to each financial statement item using the worksheet below. Please use a scale of 1 to 5. The interpretation of the scale values is given after the worksheet.

Accounts receivable-Product A
Accounts receivable-Product B

Cash Sales
Cash Receipts on Account-Product A
Cash Receipts on Account-Product B

Cash balances

Sales on Account-Product A
Sales on Account-Product B

Allowance for Doubtful Accounts-Product A
Allowance for Doubtful Accounts-Product B

Writeoffs-Product A
Writeoffs-Product B

Returns

1 = Target risks would not be achieved for any of the financial statement item assertions.

2 = Target risks would not be achieved for most critical and most noncritical financial statement item assertions.

3 = Target risks would be achieved for most critical and some noncritical financial statement item assertions.

4 = Target risks would be achieved for all critical and most noncritical financial statement item assertions.

5 = Target risks would be achieved (or exceeded) for all financial statement item assertions.

PART 3

Please indicate your assessment of the overall effectiveness of the plan by choosing the statement which best describes the plan's effectiveness at the financial statement level.

1 = Target risks would not be achieved for any financial statement item assertions.

2 = Target risks would not be achieved for most financial statement item assertions.

3 = Target risks would be achieved for some critical and some noncritical financial statement item assertions.

4 = Target risks would be achieved for all critical and most noncritical financial statement item assertions.

5 = Target risks would be achieved (or exceeded) for all financial statement item assertions.

QUESTION 2
Plan Efficiency

PART 1

Please assess the efficiency of the plan with respect to each financial statement item assertion on a scale of 1 to 5 by filling out the worksheet below. The interpretation of the scale is given in the worksheet below.

Accounts receivable-Product A
Accounts receivable-Product B

Cash Sales
Cash Receipts on Account-Product A
Cash Receipts on Account-Product B

Cash balances

Sales on Account-Product A
Sales on Account-Product B

Allowance for Doubtful Accounts-Product A
Allowance for Doubtful Accounts-Product B

Writeoffs-Product A
Writeoffs-Product B

Returns

1 = There are other sets of procedures which would result in the achievement of the same level of risk with respect to the financial statement item assertion in question as that achieved by the plan at a significantly lower cost than that of the plan.

2 = There are other sets of procedures which would result in the achievement of the same level of risk with respect to the financial statement item assertion in question as that achieved by the plan at a slightly lower cost than that of the plan.

3 = Any alternative set of procedures which would result in the achievement of the same level of risk with respect to the financial statement item assertion in question as that achieved by the plan would have the approximately the same cost as that of the plan.

4 = Any alternatives set of procedures which would result in the achievement of the same level of risk with respect to the financial statement item assertion in question as that achieved by the plan would have a cost slightly greater than that of the plan.

5 = Any alternative set of procedures which would result in the achievement of the same level of risk with respect to the financial statement item assertion in question as that achieved by the plan would have a cost which was significantly greater than that of the plan.

PART 2

Please assess the efficiency of the plan with respect to each financial statement item on a scale of 1 to 5 by filling out the worksheet below. The interpretation of the scale values is given below the worksheet.

Accounts receivable-Product A
Accounts receivable-Product B

Cash Sales
Cash Receipts on Account-Product A
Cash Receipts on Account-Product B

Cash balances

Sales on Account-Product A
Sales on Account-Product B

Allowance for Doubtful Accounts-Product A
Allowance for Doubtful Accounts-Product B

Writeoffs-Product A
Writeoffs-Product B

Returns

1 = There are other sets of procedures which would result in the achievement of the same level of risk with respect to all financial statement item assertions as that achieved by the plan at a significantly lower cost than that of the plan.

2 = There are other sets of procedures which would result in the achievement of the same level of risk with respect to all financial statement item assertions as that achieved by the plan at a slightly lower cost than that of the plan.

3 = Any alternatives set of procedures which would result in the achievement of the same level of risk with respect to all financial statement item assertions as that achieved by the plan would have approximately the same cost as that of the plan.

4 = Any alternative set of procedures which would result in the achievement of the same level of risk with respect to all financial statement item assertions as that achieved by the plan would have a cost slightly greater than that of the plan.

5 = Any alternative set of procedures which would result in the achievement of the same level of risk with respect to all financial

statement item assertions as that achieved by the plan would have a cost which was significantly greater than that of the plan.

PART 3

Please indicate your assessment of the overall efficiency of the solution plan by choosing the statement listed below which best describes the efficiency of the plan at the financial statement level.

1 = There are other sets of procedures which would result in the achievement of the same level of overall risk as that achieved by the plan at a significantly lower cost than that of the plan.
2 = There are other sets of procedures which would result in the achievement of the same level of overall risk as that achieved by the plan at a slightly lower cost than of the plan.
3 = Any alternative set of procedures which would result in the achievement of the same level of overall risk as that achieved by the plan would have approximately the same cost as that of the plan.
4 = Any alternative set of procedures which would result in the achievement of the same level of overall risk as that achieved by the plan would have a cost slightly greater than that of the plan.
5 = Any alternative set of procedures which would result in the achievement of the same level of overall risk as that achieved by the plan would have a cost which was significantly greater than that of the plan.

QUESTION 3
Plan Acceptability

PART 1

Please assess the acceptability of the solution plan by choosing a statement which best describes the overall acceptability of the plan to you.

1 = The plan is fundamentally unacceptable and even major revisions cannot change this conclusion.

2 = The plan is unacceptable and can only be made acceptable through major revisions.

3 = The plan is generally acceptable but some significant revisions are necessary.

4 = The plan is generally acceptable but some minor revisions are necessary.

5 = The plan is acceptable without any revisions being required.

PART 2

If you have chosen statement 2, 3, or 4 in the above assessment please indicate below the revisions that you would make to the solution plan to make it acceptable. Beside each revision please indicate the reason(s) for making it.

Revision   Reason(s)

QUESTION 4
The Competence of the Plan Preparer

Please assess the competence of the preparer of the plan by checking the cell in the matrix below which best describes your assessment of the seniority and experience of the preparer of the plan.

	SENIORITY	PARTNER	MANAGER	STAFF	JUNIOR
Experience					
Extensive Industry but not this client					
No experience of this industry					

QUESTION 5
Missing and Redundant Procedures

Please list any procedures which are missing from the solution plan and that you believe should be included in any solution plan for the client in question.

Please list any procedures which are included in the solution plan which you consider to be redundant.

Please indicate any procedures which are included in the solution plan that you would consider necessary but should be carried out with smaller sample sizes (smaller confidence factors).

Please indicate any procedures which are included in the solution plan that you would consider necessary but should be carried out with larger sample sizes (larger confidence factors).

APPENDIX C

DETAILED RESPONSES BY CAPEX VALIDATORS

In all the tables, scores above 2 indicate that portion of the plan is at least as efficient or effective as any other alternative of which the assessor is aware. In contrast, scores of 1 or 2 represent judgments by the assessor that the plan is less effective or less efficient than any alternative plan. The explanations of abbreviations used are provided below.

Abbreviations used for financial statement items in Manufacturing Cases 1 and 2

A/R A	=	Accounts receivable type A
A/R B	=	Accounts receivable type B
CS	=	Cash sales
CR A	=	Cash receipts relating to type A sales
CR B	=	Cash receipts relating to type B sales
SA A	=	Type A sales on account
SA B	=	Type B sales on account
AD A	=	Allowance for doubtful accounts relating to type A sales on account
AD B	=	Allowance for doubtful accounts relating to type B sales on account
W A	=	Writeoffs relating to type A sales on account
W B	=	Writeoffs relating to type A sales on account
R	=	Sales returns

Abbreviations used for financial statement items in Retail Cases 3 and 4

A/R NCC	=	Accounts receivable national credit card sales
A/R SCC	=	Accounts receivable store credit card sales
A/R W	=	Accounts receivable wholesale sales on account
CS	=	Cash sales
CR NCC	=	Cash receipts relating to national credit card sales
CR SCC	=	Cash receipts relating to store credit card sales
CR W	=	Cash receipts relating to wholesale sales on account
CB	=	Cash balances
SA NCC	=	National credit card sales
SA SCC	=	Store credit card sales
SA W	=	Wholesale sales on account

AD SCC = Allowance for doubtful store credit card accounts
AD W = Allowance for doubtful wholesale sales on account
R = Returns
M = Markdowns

Abbreviations used for financial statement items in
Banking Cases 5 and 6

BTIfx Pd = Balance of fixed interest term loans paid down during the present period
BTIfx Ex = Balance of fixed interest term loans extended during the previous period
BTIfx Adv= Balance of fixed interest term loans extended during the present period
BTIfl Pd = Balance of floating interest term loans paid down during the present period
BTIfl Ex = Balance of floating interest term loans extended during the previous period
BTIfl Adv = Balance of floating interest term loans extended during the present period
BOI Pd = Balance of operating loans paid down during the present period
BOI Ex = Balance of operating loans extended during the previous period
BOI Adv = Balance of operating loans extended during the present period
BMI Pd = Balance of mortgage loans paid down during the present period
BMI Ex = Balance of mortgage loans extended during the previous period
BMI Adv = Balance of mortgage loans extended during the present period

ITIfx Pd = Interest revenue on fixed rate loan paid down during the present period
ITIfx Ex = Interest revenue on fixed rate loan extended during the previous period
ITIfx Adv = Interest revenue on fixed rate loan extended during the present period
ITIfl Pd = Interest revenue on floating rate balance loan paid down during the present period
ITIfl Ex = Interest revenue on floating rate loan extended during the previous period
ITIfl Adv = Interest revenue on floating rate loan extended during the present period
IOI Pd = Interest revenue on operating loan paid down during the present period
IOI Ex = Interest revenue on operating loan extended during the previous period
IOI Adv = Interest revenue on operating loan extended during the present period
IMI Pd = Interest revenue on mortgage loan paid down during the present period
IMI Ex = Interest revenue on mortgage loan extended during the previous period
IMI Adv = Interest revenue on mortgage loan extended during the present period

AITIfx Ex = Interest revenue accrued on fixed rate loan extended during the previous period
AITIfx Adv= Interest revenue accrued on fixed rate loan extended during the present period
AITIfl Ex = Interest revenue accrued on floating rate loan extended during the previous period
AITIfl Adv= Interest revenue accrued on floating rate loan extended during the present period
AIOI Ex = Interest revenue accrued on operating loan extended during the previous period

AIOI Adv =	Interest revenue accrued on operating loan extended during the present period
AIMI Ex =	Interest revenue accrued on mortgage loan extended during the previous period
AIMI Adv =	Interest revenue accrued on mortgage loan extended during the present period
ML Lp =	Mortgage loan loss provision
BL Lp =	Business loan loss provision
CR =	Cash receipts
CD =	Cash disbursements
CB =	Cash balances

1. ASSESSMENTS BY CASE WRITERS

TABLE C.1
Case Writer's Ratings of CAPEX Solutions to Manufacturing Cases

		A/R A	A/R B	CS	CR A	CR B	CB	SA A	SA B	AD A	AD B	WA	W B	R
Effectiveness	Case 1	3	3	5	5	5	5	4	4	3	3	4	4	3
	Case 2	2	2	.	2	2	2	2	2	.	.	.	.	3
Efficiency	Case 1	3	3	3	3	3	3	3	3	3	3	2	2	3
	Case 2	3	3	.	3	3	3	3	3	.	.	.	.	3

Note: The dots in Table C.1. indicate that the corresponding financial items were not material in Case 2.

Note: The dots in Table C.1. indicate that the corresponding financial items were not material in Case 2.

In connection with the two Manufacturing cases, the case writer judged the effectiveness of the CAPEX-produced plan for Case 2 to be slightly lower than required to meet the target level of audit risk. Based on the case writer's comments in response to question 3, part 2 (see Appendix B), it appears that CAPEX did not recognize (1) circumstances in Case 2 that called for the use of year-end positive confirmations rather than interim positive confirmations, and (2) the need for positive confirmations of billings and receipts.

In addition, the case writer judged the efficiency of the plan for verifying Writeoffs in Case 1 to be slightly less efficient than an alternative set of procedures, primarily because he felt that, given the circumstances of Case 1, no such work was required.

TABLE C.2
Case Writer's Ratings of CAPEX Solutions to Retail Cases

		AR NC C	AR SC C	AR W	CS	CR NC C	CR SC C	CR W	CB	SA NC C	SA SC C	SA W	AD SC C	AD W	R	M
Effectiveness	Case 3	5	5	3	5	5	5	5	5	5	5	5	5	5	3	5
	Case 4	5	3	3	3	5	5	5	5	5	5	5	5	5	5	5
Efficiency	Case 3	3	3	3	3	3	3	3	3	3	3	3	3	3	3	3
	Case 4	3	3	3	3	3	3	3	3	3	3	3	3	3	3	3

The case writer judged that the CAPEX-generated plans for the retail cases Case 3 and Case 4 would result in the target levels of assurance being achieved or exceeded for all relevant financial statement item assertions. With respect to the efficiency of both plans he had no significant concerns.

TABLE C.3
Case Writer's Ratings of CAPEX Solutions to Banking Cases

		Bdfx Pd	BTIfx Ex	BTIfx Adv	BTII Pd	BTII Ex	BTII Adv	BOI Pd	BOI Ex	BOI Adv	BMI Pd	BMI Ex	BMI Adv
Effectiveness	Case 5	5	5	5	5	5	5	5	5	5	5	5	5
	Case 6	5	5	5	5	5	5	5	5	5	5	5	5
Efficiency	Case 5	4	4	4	4	4	4	4	4	4	4	4	4
	Case 6	2	2	2	2	2	2	3	3	3	2	2	2

TABLE C.4
Case Writer's Ratings of CAPEX Solutions to Banking Cases (cont'd)

		mfx Pd	mfx Ex	mfx Adv	mII Pd	mII Ex	mII Adv	IOI Pd	IOI Ex	IOI Adv	IMI Pd	IMI Ex	IMI Adv
Effectiveness	Case 5	5	5	5	5	5	5	5	5	5	5	5	5
	Case 6	5	5	5	5	5	5	5	5	5	5	5	5
Efficiency	Case 5	5	5	5	5	5	5	5	5	5	5	5	5
	Case 6	4	4	4	4	4	4	4	4	4	4	4	4

TABLE C.5
Case Writer's Ratings of CAPEX Solutions to Banking Cases (cont'd)

		AITI fx Ex	AITI fx Adv	AITIa Ex	AITIa Adv	AIOI Ex	AIOI Adv	AIMI Ex	AIMI Adv	MI Lp	BI Lp	CR Ex	CD Adv	CB
Effectiveness	Case 5	5	5	5	5	5	5	5	5	4	4	5	5	5
	Case 6	5	5	5	5	5	5	5	5	5	5	5	5	5
Efficiency	Case 5	4	4	4	4	4	4	4	4	4	4	5	5	4
	Case 6	4	4	4	4	4	4	4	4	4	4	4	4	4

In connection with the Banking cases, the case writer judged the efficiency of the plan for verifying most of the various types of loan balances in Case 6 to be slightly less efficient than an alternative set of procedures, primarily because he felt the testing extents were too high.

II. ASSESSMENTS BY INDEPENDENT EXPERTS

Manufacturing Cases

TABLE C.6
Independent Experts' Ratings of CAPEX and Human Solutions to Manufacturing Case 1

		AR A	AR B	CS	CR A	CR B	CB	SA A	SA B	AD A	AD B	WA	WB	R
Manufacturing Case 1														
Effectiveness	Auditor 1	4,4	4,4	4,4	4,4	4,4	4,4	4,4	4,4	4,4	4,4	4,4	4,4	4,4
	Auditor 2	2,2	2,2	3,3	3,3	3,3	2,3	3,3	3,3	2,1	2,1	2,3	2,3	2,2
Efficiency	Auditor 1	3,3	3,3	3,3	3,3	3,3	3,3	3,3	3,3	3,4	3,4	3,3	3,3	3,2
	Auditor 2	3,3	3,9	3,3	3,3	3,3	3,3	3,3	3,3	3,3	3,3	3,3	3,3	3,3

Note: Each cell contains the expert's rating of the solutions as (Human,CAPEX).

Note: Each cell contains the expert's rating of the solutions as (Human, CAPEX)

Auditor 1 did not distinguish between the human solution to Case 1 and the CAPEX solution from the standpoint of effectiveness. The reason why he did not assign a score of 5 appeared to be because he felt a little uneasy with the assessment approach and because he considered that sample sizes were, on the whole, too small.

Auditor 2 did make some distinction between the two plans. In all respects the CAPEX solution was judged by her to have equal or greater effectiveness than the human solution. However, she did have some significant concerns with respect to strength of evidence which would be provided concerning both types of account receivable. Her principal concern was that the sample sizes planned for the procedures were far too small.

With respect to her assessments of the evidence available with respect to writeoffs and returns she considered that it was necessary to actually sample recorded writeoffs and returns procedures which the case writer did not specify but CAPEX did. Auditor 2 consistently rated BOTH solutions as being less effective than the ratings provided by Auditor C. There is also considerable variation in the assessments made by Auditor 1 and Auditor 2.

TABLE C.7
Independent Experts' Ratings of CAPEX and Human Solutions to Manufacturing Case 2

Manufacturing Case 2		A/R A	A/R B	CRA	CRB	CB	SAA	SAB	R
Effectiveness	Auditor 1	4,5	4,5	4,4	4,4	4,4	4,4	4,4	4,4
	Auditor 2	3,2	3,2	5,3	5,3	3,4	5,2	5,2	2,2
Efficiency	Auditor 1	3,2	3,2	2,2	2,2	3,2	2,2	2,2	3,3
	Auditor 2	3,1	3,1	3,1	3,1	3,1	3,1	3,1	3,1

Note: Each cell contains the expert's rating of the solutions as (Human,CAPEX).

Note: Each cell contains the expert's rating of the solutions as (Human, CAPEX)

Auditor 1 did not distinguish between the effectiveness of the two solutions except with respect to accounts receivable. With respect to both types of accounts receivable the CAPEX plan was rated as being more effective.

Auditor 2 was much more critical of both plans. Her assessments were well below those of Auditor C. In addition, she considered that the CAPEX solution was ineffective for over half of the financial statement items.

With respect to accounts receivable, she expressed confusion that CAPEX scheduled both interim and year-end confirmations while the case writer's solution only scheduled year-end confirmations.

With respect to sales on account, CAPEX did not schedule any specific procedures while the case writer did. It appears that this problem relates to the way in which CAPEX represents the evidence which can be derived from substantive analysis techniques when there is very significant variability in the independent variable.

The assessors' concern with the effectiveness of CAPEX with respect to cash receipts on account also appears to be related to its failure to provide for procedures directed towards sales since, in the case writer's solution, these procedures provided evidence with respect to cash receipts as well as billings.

The assessments provided by Auditor 2 are broadly consistent with the assessments of the CAPEX solution provided by the case writer. He considered that CAPEX derived too much assurance from analytic review procedures directed towards sales.

Auditor 1 rated the efficiency of the human and CAPEX solutions as being quite similar except with respect to one type of accounts receivable, cash balances and returns. The assessment concerning the second type of account receivable appeared to result from the fact that CAPEX scheduled a review of subsequent cash receipts on account and the case writer didn't.

One of the problems highlighted by the preceding assessments is that the scale provided for effectiveness assessments did not allow the assessor to indicate where a particular plan would result in risks significantly lower than target risks at the financial statement item level.

Auditor 2 did not distinguish between the efficiency of the two solutions except with respect to returns. She gave no indication as to why she considered the case writer's plan to be more efficient.

Auditor 1 rated the efficiency of the human and CAPEX solutions as being quite similar except with respect to both types of accounts receivable and cash balances. He considered CAPEX's plan to be less efficient with respect to achieving audit objectives for these financial statement items than the case writer's plan. Auditor 1 did not explain the reasons for these assessments. However, they can probably be explained by the fact that CAPEX scheduled interim confirmations in addition to year-end confirmations while the case writer did not.

Auditor 2 essentially rejected the CAPEX solution as being extremely inefficient, while assessing the human solution as being relatively efficient. Her concern was that too much work was being scheduled, in particular, interim and year-end confirmations. This assessment may also have had a 'halo' effect with respect to her other assessments, leading her to consider CAPEX as being generally inefficient at satisfying any of the required audit objectives.

Retail Cases [22]

TABLE C.8
Independent Expert's Ratings of CAPEX and Human Solutions to Retail Cases 3 & 4

		AR NCC	AR SCC	AR W	CS	CR NCC	CR SCC	CR W	CB	SA NCC	SA SCC	SA W	AD SCC	AD W	R	M
Effectiveness	Case 3	2,1	2,1	3,3	2,1	2,1	2,1	2,1	5,5	2,2	2,2	2,2	3,3	3,3	5,5	1,3
	Case 4	2,2	4,2	2,2	3,3	3,3	3,3	3,3	5,5	3,3	3,3	3,3	2,2	2,2	5,5	1,2

Note: Each cell contains the expert's rating of the solutions as (Human,CAPEX).

Note: Each cell contains the expert's rating of the solutions as (Human, CAPEX)

Generally speaking, Auditor 3 rated both the human and the CAPEX solution plans as being ineffective except with respect to cash balances and returns. The human solution plan was assessed as being more effective than the CAPEX solution though this is somewhat surprising in the case of accounts receivable since the sample sizes are very similar in both solutions.

Auditor 3 also considered that the case writer's solution was more effective with respect to cash sales and cash sales on account. This is to be expected because CAPEX did not schedule procedures directed towards these financial statement items whereas the case writer did.

In the judgment of Auditor 3 the solutions to Case 4 were considered to be superior to those for Case 3. With the exception of accounts receivable relating to store credit card accounts, both the human and the CAPEX solutions are rated equally with respect to effectiveness. This variation in assessments for the single type of accounts receivable may have arisen from the fact that the sample size of the interim positive confirmation of this item is only 5 for CAPEX and 35 for the case writer's solution.

Banking Cases[23]

TABLE C.9
Independent Expert's Ratings of CAPEX and Human Solutions to Banking Cases 5 & 6
(all the relevant types of loan balances)

		Bdfx Pd	BTIfx Ex	BTIfx Adv	BTIΩ Pd	BTIΩ Ex	BTIΩ Adv	BOI Pd	BOI Ex	BOI Adv	BMI Pd	BMI Ex	BMI Adv
Effectiveness	Case 5	2,4	2,4	3,4	3,4	2,4	4,4	3,4	3,4	3,4	2,3	2,3	2,3
	Case 6	2,2	2,2	2,2	2,2	2,2	2,2	3,4	3,4	3,4	4,2	4,2	4,2
Efficiency	Case 5	3,3	3,3	3,3	3,3	3,3	3,3	4,3	4,3	4,3	4,3	4,3	4,3
	Case 6	2,2	2,2	2,2	2,2	2,2	2,2	3,3	3,3	3,3	2,3	2,3	2,3

Note: Each cell contains the expert's rating of the solutions as (Human,CAPEX).

TABLE C.10
Independent Expert's Ratings of CAPEX and Human Solutions to Banking Cases 5 & 6
(cont'd: all relevant types of interest income derived from all the types of loans)

		ITIfx Pd	ITIfx Ex	ITIfx Adv	ITIΩ Pd	ITIΩ Ex	ITIΩ Adv	IOI Pd	IOI Ex	IOI Adv	IMI Pd	IMI Ex	IMI Adv
Effectiveness	Case 5	3,3	3,3	2,3	2,3	2,3	2,3	3,3	3,3	3,3	3,3	3,3	3,3
	Case 6	3,3	3,3	3,3	3,3	3,3	3,3	3,3	3,3	3,3	3,3	3,3	3,3
Efficiency	Case 5	3,3	3,3	3,3	3,3	3,3	3,3	4,3	4,3	4,3	4,3	4,3	4,3
	Case 6	2,2	2,2	2,2	2,2	2,2	2,2	3,3	3,3	3,3	2,3	2,3	2,3

Note: Each cell contains the expert's rating of the solutions as (Human,CAPEX).

TABLE C.11
Independent Expert's Ratings of CAPEX and Human Solutions to Banking Cases 5 & 6
(cont'd: all relevant categories of accrued interest, loan provisions, cash balances, cash disbursements, and cash receipts)

		AITIx x Ex	AITIx x Adv	AITIx x Ex	AITIΩ Adv	AIOI Ex	AIOI Adv	AIMI Ex	AIMI Adv	MI Lp	BI Lp	CR Ex	CD Adv	CB
Effectiveness	Case 5	2,4	2,4	2,4	2,4	3,4	3,4	3,4	3,4	3,5	3,5	2,4	2,4	2,4
	Case 6	4,2	4,2	4,2	4,2	4,2	4,2	4,2	4,2	2,3	2,3	2,2	2,2	2,2
Efficiency	Case 5	3,3	3,3	3,3	3,3	3,3	3,3	3,3	3,3	2,4	2,4	3,2	3,2	3,2
	Case 6	3,2	3,2	3,2	3,2	3,2	3,2	3,2	3,2	4,3	4,3	4,2	4,2	4,2

Note: Each cell contains the expert's rating of the solutions as (Human,CAPEX).

Note: Each cell contains the expert's rating of the solutions as (Human, CAPEX)

Both the case writer's and CAPEX's solutions received mixed assessments. Auditor 4 considered that target levels of assurance would be achieved by both solution plans with respect to all relevant assertions relating to loan balances, accrued interest, cash balances, interest income, and loan loss provisions. Further, with respect to all financial statement items, Auditor 4 considered that the CAPEX solution was more effective than the human generated plan.

Both the case writer's and CAPEX's solutions received mixed assessments. As with the CAPEX solution to Case 5 the assessor considered that it did not provide sufficient evidence with respect to mortgages. He also considered that it failed to address the risks associated with accrued interest. One explanation for this failure is that CAPEX derives too much assurance from substantive analysis procedures. The auditor who failed to complete the banking assessments indicated this as a serious problem and one of the reasons why she could not make complete assessments.

The efficiency assessments for both the CAPEX solution and the human solution are reasonably consistent. The assessor considered the human generated solution to be more efficient than the CAPEX solution with respect to operating loans and mortgages, mainly as a result of the fact that the human solution specified smaller sample sizes.

There is some concern with the reliability of the assessments for Case 6, since Auditor 4 differentiated between the efficiency AND effectiveness of the two plans in addressing risks with respect to loan loss provisions. In actual fact, both plans scheduled exactly the same set of procedures with the same extents to provide evidence to reduce these risks.

The CAPEX plan was considered to be less efficient with respect to the accrued interest assertions, but ranked reasonably well with the human solution except in the case of the efficiency of procedures directed towards cash balances, receipts, and disbursements. The main concern in these areas was probably related to the relatively large sample sizes scheduled by CAPEX, compared to those scheduled by the case writer.

ENDNOTES

1. CAPEX (Canadian Audit Programming Expert System) was developed by Efrim Boritz and Anthony Wensley and is described in detail in Boritz and Wensley [1989], Boritz and Wensley [1990], and Wensley [1989]. The work described in this paper would not have been possible without the assistance of a very large number of people. We would particularly like to thank many partners and managers of Peat Marwick Canada and Peat Marwick Main who provided substantial support in the construction of the system and its subsequent testing: David Knight, Dennis Hogarth, Julia Lelik, John Willingham, Richard Webb, Reinhard Dotzlaw, Garth Pudwell, Brian Reel, Al Schope, Tim Gunther and several managers in Montvale, New Jersey who provided invaluable assistance in testing CAPEX in its many incarnations. Funding for the project has been provided by Peat Marwick, Canada and the Ontario Government through its URIF matching grant program. In addition, Jerry Whelan and Jeff Trost of Price Waterhouse, Canada, assisted in some of the validation experiments. We also wish to acknowledge the technical and research assisstance provided by Glenn Wettlaufer, Nick Favron, Cindy Ditner and Michelle Lynch.

2. For instance, O'Leary [1986, p. 8] states: "Verification is defined as an attempt to find errors by executing a program in a simulated environment. Validation is defined as an attempt to find errors by executing a program in a real environment. Testing [assessment] is the process of executing a program to find errors."

3. Finlay, *et al.* [1988] and Hollnagel [1989] make some reference to problems discussed in this section, however.

4. Issues relating to expert systems verification in general and the verification of CAPEX are considered in detail in Wensley [1989] and Wensley [1990].

5. Though the work of Shpilberg and Graham [1986] involves a very careful analysis of the types of information which experts consider to be relevant to tax accrual planning and the design of an expert system to process only relevant knowledge.

6. In this context the term 'valid' may be interpreted as 'being acceptable to domain experts'. The notion of "acceptability" is intentionally vague. It may mean acceptable as a way for an individual with expertise level X could possibly generate a particular behavior or it may mean acceptable to the extent that the process makes "sense", does not involve any obvious contradictions, or invalid inferences. The second definition of acceptable relies on

relatively formal properties of the process which generates the behavior in question.

7. For further discussion of this point, see Finlay, *et al.* [1988].

8. Specific areas in which information was missing were: Previous period's working papers, descriptions of the inherent risk assessment, descriptions of the control risk assessment, and detailed information concerning the environment in which the client operates. The case material provided to the assessors contained control risk and inherent risk assessments and summary information concerning the client being audited.

9. Since this document is considered to be confidential by the firm it is not possible to reproduce it in detail.

10. The term "significant" indicates accounts which have proved to be suspect in the past, are very large, or have characteristics which are particularly difficult to assess. The term "critical" indicates accounts whose misstatement would lead to substantial negative consequences for the accounting firm.

11. For example, some of the changes which were made:

   • The cases were revised to identify the clients as first time audits for the audit firm. This provided an "explanation" for the lack of prior information. The cases were also revised to indicate that prior audits conducted by other auditors had not generated any abnormal results.

   • The case material was revised to have participants indicate how any missing information was to be used. Hence, if a request was made for information concerning prior period sales, the participant might indicate that it would be used in a substantive analysis procedure to identify unusual fluctuations in sales.

   • If some information item appeared to confuse participants in pretesting phases it was discussed with the case writers. They made the decision as to whether it was appropriate to provide additional information and/or whether the relevant section of the case should be clarified. In a number of instances of confusion on the part of the participants, the case writers did not change the information presented in the case. They considered that to do so would remove the necessity for making judgments which they felt were particularly important.

   • Some information items were deleted from the case material.

This was done either because the test participants did not make use of the information or it was judged, by the case writers, to bias their selection of procedures in a manner which was atypical of the normal audit planning task.

- In early versions of each case an indication was given of relationships between variables which were plausible and hence could be used in the design of substantive analysis procedures. The case writers ultimately concluded that this information unnecessarily constrained the participants. They also felt that there was sufficient information in the cases to enable participants to identify potentially plausible relationships between accounting and nonaccounting variables and design substantive analysis procedures based on such relationships.

12. A partial description of the knowledge base can be found in Boritz and Wensley [1990]. The complete specification of the knowledge base can be found in Wensley [1989].

13. This modification of the knowledge structure is only legitimate in certain circumstances and must be accompanied by further independent validation tests. In the current research, the knowledge structure was only refined if a number of experts indicated deficiencies in the existing structure.

14. It is interesting to note that the types of mistakes an individual makes in solving a particular problem are often indicative of the level of expertise attained by the individual. Thus, it is important not to ignore the failures of the system to achieve its objectives since they may both provide a rich source of information about the performance of the system and insights into how such performance might be improved.

15. As will be noted later, there is some indication of this type of bias with respect to the assessment of the proposed solutions to the banking cases. One assessor objected to the structured approach to generating an audit program plan for banking clients and for all intents and purposes, refused to make any assessments.

16. In fact, they were also asked to provide assessments concerning the efficiency and effectiveness with which a given plan achieved target risks for every relevant item in the financial item assertion.

17. Unfortunately, one of these auditors was unable to provide the researchers with useable responses.

18. The participating auditors were not made aware that they were participating in the evaluation of an expert system. They were told

that each of the case solutions was the work of a human auditor. This type of approach to the blinding of validation tests is somewhat loosely referred to as a Turing test [O'Leary, 1988]. A true Turing test would allow for the interrogation of both the system and experts by the evaluators.

19. This fact, in and of itself, would cause assessors to be suspicious about the source of the solution plans.

20 If a particular solution audit program plan were identified as being the work of an audit partner with extensive industry experience the subjects might well anchor on such a plan. Such anchoring would be considered to be even more likely if the subject were told that a plan was the work of the writer of the case in question. In contrast, if they were told that a particular solution was produced by an expert system they may anchor more strongly on their own proposed solution because they feel that their solution must be superior to one generated by a computer.

21. For a complete presentation and discussion of the validation results see Wensley [1989].

22. Somewhat limited results were obtained from the auditor who assessed the human and CAPEX solutions to the retail cases. She considered BOTH the human and CAPEX solutions to be very ineffective. As a result she was not prepared to make assessments with respect to the efficiency of either of these solution plans.

23. Unfortunately, in spite of considerable pretesting of both the banking cases and assessment forms, one of the auditors selected to assess the solutions to the banking cases declined to provide assessments for most financial statement items. As a result, only one auditor provided meaningful assessments of the efficiency and effectiveness of human and CAPEX generated solutions to the two banking cases.

REFERENCES

Ashton, R.H., *Human Information Processing*, Accounting Studies in Accounting Research, No. 17, Sarasota, Florida: American Accounting Association, 1982.

Bailey, A.D., Jr., Hackenbrack, K., De, P., and J. Dillard, "Auditing Intelligence, Cognitive Science, and Computational Modeling in Auditing Research: A Research Approach", *The Journal of Information Systems*, Vol. 1, No. 2, Spring 1987, pp. 20-40.

Benbasat, I., and B. R. Nault, "Empirical Research in Decision Support and Expert Systems: An Examination of Research to date and Emerging Topics," in A. Bailey (ed.) Auditor Productivity in the Year 2000: 1987 Proceedings of the Arthur Young Professors' Roundtable, Reston, Va: Arthur Young, 1988.

Bonnet, A., Haton, J.P., and J-M. Truong-Ngoc, *Expert Systems,* Prentice Hall, 1988.

Boritz, J.E., and A.K.P. Wensley, "Structuring the Assessment of Audit Evidence: An Expert Systems Approach," *Auditing: A Journal of Practice and Theory* (forthcoming, 1990).

————, and ————, CAPEX Technical Manual Version 1.0, unpublished manuscript, School of Accountancy, University of Waterloo, Waterloo, Ontario, NFL 3G1, Canada, 1989.

Brinberg, D., and J.E. McGrath, *Validity and the Research Process,* London, England: Sage, 1985.

————, and J.E. McGrath, "A Network of Validity Concepts Within the Research Process," in *Forms of Validity in Research.,* Brinberg, D., and L.H. Kidder (eds.), Jossey Bass Inc., 1982, pp. 5-22.

Dungan, C., A Model of an Audit Judgment in the Form of an Expert System, Ph.D. dissertation, University of Illinois, 1983.

Finlay, P.N. Forsey, G.J., and J.M. Wilson, 'The Validation of Expert Systems-Contrasts with Traditional Methods," *Journal of the Operational Research Society,* Vol. 39, No. 10, pp. 933-938, 1988.

Geissman, J.R., and R.D. Schultz, "Verification and Validation of Expert Systems, "*AI Expert,* Vol. 3, No. 2, February, 1988, pp. 26-35.

Hickam, D.H., Shortliffe, E.H., Bischoff, M.B,. and C.D., Jacobs, "The Treatment Advice of a Computer-Based Cancer Chemotherapy Protocol Advisor," *Annals of Internal Medicine,* 103(6): 928-936.

Hollnagel, E., "Evaluation of Expert Systems, in Guida, G., Tasso, C.(eds.), *Topics in Expert System Design,* New York: North-Holland, 1989, pp. 377-416.

Kahneman, D., and A. Tversky, "Judgment Under Uncertainty," in *Judgment Under Uncertainty: Heuristics and Biases,* Kahneman, D., Slovic, P., and A. Tversky (eds.), Cambridge University Press, 1982

Klein, M., and L.B. Methlie, *Expert Systems: A Decision Support Approach,* Addison-Wesley, 1990.

Martin, J., and C. McClure, *Structured Techniques for Computing,* Prentice Hall, 1985.

O'Leary, D., "Methods of Validating Expert Systems," *Interfaces,* **18,**

No. 6, November–December, 1988, pp. 72-79.

————, "Validation of Expert Systems," *Decision Sciences*, Vol. 18, No. 3, Summer. 1987, pp. 468-486.

————, "Validation of Business Expert Systems," *Symposium on Expert Systems and Audit Judgement*, University of Southern California, February, 1986.

Shannon, R.E., *Systems Simulation: The Art and the Science*, Prentice Hall, 1975.

Shooman, M.L., *Software Engineering*, McGraw Hill, 1983.

Shortliffe, E.H *Computer-based Medical Consultations: MYCIN*, Elsevier, 1976.

Shpilberg, D., and L.E. Graham, "Developing ExperTAP: An Expert System for Corporate Tax Accrual and Planning," *Auditing: A Journal of Practice and Theory*, Vol. 6, No. 1, Fall 1986, pp. 75-94.

Steinbart, P., "Materiality: A Case Study Using Expert Systems," *The Accounting Review*, Vol. LXII, No. 1, January 1987, pp. 97-116.

Sviokla, J.J., PLANPOWER, XCON, and MUDMAN: An In-depth Analysis Into Three Commercial Expert Systems in Use," Unpublished DBA Dissertation, Graduate School of Business Administration, Harvard University, 1986.

Wensley, A.K P., 'The Feasibility of Developing A Computational Model of Assertion-Based Audit Planning Using Expert Systems Methodology," unpublished Ph.D. thesis, Department of Management Sciences, University of Waterloo, Waterloo, Ontario, Canada, 1989.

————, "Expert Systems Validation: Some Issues", unpublished manuscript, Faculty of Management, University of Toronto, 1990.

Yu, V.L., Fagan, L., Wraith S., Clancey, S.W., Scott, W.J., Hannigan, A.C., Blum, R., Buchanan, B.G., and S.N. Cohen, "Antimicrobial Selection by Computer. A Blinded Evaluation by Infectious Disease Experts, *Journal of the American Medical Association*, Vol. 241, No. 12, 1979, pp. 1279-1282.

A Basic Introduction to Neural Networks for Accountants

THERESE GRAHN MASSAAD AND
LESLIE RICHESON WINKLER

Preface

Neural net technology is based on the concept of a biological nervous system. Using a computer to simulate the nervous system's activity, this technology attempts to mimic the human brain's associative reasoning capabilities.

Introduction

What is a neural net? How can a computer simulate a neural net? Why is it important to accounting? The purpose of this paper is to answer these three questions. Part one reviews the concept of biological neural networks. Part two shows how the biological concept is translated into a conceptual computer model. Finally, the importance of neural nets to accounting is examined in part three: two auditing applications are explored.

Many different methods can be used to simulate a biological neural net on a computer. This paper is limited to software simulation (as opposed to hardware simulation) and explains only one possible method of modeling a neural net.

Concept of a Biological Neural Network

The central nervous system of the human body is an assembly of cells connected by an immense number of communication lines

(Kuffler, 1976). This assembly (or network) receives information from the external environment, processes that information, and arrives at a decision. The nerve cells in the network (called neurons), and the communication lines (connected by synapses), perform specialized functions that contribute to the final decisions made by the network.

Neurons

A representation of a pyramidal neuron found in the brain and a simplified version of how neurons are connected are shown in Figure 1. The dendrites of the neuron receive stimulus from the outside environment or from other neurons. This stimulus travels from the dendrite to the soma. Within the soma, an electrochemical potential exists. This potential tells the neuron whether or not to fire (emit an impulse). As the soma receives incoming stimuli, the potential is either raised or lowered. When the potential reaches its threshold level, it fires, passing an impulse down the axon to the external environment, another neuron's dendrite, or directly to another neuron's soma. Neurons generally perform one of three tasks: sensing, transferring, or outputting—sometimes the tasks overlap.

Synapse

A synapse is the junction between neurons at which signals are transferred. (Kuffler, 1976) Although some synapses use electrical transfer, most synapses in the human brain use a chemical-based transfer. Chemical synapses are more complex than electrical synapses and are associated with more advanced brain functions.

Some transfers are excitatory, some inhibitory. If the incoming synaptic transfer is excitatory, it will raise the potential of the soma that receives it; if inhibitory, it will lower it.

Learning

Neurons do not reproduce. A person has the maximum number of neurons at birth; as time passes, neurons die. The synapses which connect neurons are not static and although the learning process is not fully understood, researchers generally agree that learning occurs by changes in the synaptic connections.

Synaptic connections between neurons can change; that is, they can become stronger or weaker, or, form new connections. This is called synaptic plasticity, "the capability of synapses to vary their function, to be replaced, and to increase or decrease in number when required." (Nieto-Sampedro, 1989)

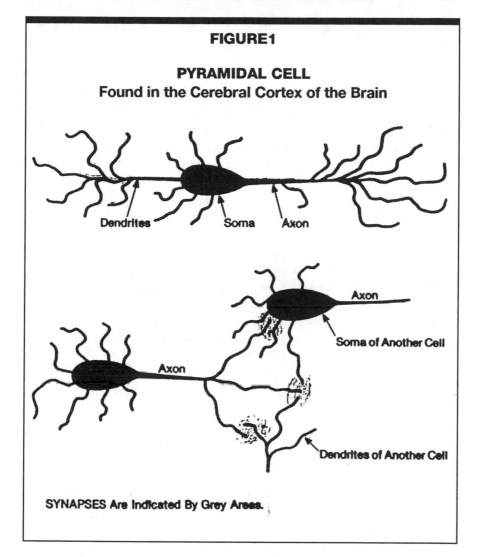

FIGURE1

PYRAMIDAL CELL
Found in the Cerebral Cortex of the Brain

Dendrites   Soma   Axon

Axon

Soma of Another Cell

Axon

Dendrites of Another Cell

SYNAPSES Are Indicated By Grey Areas.

Building a Computer Model From a Biological Concept

Representing the nervous system with a computer model can be done in various ways. In 1958 Rosenblatt published a model which he called the "Perceptron" (Rosenblatt, 1958). More recent models include Anderson's "Brain-State-in-a-Box" (Anderson, 1988), and Hopfield networks (Hopfield and Tank, 1986). Researchers, who are concerned with modeling human behavior, hope to one day develop a model that can simulate human thinking. For others, who hope to find practical applications for computer models, performance of computer models in specific areas is the main focus.

Conceptual Framework

Since the human nervous system is a very complex network of neurons and synapses, a computerized network using nodes and relational connections can represent the biological system. Figure 2 is a simple model of a three-layered neural net. A neural net can have one layer or many layers; the number of nodes in each layer can vary too. The output layer in this figure has only one node so that the model produces as yes or no output. Neural net models can also have multiple output nodes. The structure will depend on the application.

Network Concept

Each node represents a neuron. Arrows represent relational connections (dendrites and synapses) between nodes and show the direction of information flow. Inputs into the first layer of nodes is the equivalent of sensory neurons receiving information from the external environment. When a node receives inputs, the node processes the inputs (like the potential within the soma); compares the processed inputs to its preprogrammed threshold; and emits a binary output, a one if the processed inputs exceed the threshold, a zero if not. This nodal output channel is equivalent to an axon. In Figure 2, it is connected to other nodes (neurons) in the first and second layers, and to the external environment in the third layer.

A biological neuron's input varies in intensity, but the output is either an impulse or nothing. This is analogous to a computer system that receives analog inputs and emits digital outputs. Since this neural net model is assumed to operate on a digital system, it must have a way of simulating those analog inputs.

The small circles in Figure 2, between the arrowheads and the nodes, represent assigned weights (synaptic strength). Before the inputs enter the node to be added to or subtracted from the potential, they will be multiplied by the weights that are contained in those circles. This stimulates the intensity of a biological neuron's input stimulus. To simulate the excitatory and inhibitory synapses, the white circles (excitatory) are positive numbers, the black circles (inhibitory) are negative numbers.

Learning Concept

As already mentioned, learning occurs either because of changes in

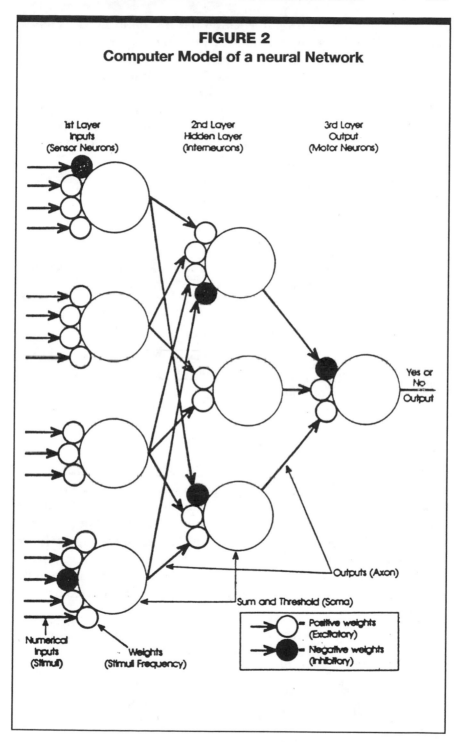

FIGURE 2
Computer Model of a neural Network

synaptic connections or from formation of new connections (synaptic plasticity). This learning occurs with repeated exposure to certain conditions or "learning from experience". To simulate this in a computer model, the model must be shown many episodes of a condition. These episodes must include the inputs and the corresponding correct outputs. The system must also have a way of adjusting its connection weights and nodal connections so it will recognize those same inputs—if it sees them again—and produce the correct output. In effect, the model must learn.

To teach the model, a method called back propagation is used to adjust the connection weights (Rumelhart *et al,* 1985).

This method entails several steps:

1. The inputs are entered into the network for processing,

2. The network output is compared with the "correct answer" to determine the error, and

3. Moving backward through the network, the connection weights are adjusted in order to reduce or eliminate the error.

Back propagating through the network does not necessarily mean that all network weights will be adjusted. Only those weights that are connected to error-producing nodes will be affected. Figure 3 shows back-propagation paths for a network that has two output nodes.

COMPUTATIONAL FRAMEWORK

Two basic algorithms are used in this model to demonstrate the computational framework. The processing algorithm converts node inputs into node outputs (moving in the direction of the arrows as shown in Figures 2 and 3) and the learning algorithm adjusts the connection weights between the nodes during the learning process (moving backward through the network as shown in Figure 3).

The processing algorithm, referred to by Anderson as a generic neural network computing element, is based on Rosenblatt's description of the perceptron:

> If the algebraic sum of excitatory and inhibitory impulse intensities is equal to or greater than the threshold of the A unit [node], then the A unit [node] fires. . . (Rosenblatt, 1958)

The learning algorithm is based on Rumelhart, Hinton, and

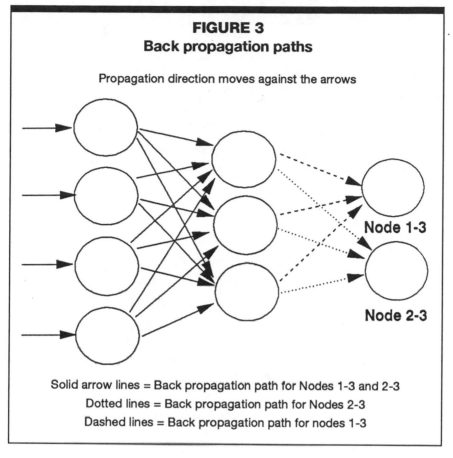

FIGURE 3
Back propagation paths

Propagation direction moves against the arrows

Node 1-3

Node 2-3

Solid arrow lines = Back propagation path for Nodes 1-3 and 2-3
Dotted lines = Back propagation path for Nodes 2-3
Dashed lines = Back propagation path for nodes 1-3

William's concept of error propagation (Rumelhart et al, 1985). This method is used because of its ability to accommodate hidden layers (i.e., the layers between the input layer and output layer). The state of the model at any given point in time is represented by matrices: one matrix to represent nodal connection weights and another to represent node outputs.

Matrices

The processing algorithm will use network inputs and Matrix 1 to compute Matrix 2. The second algorithm (only used during learning) will adjust weights by taking the desired Matrix 2 outputs and re-computing Matrix 1. To better understand this concept, the following matrix is used to illustrate how a person can be represented by an output matrix of physical characteristics (equivalent to Matrix 2).

COLOR	COLOR	SEX
Blue	Brown	Female
Brown	Black	Male
Green	Blond	Other
Hazel	Red	Other

Each column represents a physical characteristic; each row represents a choice for that characteristic. The choice is either yes or no, depending on the particular person's physical characteristics. Remember that Rosenblatt's "Perceptron" either fires or doesn't fire. Since the choice is binary, the matrix definition will use the number 1 for yes (fire) and 0 for no (doesn't fire). Every person can now be defined by a matrix. Thus, a green-eyed, brown-haired, female, is represented by the following matrix.

$$\begin{bmatrix} 0 & 1 & 1 \\ 0 & 0 & 0 \\ 1 & 0 & 0 \\ 0 & 0 & 0 \end{bmatrix}$$

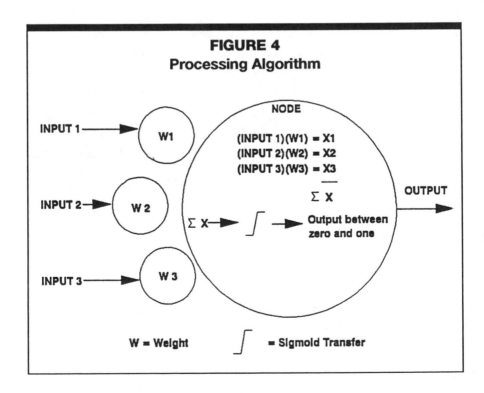

FIGURE 4
Processing Algorithm

INPUT 1 → W1

NODE

(INPUT 1)(W1) = X1
(INPUT 2)(W2) = X2
(INPUT 3)(W3) = X3

$\overline{\Sigma\ X}$

OUTPUT

INPUT 2 → W 2

$\Sigma\ X$ → ∫ → Output between zero and one

INPUT 3 → W 3

W = Weight   ∫ = Sigmoid Transfer

The Processing Algorithm

The algorithm used to process node inputs into node outputs is shown in Figure 4. Each input is multiplied by its corresponding weight; these products are then summed and entered into a sigmoid transfer function (STF). The STF limits the range of the sum to a value that falls between zero and one (Figure 5). The STF is the first step toward converting inputs into a zero or one output. The learning algorithm then converts the values falling between zero and one into outputs that are either zero or one.

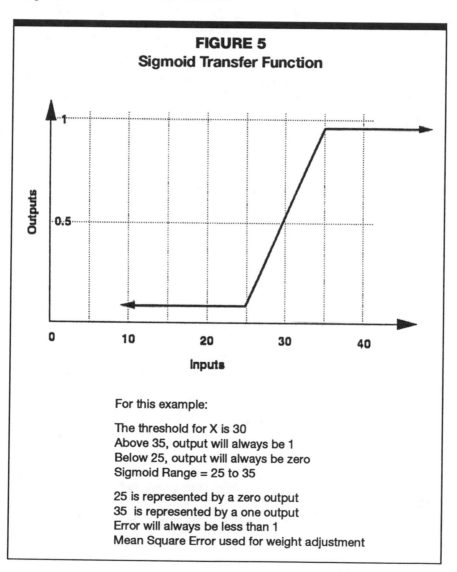

FIGURE 5
Sigmoid Transfer Function

For this example:

The threshold for X is 30
Above 35, output will always be 1
Below 25, output will always be zero
Sigmoid Range = 25 to 35

25 is represented by a zero output
35 is represented by a one output
Error will always be less than 1
Mean Square Error used for weight adjustment

The Learning Algorithm

A pattern results from applying the processing algorithm to a set of inputs. The difference between the actual pattern output and desired pattern output is the error for that pattern. The learning algorithm squares that error (to ensure a positive number) and computes the mean square error (MSE) for all patterns presented. The adjustment of weights is based on this MSE. To control the speed of adjustment, the MSE is then multiplied by a learning rate. The learning rate is determined by the network builder. The product of the MSE and learning rate is the amount of aggregate change in weights that must occur at that node. The aggregate change must then be apportioned between the weights associated with that node. This is done by using the derivative of the processing algorithm. During back propagation, the error in the output layer is used with the derivative to proportionally calculate the individual weight changes (Figure 6). When the weights in the output layer have been recalculated, the error is propagated back to the previous layer to calculate the new weights in that layer. This continues until the error is propagated back to all layers that have weights associated with their nodes.

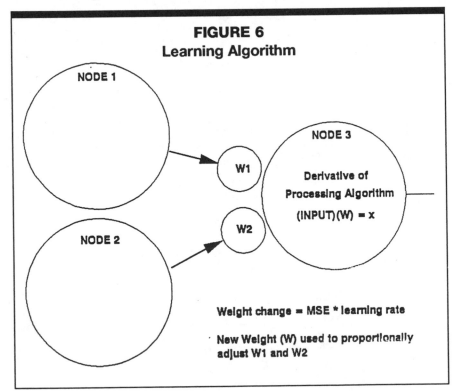

FIGURE 6
Learning Algorithm

NODE 1

NODE 3

W1

Derivative of
Processing Algorithm

(INPUT)(W) = x

W2

NODE 2

Weight change = MSE * learning rate

New Weight (W) used to proportionally
adjust W1 and W2

It is important to note that back propagation is an iterative process. When the output from a node falls within the sigmoid range, it means the node has not decided whether to produce a zero or a one. The purpose of the iterative MSE adjustment is to pull the node toward one of the two choices.

In the example shown in Figure 5, the threshold of 30 is represented by 0.5 in the STF. If a node outputs a 0.5 and the desired output is 1, the MSE adjustment will pull the node sum toward 35 by adjusting its positive weights up and negative weights down. Remember that the error will always be less than 1, making the MSE adjustment less than the error amount. This causes the adjustment to become exponentially small as it approaches 1. Through many iterations, the node sum will eventually converge toward 35, causing it to rise above the sigmoid range and consistently produce an output of 1.

While the learning algorithm changes the connecting weights within the network, the biological neural net also learns by changing the connection paths between neurons. Since nodal connection paths are part of the network architecture, they must be changed manually by the person building the system. This should not be a weakness or a problem because the person mapping out the network can connect each node to all other nodes in the next layer using an initial weight of zero; back propagation will determine if a connection exists. If the builder does not want a connection between all nodes in the network, some weights can be permanently set to zero.

Using back propagation, the model will learn by adjusting the weights in each layer. By using a derivative of the processing algorithm, back propagation allows the system to chain these weight adjustments so that the weights in each layer will be adjusted by a factor that includes the function of the nodes in that layer as well as the output error in the next layer.

It is important to understand that weight readjustment occurs in the exact opposite direction that the network processes information. Thus, learning and processing cannot be done simultaneously. The network must be in a learning mode for back propagation to occur and a running mode for information processing to occur.

Neural Networks and Accounting

Decisions involving judgment consume much of an accountant's or auditor's time and effort. Good judgment is the result of years of experience. One aspect of experience is the associative reasoning and pattern recognition capabilities discussed in part one. This section first discusses an expert system project that simulated an auditor's reasoning process in recognizing a going concern problem. Then some of the limitations of this approach are presented. Finally two potential neural network auditing applications along with suggestions about how to determine variables and proceed in development are discussed.

THE GCX PROJECT

Selfridge and Biggs (1988) modeled the going concern decision in the GCX project. Using an audit expert and knowledge-acquisition techniques, they built an expert system to simulate an auditor's reasoning in

1. Recognizing a going concern problem

2. Determining the cause,

3. Evaluating management plans to mitigate the problem, and

4. Rendering a going concern judgment.

The project was a success within its scope of study, but it exposed many shortcomings that rule-based and frame representation models have: inability to deal with complexity, domain and solution limitations, and problems with knowledge engineering techniques (Selfridge and Biggs did not address the problems of knowledge acquisition).

We believe neural nets provide a means to overcome many of these shortcoming, especially in the areas of problem recognition, dynamic environment, size, focus, and data relationships.

Recognizing a Problem and its Cause

Given the large volume of factors that must be considered and weighed against each other, the auditor may not recognize that a problem exists; or recognizing that a problem exists, the auditor may not be able to determine the cause. A neural net recognizes a problem because it is trained to find similar patterns in historical data. To find the source of the problem, the user can examine the weight matrices to determine which inputs have the greatest influence on the final output.

Dynamic Decisions

Changing business and economic environments can cause an auditor's knowledge to become obsolete. This is also true of rule-based expert systems. Auditors must constantly update their expertise. Rule-based expert systems must be maintained through ongoing iterative development. Updating rule-based expert systems is expensive because of the expert's and knowledge engineer's time. Neural nets do not use experts. As the world changes, data patterns change. It is fairly easy to retrain a neural net with new data as it becomes available.

Size

The large volume of rules needed to solve complex problems can become unmanageable in both the development and maintenance stages of expert systems. Furthermore, when an inference engine chains through a large number of rules it utilizes more time finding a solution. Neural nets overcome this problem because they use parallel distributed processing. Knowledge and information processing are distributed among all the nodes in the network, causing inputs to be processed simultaneously instead of serially. (One drawback that should be noted here is that neural nets are known for utilizing large amounts of RAM.)

Focus

The GCX project models a going concern expert system using a troubled company. Training a neural net with historical data, the network builder will use data that indicates viability as well as data that indicates problems. This enables the neural net to learn the patterns associated with a troubled company and the patterns that constitute a viable company.

Interrelationships of Data

When an auditor uses large volumes of interrelated data, the strength of those relationships are not always clear, even to an expert. Neural nets calculate those relationships through iterative learning. Given a set of pattern inputs and correct outputs, a neural net uses its learning algorithm to keep adjusting its weight matrices until it settles into a stable state. At this point it can make predictions based on the training patterns.

THE GOING CONCERN JUDGMENT

An example of an audit application of neural networks is the determination of the viability of a company. Statement on Auditing Standards #59 requires the auditor evaluate a client's ability to continue for a reasonable period of time:

> The auditor considers whether the results of his procedures performed in planning, gathering evidential matter relative to the various audit objectives, and completing the audit identify conditions and events that, when considered in the aggregate, indicate there could be substantial doubt about the entity's ability to continue as a going concern for a reasonable period of time. It may be necessary to obtain additional information about such conditions and events, as well as the appropriate evidential matter to support information that mitigates the auditor's doubt. (AICPA SAS #59 para. 3a, 1988)

It also lists conditions and events that an auditor should consider when making an evaluation. Figure 7 is a example of a neural net model that uses those conditions and events as inputs to determine an entity's viability as a going concern. It is only a starting point for a net-

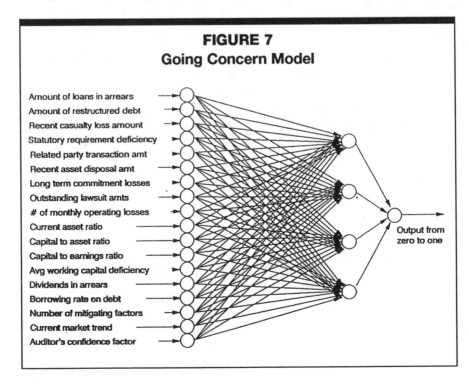

FIGURE 7
Going Concern Model

Amount of loans in arrears
Amount of restructured debt
Recent casualty loss amount
Statutory requirement deficiency
Related party transaction amt
Recent asset disposal amt
Long term commitment losses
Outstanding lawsuit amts
# of monthly operating losses
Current asset ratio
Capital to asset ratio
Capital to earnings ratio
Avg working capital deficiency
Dividends in arrears
Borrowing rate on debt
Number of mitigating factors
Current market trend
Auditor's confidence factor

Output from zero to one

work builder. When fully developed, the model would include all inputs that affect the going concern judgment (or all the inputs that are available). An audit firm can use its own historical client data or published data to train the network to recognize conditions indicating bankruptcy or liquidation. The network serves as an expert system, giving a prediction as to the client's viability. If the model's output is one, the client's viability is good with a very low risk factor; if output is zero, the client is predicted to fail. If the output is between zero and one, for example, .8, then the model indicates with an 80% confidence that the client will remain a going concern.

LIABILITY ESTIMATION

Liability estimation is a second possible audit application of neural networks. Manufacturers must estimate how much will be paid out in future years to cover warranties to the buyers. The amount is then expensed on current financial statements in order to comply with GAAP. The auditor, who examines the company's financial records, has the responsibility to verify those estimates:

> In evaluating the reasonableness of an estimate, the auditor normally concentrates on key factors and assumptions that are—
>
> a. Significant to the accounting estimate.
> b. Sensitive to variations.
> c. Deviations from historical patterns.
> d. Subjective and susceptible to misstatement and bias.
>
> The auditor normally should consider the historical experience of the entity in making past estimates as well as the auditor's experience in the industry (AICPA, SAS 57, para. 9, 1988)."

A company is concerned with keeping the estimate as low as possible in order for the financial statements to appear more profitable. The auditor, on the other hand, is concerned with obtaining the most accurate estimation of warranties. Too high of a figure will anger the client; too low of a figure might expose the auditor to lawsuits filed by third parties. The AICPA states that "Based on the auditor's understanding of the facts and circumstances, he may independently develop an expectation as to the estimate by using other key factors or alternative assumptions about those factors". Neural nets can assist the auditor. An estimation liability neural network can be trained with

data most likely to affect warranty costs. The variables include historical company liabilities, sales volume, consumer trends, percent of sales
dollars spent on quality control, and average competitor guarantees.
In order to test the effectiveness of such a network, the neural net's
estimates can be compared with the company's past estimates to determine if it comes closer to the actual amounts. If neural net estimates
significantly outperform the company's estimate, the auditor may
decide the neural net is a useful tool for estimation.

HOW TO BEGIN

Building a network requires mapping out node layers and determining what the inputs and outputs will be. This is the most difficult
and most critical part of network construction. To build a liability estimation model, all inputs that affect that estimation should be identified first. These are the inputs to the nodes in the first layer. Figure 8
is a hypothetical example of how a builder might begin mapping out a
network for liability estimation.

At this early stage, the third layer will act as an output layer. Since
liability estimates for sales can be expressed as a percentage of sales,

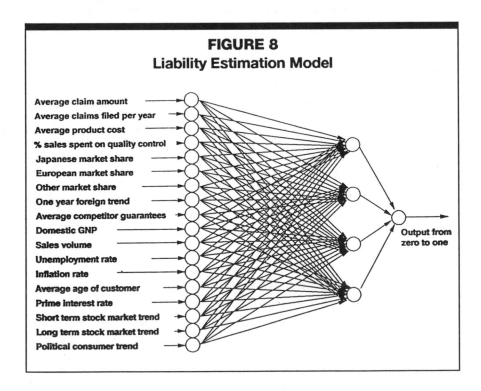

FIGURE 8
Liability Estimation Model

this model will not use a binary output but rather a value between zero and one to represent the percentage of sales that must be expensed as warranty costs. To train the network, historical data in the same form as the inputs will be fed into the system and compared with the actual warranty costs for those years. Through iterative learning the network will learn to recognize the historical patterns and after training will be able to predict future costs.

Figures 7 and 8 illustrate starting points for building a neural net. During testing and evaluation, the network inputs and node positions may change. The final network may differ from the initial network map.

Conclusion

Interest in applying the concept of neural networks has increased in recent years. The paper suggests two possible applications that accountants can use to improve decision making. Several paradigms are readily available to train a neural network. An easy to understand and widely used method is back-propagation.

Neural computing differs from traditional computing. Computerized neural networks are based on the concept of biological neurons—the building blocks of the brain. Will they ever replace traditional computers? Probably not. What role will they play? James Anderson, a leading authority on neural nets, predicts a future symbiotic relationship between the two:

> Neural net systems have pronounced strengths and weaknesses. These must be acknowledged and used. Neural nets are complementary to traditional computers. They have strengths where traditional computers are weak but they also have severe weaknesses where traditional computers are strong. They will never replace traditional computers. If the technology evolves successfully, however, they will powerfully supplement traditional computers.

The future of neural computing in the accounting profession is yet to be defined. The most promising applications are probably in areas where traditional rule-based systems don't work—areas where the rules are fuzzy, the strength of relationships between inputs and outputs is unclear, or where large databases of information are involved.

REFERENCES

AICPA, Statements on Auditing Standards (SAS), No. 57, paragraphs 9 and 12. No. 59, paragraph 3a,.New York: American Institute of Certified Accountants, 1988.

Anderson, James A., What Neural Nets Can Do, Lawrence Erlbaum Associates, 1988, p. 7.

Hopfield, John J., and David W. Tank, "Computing with Neural Circuits: A Model," Science, Vol. 233, 1986, pp. 625-633.

Kuffler Stephen W. and John G. Nicholls, From Neurons to Brain: A Cellular Approach to the Function of the Nervous System, Sinauer Associates, 1976, pp. 3-15.

Nieto-Sampedro, Manuel and Carl W. Cotman "Synaptic Plasticity," Learning and Memory: Readings from the Encyclopedia of Neuro-science, Richard F. Thompson, Ed., Birkhauser Boston,

Rosenblatt, F., "The Perceptron: A Probabilistic Model for Information Storage and Organization in the Brain," Psychological Review, Vol. 65, 1958. pp. 386-408.

Rumelhart, D.E., G.E. Hinton, and R.J. Williams, "Learning Internal Representations by Error Propagation," Parallel Distributed Processing: Explorations in the Microstructure of Cognition, Volume 1: Foundations, MIT Press, 1985, pp.318-361.

Selfridge, M. and S. Biggs, "GCX, A computational Model of the Auditor's Going-Concern Judgment", paper presented at the Audit Judgement Symposium, University of Southern California, Los Angeles, California, February 15, 1988.

III

AI/ES In
Audit Practice

Expert Systems in Public Accounting: Current Practice and Future Directions

CAROL E. BROWN

1. INTRODUCTION

The use of Artificial Intelligence techniques, including expert systems, as decision aids and for solving accounting problems has been growing at a phenomenal rate (Brown, 1989). The following major international accounting firms are currently using expert systems:

- Arthur Andersen & Company;
- Coopers & Lybrand;
- Deloitte & Touche;
- Ernst & Young;
- KPMG Peat Marwick;
- Price Waterhouse.

These firms use expert systems to assist with a variety of tasks in their tax (Brown, 1988; Brown, Black, Buehler, & Royers, 1988; Black, Carroll, & Rex, 1990), audit (Brown & Murphy, 1990; Harmon, 1988, Messier & Hansen, 1988; O'Leary & Watkins, 1989), personal financial planning (Brown, Nielson, & Phillips, 1990; Phillips, Brown, & Nielson, 1990; Behan & Lecot, 1987), and consulting (Harmon, 1988) practices. Expert systems are rapidly pervading public accounting.

Current use of expert systems in public accounting by the six major international accounting firms is described based on interviews and correspondence with more than 30 firm professionals over a period of 3 years (see Table 1). Section 5 discusses future direction of expert sys-

TABLE 1
Firm Contacts

Firm Contact	Dates	Form of Contact	Firm and Location
Barbee, George	1989–1990	Interviews	Price Waterhouse: Waltham, MA
Barlett, Andrew	1990	Letter	Ernst & Young: London, UK
Black, Robert	1990	Interview and Letter	Coopers & Lybrand: Washington, DC
Bouten, Adriaan	1988	Interview	Arthur Young: New York
Bickerstaff, Mollie	1990	Letter	Coopers & Lybrand Deloitte: London, UK
Brady, Anthony	1990	Interview and Letter	Ernst & Young: Washington, DC
Buehler, Steven E.	1988–1990	Interviews	Price Waterhouse: Chicago, IL
Carroll, Tom	1988–1989	Interviews	Coopers & Lybrand: Washington, DC No longer with the firm.
Carter, Joe	1988–1990	Interviews and Letter	Arthur Andersen & Co.: Chicago, IL
DeSalvo, Joseph J.	1988–1990	Interviews	Coopers & Lybrand: New York, NY
Drew, Patrick	1989	Interviews and Letter	Arthur Andersen & Co.: Houston, TX
Fikes, Richard	1990	Interview	Price Waterhouse: Menlo Park, CA
Goldberg, Paul S.	1988–1990	Interviews and Letter	KPMG Peat Marwick: Montvale, NJ
Glettner, Warren	1990	Interview	Price Waterhouse: San Francisco, CA
Graham, Harvey	1990	Interview	Price Waterhouse: Toronto, Canada
Graham, Lynford E.	1990	Interviews	Coopers & Lybrand: New York, NY
Hayle, Dan	1988–1990	Interviews	Arthur Andersen & Co.: Chicago, IL
Haner, John	1988–1990	Interview and Letter	Arthur Andersen & Co.: Chicago, IL
Head, Wallace	1989–1990	Interviews	Arthur Andersen & Co.: Chicago, IL
Hodgson, David	1989–1990	Interviews and Letter	Price Waterhouse: Morristown, NJ
Kennamer, Walt	1988–1990	Interviews	Ernst & Young: Cleveland, OH No longer with the firm.
Laube, Sheldon	1988	Interviews	Price Waterhouse: Waltham, MA
Maguire, Ben	1989	Interviews and Letter	Deloitte & Touche: Seattle, WA
Marney, David	1988–1990	Interview	Deloitte & Touche: Washington, DC
Nigro, Laura	1988	Interview	Arthur Young: Portland, OR
Ribar, Gary S.	1988–1990	Interviews	KPMG Peat Marwick: Montvale, NJ
Scott, David	1989	Interview and Letter	Price Waterhouse: Morristown, NJ
Shapiro, Alan	1988	Interview	Touche Ross: Washington, DC
Sparks, Wayne	1988	Interview	KPMG Peat Marwick: Montvale, NJ
Stott, Ken	1988–1990	Interviews	Deloitte & Touche: Princeton, NJ
Subisarette, Jim	1989	Interviews	Exxon: Houston, TX
Walsh, Andy	1990	Interview	Ernst & Young: Cleveland, OH
Wong, Stanley	1988	Interview	KPMG Peat Marwick: New York, NY
Yarnall, Kent	1988–1990	Interviews	Touche Ross: New York, NY

tems development from both technical and applications perspectives.

2. Practice Areas

A taxonomy of expert systems currently in use by public accounting firms is shown in Figure 1. The major categories of applications include audit, tax, consulting, and computer support. Related subcategories are shown with dashed lines.

2.1. AUDIT CATEGORIES

2.1.1. *Work Program Development.* These systems plan comprehensive audit programs for specific audit clients. Audit programs produced by these expert systems include specific tests and procedures to be used

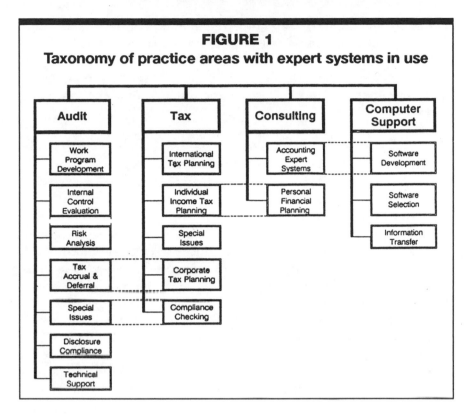

FIGURE 1
Taxonomy of practice areas with expert systems in use

in performing the audit and a level of confidence provided by the audit program. Two basic development approaches are used in this area: (1) embedded expert systems within traditional software that enhance the software's ability to deal with particularly difficult issues; and (2) an expert system that controls the audit planning process.

2.1.2. *Internal Control Evaluation.* These systems assist auditors in evaluating the reliability of a client's internal controls. Some of these systems provide assistance for evaluating very specific computer environments, while others are more general. Some systems address only internal control evaluation, while others also address estimation of audit risk.

2.1.3. *Risk Analysis.* These systems may estimate audit risk relying on an independently performed evaluation of internal controls or may combine internal control evaluation and risk analysis.

2.1.4. *Tax Accrual.* These systems assist auditors in calculating a client's income tax accrual and deferred amounts. Some systems combine tax accrual calculations with corporate tax planning functions.

2.1.5. Disclosure Compliance. These systems assist the auditor in determining whether a client is making all the required financial statement disclosures.

2.1.6. Special Audit-Related. These systems include expert systems developed to assist auditors with a variety of accounting topics such as loan loss reserve estimation and the treatment of foreign currency transactions.

The environment in which accountants operate is rapidly increasing in complexity. Interpretive aids are being developed to assist with understanding and interpreting pronouncements. Some interpretive aids currently in use are stand-alone expert systems that address individual accounting pronouncements. The proliferation of authoritative pronouncements increases the need for such interpretive aids. Because of the complex interrelationships between pronouncements, general-purpose aids should be developed that recognize these interrelationships. A number of CD-ROM databases are currently in use to assist accountants in accessing the relevant literature (Brown & Phillips, 1989). Interpretive aid expert systems will increasingly use existing hypertext and CD-ROM technology to expand interpretive assistance.

2.1.7. Technical Audit Support. These systems assist auditors with the non-accounting aspects of the audit such as determining sample size and finding applicable SEC regulations.

2.2. TAX CATEGORIES

2.2.1. Comprehensive Corporate Tax Planning. These systems assist accountants in structuring transactions and choosing accounting methods to minimize federal and state income taxes. They may also assist auditors in determining tax accruals. Systems that assist with specific corporate tax planning topics rather than doing comprehensive planning are included in the special issues category.

2.2.2. Comprehensive International Tax Planning. These systems assist with structuring organizations and international transactions to minimize total taxes. They consider the domestic tax laws of numerous countries as well as international tax treaties. Systems that assist only with a specific international issue are included in the special issues category.

2.2.3. *Comprehensive Individual Income Tax Planning.* These systems include federal income tax planning and may also include state income tax planning. Systems that address only specific individual income tax issues, like determining resident alien status, are included in the tax special issues category. Systems that perform broader comprehensive personal financial planning are also a separate category.

2.2.4. *Compliance Checking* These systems assist with the determination of a client company's compliance with specific tax regulations. Compliance checking is basically a process of interpretation and classification. Information about a particular situation is interpreted with regard to a set of rules to determine how the particular instance being analyzed should be classified (e.g., a regulated investment company or not). For example, systems have been developed to determine if a client company is in compliance with the requirements for tax exempt status, the COBRA rules, or the British value-added tax regulations. These systems will continue to be the first response to particularly cumbersome or complicated new tax laws, government regulations, and financial reporting standards. If successful, the systems developed in this way will eventually be integrated as part of larger more comprehensive systems.

2.2.5. *Special Tax Issues.* These systems deal with specific tax issues such as whether an individual is a resident alien, and how preferred shares are treated under Canadian tax law.

2.3. CONSULTING PRACTICE CATEGORIES

2.3.1. *Accounting Expert Systems.* These include expert systems that have been developed by accounting firms for clients. (See Tables 2-8.) The systems included in Tables 3 through 8 do not constitute a complete list. Only a few of the expert systems developed on a consulting basis for clients are listed. Client confidentiality prevents discussion of many others.

2.3.2. *Personal Financial Planning.* These systems produce comprehensive personal financial plans for individuals or families. They sub-

TABLE 2
Expert Systems by Firm and Practice Area

Practice Area	Arthur Andersen	Coopers & Lybrand	Deloitte & Touche	Ernst & Young	KPMG Peat Marwick	Price Waterhouse
Audit						
Work Program Development	EASY	Expertest	Audit Planning Advisor	EY Decision Support		COMPAS
Internal Control Evaluation		C&L Control Risk Assessor	Internal Controls Expert	Flow Eval CCR/36 Advisor	Inherent Risk Analysis	Detailed Planning Practice Aid Systematic AS/400 Expert
Risk Analysis		Risk Advisor		Flow Eval CCr/36 Advisor	Inherent Risk Analysis	Risk Assessment
Tax Accrual & Deferral		ExperTAX	FAS96			US Tax Planning & Tax Provision Checklist
Disclosure Compliance	Financial Disclosures	Statutory Accounts Checker				Professional Disclosure Requirements
Special Issues		ExempTAX		VATIA PANIC	Loan Probe SFAS80 SFAS91 Bank Failure Prediction SEC-AID	Automated Analytics RIC Checklist COBRA
Technical Support		Sample Sizer				
Tax						
Corporate Tax Planning		ExperTAX			Corporate Tax Analysis Tool	US Tax Planning & Tax Provision Check List
International Tax Planning			World Tax Planner			International Tax Advisory System
Individual Income Tax Planning	AAFINPLAN	CLINTE			PEAT/1040	Personal Financial Analysis
Compliance Checking		ExempTAX				
Special Issues				VATIA PANIC UCRadvisor	ALIEN PEAT/EXPATRIATE	RIC Checklist COBRA Golden Parachutes Section 367 Preferred Shares
Consulting						
Personal Financial Planning	AAFINPLAN ICOR PRA					Personal Financial Analysis
Expert System Development		AShell	Buyers Workbench			
Computer Support						
Software Development		QShell AShell	D&T Expert			The Automated Checklist Tool
Software Selection	Soft Sel					
Information Transfer				Micro DataCentre Conversion Advisor		
References & Descriptions	Table 3	Table 4A & B	Table 5	Table 6	Table 7	Table 8

TABLE 3
Arthur Anderson & Co. Expert Systems

Name	Function	Use	Contacts (Table 1)	References	Description
AAFINPLAN	Personal Financial Planning	Field use 1990	Head, 1990	Phillips, Brown, & Nielson, 1990; Brown, Nielson, Phillips, 1990; McKell, Jenkins, & Farr, 1988	AFFINPLAN is a modified version of PLANMAN that Arthur Andersen & Co. has developed with Sterling Wentworth Corporation for providing personal financial planning to individuals and members of employee groups.
Financial Disclosures	Audit—Compliance Checking	Field use 1989	Haley, 1988–1990		Arthur Andersen has developed an expert system to help auditors determine whether all required and appropriate financial disclosures are being made by client companies.
EASY	Audit—Work Program Development	Field use 1988	Haley, 1988–1990	Murphy & Brown, 1991	A smart questionnaire embedded in Arthur Andersen's Engagement Administration System, EASY, software to assist in the design of audit work programs.
SoftSel	Computer Support—Software Selection	No longer in use	Haley, 1988–1990		SoftSel recommended the most appropriate in-house and third-party software products for a particular audit engagement and the associated field hardware needed. This system is no longer in use.
ICOR	Consulting Practice	Developed 1986, Customized 1989	Andersen Consulting Carter, 1988–1990; Drew, 1989; Subisaretta, 1989		ICOR was developed with ARCO and customized for Exxon. The knowledge bases of the ICOR Materials Subsystem determine prices, sales tax, and use tax for inventory and equipment transferred, and for use in preparing the journal entries.
PRA (Passenger Revenue Accounting)	Consulting Practice	Developed 1989–1990	Andersen Consulting Carter, 1988–1990		PRA has integrated expert systems into an image processing system that automatically checks each tickets sale price, enters the transaction in the general ledger, and verifies that the agent commission and sales tax are appropriately calculated and paid.

TABLE 4A
Coopers & Lybrand Expert Systems

Name	Function	Use	Contacts (Table 1)	References	Description
ExperTAX	Tax—Corporate Tax Planning / Audit—Tax Accrual & Deferral	Field use 1986	Black, 1990; Carroll, 1988–1989	Brown, 1988; Brown & Streit, 1988; Schatz et al., 1987; Shpilberg et al., 1986; Shpilberg & Graham, 1986	ExperTAX uses over 3,000 rules in the form of an intelligent questionnaire to help auditors and tax professionals gather and review data for tax accrual and tax planning purposes. ExperTAX has improved the productivity of staff accountants, the information is higher quality, and the training process for staff accountants has accelerated. ExperTAX enhances the analysis functions by uncovering and describing tax accrual and planning issues and alternatives. Insurance ExperTAX and Oil & Gas ExperTAX are companions to ExperTAX for use with client companies in those industries because of the unique tax laws that apply.
Insurance ExperTAX Oil & Gas ExperTAX	Tax—Industry Specific Corporate Tax Planning Audit—Tax Accrual & Deferral	Field use 1988 (Insurance) Field use 1989 (Oil & Gas)	Black, 1990; Carroll, 1988–1989	Brown, 1988; Coopers & Lybrand, 1988b	
ExempTAX	Tax—Special Issues	Field use 1990	Black, 1990; Carroll, 1988–1989	Brown, 1988	ExempTAX is a diagnostic expert system for tax exempt organizations that evaluates exposure to the unrelated business income tax and pitfalls to maintaining tax exempt status, among other tax-related topics for exempt organizations.
Risk Advisor	Audit—Risk Analysis	Field use 1989	Graham, 1990	Graham, Damens, & Van Ness, 1990; Murphy & Brown, 1991	Risk Advisor is an expert system designed to interpret the client's financial and nonfinancial information in order to highlight and quantify potential inherent risks. Risk Advisor accesses an on-line database to get industry information for comparison.
QShell	Expert System Development Shell	Field use 1986	Graham, 1990	Shpilberg et al. 1986; Shpilberg & Graham, 1986	QShell, which was used in the development of ExperTAX, is a special expert system shell. A knowledge base maintenance system (KBMS) has been constructed for maintaining the knowledge bases of systems developed with QShell.
AShell	Expert System Development Shell	Field use 1988	DeSalvo, 1988–1990	Nielson & Brown, 1989; Coopers & Lybrand, 1988a	AShell is used to develop and maintain auditing expert systems. AShell's PC-based core expert system for the audit process is a comprehensive system that covers the entire audit process—planning, execution, and the automatic generation of workpapers and audit reports.

TABLE 4B
Coopers & Lybrand Expert Systems

Name	Function	Use	Contacts (Table 1)	References	Description
Expertest	Audit—Work Program Development	Field use 1987	Bickerstaff, 1990	Brown & Murphy, 1990; Bickerstaff, 1988; Murphy & Brown, 1991	Expertest uses information about the client's business and identified audit strategy decisions to tailor an individual audit program for a client from 19 general audit programs embedded in its knowledge base.
C&L Control Risk Assessor	Audit—Internal Control Evaluation	Field use 1987	Bickerstaff, 1990	Brown & Murphy, 1990; Bickerstaff, 1988; Murphy & Brown, 1991	C&L Control Risk Assessor is an automated questionnaire designed to assist auditors in assessing internal control. Answers to early questions determine the flow of subsequent questions.
Statutory Accounts Checker	Audit—Compliance Checking	Field use 1989	Bickerstaff, 1990		The Statutory Accounts Checker is an interactive questionnaire to improve efficiency in checking compliance of company accounts with United Kingdom statutory and other disclosure requirements.
Sample Sizer	Audit—Technical Support	Field use	Bickerstaff, 1990	Bickerstaff, 1988	Sample Sizer recommends optimal sample sizes and gives the corresponding range of materiality and tolerable error using overall numeric information about the audit area and auditor estimates of audit assurance and error.
CLINTE	Tax—International tax planning	Field use 1987		Gleeson & West, 1988; Brown, 1988	CLINTE attempts to optimize the international tax position of a corporation within user defined constraints. The system uses two basic models: the corporate model and the international model. The corporate model is a hierarchy of companies. The international model has the information about tax laws and how they apply to multinationals.

TABLE 5
Deloitte & Touche Expert Systems

Name	Function	Use	Contacts (Table 1)	References	Description
FAS96	Audit—Tax Accrual & Deferral	Field use 1989	Stott, 1988–1990		FAS96, developed using D&T Expert, is an expert system for tax accrual determination under Financial Accounts Standards Board Statement 96. This program was originally developed at Deloitte, Haskins & Sells.
Internal Controls Expert	Audit—Internal Control Evaluation	Field tests 1990	Stott, 1990	Brown & Murphy, 1990; Murphy & Brown, 1991	Internal Controls Expert assists the auditor in documenting and evaluating internal controls and forming an opinion on the degree of engagement risk. The expert system integrates Firm Audit Standards and the relevant generally accepted audit standards on CD-ROM with information entered by the auditor to dynamically prepare a customized hypertext report specifically for that audit engagement.
D&T-Expert (previously DH&S-Expert)	Computer Support—Software Development	Field use 1988	Stott, 1988–1990		D&T-Expert is an internally developed expert system shell geared specifically to auditing applications. The auditor can override the conclusions of the expert system by returning to a prior node in a rule chain and entering the appropriate result as the knowledge base is processed. D&T-Expert produces a text file documenting the line of reasoning which can be edited and included in the workpapers. D&T-Expert was originally developed at Deloitte, Haskins & Sells.
Audit Planning Advisor (previously MAPS)	Audit—Work Program Development	Field use 1988	Yarnell, 1988–1990; Stott, 1990	Murphy & Brown, 1991	Audit Planning Advisor is a rule-based audit planner designed for use by an audit in-charge incorporating over 1,000 questions addressing both general and special areas of concern grouped by audit area which produces a detailed first draft of an audit program. Audit Planning Advisor was originally developed by Touche Ross.
World Tax Planner	Tax—International Tax Planning	Field use 1985	Marney, 1988; Shapiro, 1988	Brown, 1988	World Tax Planner is an expert assistant for international tax optimization. By some definitions it would not be considered an expert system but rather a very sophisticated or "intelligent" database. World Tax Planner was originally developed by Touche Ross.
Buyer's Workbench	Consulting Practice	Development 1989	Maguire, 1989	Brown & Phillips, 1990	The long-run goal of the project is to provide an integrated Merchandisers workbench that will assist with buying, pricing, promotion planning, assortment selection and retail space allocation. The first part of the project tackled was the Buyer's Workbench. The purpose of this project is to capture the company's buying expertise in a knowledge base.

TABLE 6
Ernst & Young Expert Systems

Name	Function	Use	Contacts (Table 1)	References	Description
EY/Decision Support (formerly AY/Decision Support)	Audit—Work Program Development	Field use	Walsh, 1990; Beuten, 1988; Nigro, 1988	Brown & Murphy, 1990; Murphy & Brown, 1991	EY/Decision Support is a rule-based expert system module in Ernst & Young's Audit Automation Library support tools which provides the auditor with an audit approach plan, an audit program, and an indication of the level of comfort provided by the audit program. EY/Decision Support was originally developed at Arthur Young & Co.
Flow Eval	Audit—Internal Control Evaluation Audit—Risk Analysis	Field use 1990	Walsh, 1990; Beuten, 1988	Brown & Murphy, 1990; Murphy & Brown, 1991	Flow Eval is the front-end for EY/Decision Support and is designed to help auditors document (flow chart) the existing internal controls, identify where control points should be, evaluate the adequacy of existing internal controls, and suggest where additional control should be. Flow Eval was originally developed at Arthur Young & Co.
CCR/36 Advisor (Computer Control Review Advisor)	Audit—Internal Control Evaluation Audit—Risk Analysis	Field use 1989	Walsh, 1990; Barlett, 1990	Murphy & Brown, 1991	CCR/36 Advisor provides a management letter, comments and suggestions for improving system controls, and a yes or no recommendation on whether the internal controls should be relied on for audit purposes in an IBM System 36 environment. CCR/36 Advisor was originally developed at Ernst and Whitney.
VATIA (Value Added Tax Intelligent Assistant)	Tax—Compliance Checking	Field use 1988	Barlett, 1990; Kennamer, 1988–1990	Susskind & Tindall, 1988; Brown, 1988;	VATIA developed primarily at Ernst & Whitney in London, assists auditors review a client's procedures for complying with the Value Added Tax laws.
PANIC (Pay As You Earn/ National Insurance Contributions Advisor)	Tax—Compliance Checking	Prototype 1990	Barlett, 1990		PANIC will assist auditors in their review of clients' Pay As You Earn and National Insurance Contribution payment compliance. This is the first expert system developed by the joint firm in their London office.
UCRadvisor	Tax—Special Issues	Field use August 1989	Brady, 1990		UCRadvisor identifies planning opportunities and additional options in applying the uniform capitalization rules and prepares the required checklists for the IRS.
Conversions Advisor	Computer Support—Information Transfer	Development 1990	Barlett, 1990		The merged firm has two different hardware platforms and different software tools for those platforms. The conversion advisor will provide auditors with assistance in converting data between the two platforms. Conversion Advisor is being developed in the London offices of Ernst & Young.
Micro DataCentre	Computer Support—Information Transfer	Field use 1988	Barlett, 1990		Micro DataCentre provides auditors with advice on how to best obtain data from a client's computer.

TABLE 7   KPMG Peat Marwick Expert Systems

Name	Function	Use	Contacts (Table 1)	References	Description
Bank Failure Prediction Thrift Failure Prediction	Audit—Special Issues	Testing (Bank), Data Gathering (Thrift) 1990	Ribar, 1990	Bell et al., 1989	This system combines neural network and statistical techniques to predict bank failure. It is scheduled for release in the fourth quarter of 1990.
Inherent Risk Analysis	Audit—Internal Control Evaluation and Risk Analysis	Data analysis 1990	Ribar, 1988–1990	Murphy & Brown, 1991	The KPMG Audit Research group is developing an inherent risk analysis expert system prototype. Data gathering was completed July 1990 and analysis has begun. The prototype will primarily focus on manufacturing and merchandising firms.
Loan Probe	Audit—Special Issues	Field use 1987	Ribar, 1988–1990	Brown & Murphy, 1990; Nielson & Brown, 1989; Willingham & Ribar, 1988; Ribar 1988a, b, 1987; KPMG, 1987a, b	Loan Probe addresses the problem of the analysis of bank loans by auditors using a knowledge base that includes more than 8,500 rules and reflects the knowledge of the firm's top banking professionals, and statistics and projections for more than 170 industries.
SFAS80—Accounting for Foreign Currency Transactions & Hedges	Audit—Special Issues	Informal training use 1986	Ribar, 1988–1990; Sparks, 1988		SFAS80 was developed to assist with accounting for foreign currency transactions and hedges. The system was developed in 1986 and is still in use for informal training and as reference and support tool for auditors.
SFAS91—Accounting for Loan Fees & Cost	Audit—Special Issues	Limited field use 1988	Ribar, 1988–1990; Sparks, 1988		Accounting for Loan Fees & Costs—SFAS91 Interpretive Aid (SFAS91) is used for informal training and as reference and support tool to help auditors understand the proper accounting treatment of loan fees and costs under SFAS91.
SEC-AID	Audit—Technical Support	Limited field use 1988	Ribar, 1988–1990		SEC-AID is an intelligent index into the SEC regulations which includes a summary of the key elements of the regulations and references to the appropriate regulation sections.
PEAT/1040	Tax—Individual Income Tax Planning	Field use 1987	Goldberg, 1988–1990	Brown & Phillips, 1990; Brown, 1988; KPMG, 1988	PEAT/1040 is a tax projection and analysis tool for individual income tax planning. PEAT/1040 comprises: a spreadsheet program in which tax calculations are performed; a planning and analysis portion; passive activities; and an automated bridge from FAST-Tax.
Coporate Tax Analysis Tool	Tax—Corporate Tax Planning Audit—Tax Accrual & Deferral	Development 1990	Goldberg, 1988–1990	Brown, 1988	Projection and Expert Analysis Tools for corporate tax planning. The extreme breadth of the subject area ha led to prolonged analysis to determine the appropriate scope and structure of the system.
ALIEN	Tax—Special Issues	Field use 1988	Goldberg, 1988–1990	Brown, 1988	Alien is a rule-based system for the determination of resident alien status. It is a relatively small system with 150 rules and no numeric calculations. Minor updates are being made in 1990.
PEAT/EXPATRIATE	Tax—Special Issues	Field use 1990	Goldberg, 1990		PEAT/EXPATRIATE projects the costs associated with sending employees to foreign countries. Comprehensive tax calculations for 56 countries are available. The system allows "what if" analysis to evaluate different reimbursement options.

TABLE 8
Price Waterhouse Expert Systems

Name	Function	Use	Contacts (Table 1)	References	Description
COMPAS (Computerized Planning Advisory System)	Audit—Work Program Development	Prototype 1990	Hodgson, 1990	Murphy & Brown, 1991	COMPAS is designed to assist auditors in the selection of the most cost-effective combination of audit procedures that will provide satisfaction that all audit assertions have been adequately addressed.
Detailed Planning Practice Aid	Audit—Internal Control Evaluation	Prototype 1989	Scott, 1989		Detailed Planning Practice Aid is designed to help auditors document where existing controls are, identify where control points should be, evaluate the adequacy of existing internal controls and suggest where additional control should be.
Systematic	Audit—Internal Control Evaluation	Beta Test May 1990	Hodgson, 1990	Murphy & Brown, 1991	Systematic assists auditors with obtaining an understanding of both the manual and computerized aspects of complex computerized information systems.
AS/400 Expert	Audit—Internal Control Evaluation	Field use 1989	Hodgson, 1990	Murphy & Brown, 1991	AS/400 Expert assists computer auditors in developing an understanding of controls related to an IBM AS/400 installation.
Risk Assessment	Audit—Risk Analysis	Field tests 1990	Scott, 1989; Hodgson, 1990; Fikes, 1990	Murphy & Brown, 1991	The first prototype was aimed at manufacturing and distribution clients. The firm plans to start work on a banking version in the summer of 1990.
RIC Checklist (Regulated Investment Company Checklist)	Audit—Compliance Checking	Field use 1988	Hodgson, 1990	Brown, 1988; Brown & Murphy, 1990; Brown et al., 1988	This intelligent questionnaire assists auditors in determining if a company is in compliance with investment company regulations, reviews the standard audit checklist for a mutual company, and provides some assistance with the tax accrual.
Professional Disclosure Requirements	Audit—Compliance Checking	Planning 1990	Hodgson, 1990		Price Waterhouse is planning an intelligent questionnaire to ensure that client financial statements comply with firm and professional disclosure requirements.
The Automated Checklist Tool	Computer Support—Software Development	Field use 1988	Scott, 1989		The Automated Checklist Tool is used to develop intelligent questionnaires. It was used to develop RIC-Checklist and will be used for other intelligent questionnaires.
US Tax Planning and Tax Provision Checklist	Audit—Tax Accrual Tax—Corporate Tax Planning	Field use 1989	Scott, 1989		Automates checklists for US tax provision and tax planning for the audit division.

TABLE 8 (Continued)

Name	Function	Use	Contacts (Table 1)	References	Description
Internationl Tax Advisory System International Tax Planning System	International Tax	Prototype 1990 (advisory) Prototype 1988 (planning)	Fikes, 1990; Buehler, 1988	Brown, 1988	International Tax Advisory System will assist with recognition of international tax issues. The system is designed to both monitor the ongoing client situation and to assist with planning for specific client transactions. International Tax Planning system was a "proof of concept" prototype that was complete in 1988 but no working model was developed.
Automated Analytics	Audit—Special Issues	Prototype 1990	Fikes, 1990		To assist auditors in monitoring and interpreting client data. This is a component of a larger envisioned business understander system to be developed over the next 5 years.
Income Tax Issues of Preferred Shares	Tax—special issues	Beta Tests 1990	Graham, 1990		This system will assist tax professionals in Canada with determining the income tax implications of preferred shares of stock, a particularly difficult area of Canadian tax law.
COBRA Expert	Tax—Special Issues	Development 1990	Glettner, 1990		COBRA Expert is being developed for use by both Price Waterhouse professionals and for use by client firms to assist with properly handling employee benefits within the COBRA rules. The system is expected to be ready for use by the end of 1990.
Golden Parachutes (no official name)	Tax—Special issues (compensation and excise tax)	Development 1990	Glettner, 1990		This system is being developed to assist in determining if compensation payment is subject to excise tax. If it is determined to be subject to excise tax then the system suggests ways to correct the form of the transaction. The system is expected to be ready for use in early 1991.
Section 387 (no official name)	Tax—Special Issues	Development 1990	Glettner, 1990		This system is being developed to determine the appropriate taxation of property transferred off shore under section 367 of the US tax code. The system is expected to be ready for use in early 1991.
Personal Financial Analysis	Personal Financial Planning	Field use	Barbee, 1989–1990; Laube, 1988	Phillips, Brown & Nielson, 1990; Brown, Nielson & Phillips, 1990	Personal Financial Analysis is a package of services based on a family of expert systems available to companies which are Price Waterhouse's clients.

sume the individual income tax planning systems. These systems are included in the consulting practice category because they are used by public accounting firms to provide personal financial planning services to client-companies' employees as an employee benefit rather than being primarily part of the tax practice.

2.4. COMPUTER SUPPORT CATEGORIES

2.4.1. *Software Development for Accounting Expert Systems.* This category includes expert system shells that have been specifically designed for accounting applications.

2.4.2. *Software Selection.* This category includes one system that assisted in the selection of the appropriate software.

2.4.3. *Information Transfer.* These systems assist with the conversion of files from one format to another or the acquisition of data from clients' computers.

3. Current Firm Practices

Both experience and interest in expert systems vary widely among the major international accounting firms. Coopers & Lybrand began developing its first expert system more than 7 years ago. Deloitte & Touche and Ernst & Young have been actively involved in this area for only a few years. Arthur Andersen & Company and Coopers & Lybrand do substantial expert systems development for clients. KPMG Peat Marwick has chosen to apply the technology to areas of internal concern. Still, this great diversity produces one central theme: expert systems are useful for solving accounting, tax, and auditing problems. The large public accounting firms have integrated expert systems into several functional areas of their audit, tax, and consulting practices.

Tables 2 through 8 provide examples of expert systems developed by the six major international accounting firms in each of these functional areas. All systems that the firms were willing to release information on are described briefly. Table 2 summarizes expert system activities by both firm and function of the systems. Tables 3 through 8 are organized by firm and provide more detailed information about each system.

4. Future Directions

Expert systems are being used successfully in a wide range of accounting, auditing, and tax related tasks. Many of the expert systems currently in use automate time-consuming manual processes that do not require a high level of expertise—tasks typically performed by staff or senior level auditors. The issue now is how to develop expert systems to maximize their payoff. A number of relatively new technologies are now being integrated into accounting expert systems for the interfacing functions. As interface functions become more efficient, the effectiveness of the expert systems will improve.

4.1. INTERFACE: DATA GATHERING AND PRESENTATION

As summarized in Figure 2, interface can be classified by the type of entities communicating and the nature of the communication (namely, whether the communication is directly with a human, with another computer program by transfer of a file, or by directly interacting with other computer programs).

4.2. COMMUNICATION DIRECTLY WITH HUMANS OR BY PRINTED DOCUMENTS

The methods of communicating with humans can be categorized as follows: intelligent questionnaires, hypertext, on-screen forms and reports, and printed questionnaires and reports. All of these methods are currently in use in accounting expert systems.

4.2.1. *Intelligent Questionnaires.* For many years, accounting firms have used questionnaires to assist auditors and tax professionals with gathering information. Traditional questionnaires can exceed 200 pages. Some of the first expert systems started out as automated versions of paper questionnaires. These automated versions are called intelligent questionnaires because they determine the relevant questions based upon the answers to previous questions and ask only those relevant questions. Building these questionnaires into an expert system adds functionality because, in addition to collecting the information, the systems perform other tasks like planning or compliance checking. Coopers & Lybrand's ExperTAX and Price Waterhouse's RIC-Checklist are examples of systems that use intelligent questionnaires for data gathering. Because automating questionnaires has proven effective, expert systems automating long questionnaires will continue to be developed for data gathering.

4.2.2. *Hypertext.* Firms are beginning to integrate hypertext into their expert systems. For example, Deloitte & Touche's D&T Expert incorporates a hypertext glossary feature. When a hypertext glossary entry is available for selected words in a question or comment and a user does not understand a term that is highlighted, an explanation can be requested directly. This simple application of the hypertext concept promises to make systems significantly easier to use and, therefore, more effective. Hypertext will become a standard feature of expert systems in the near future.

4.2.3. *On-Screen Forms and Reports.* Virtually all systems have some sort of on-screen reporting. The two most common forms are tables and text-based reports. Some systems, like KPMG Peat Marwick's Loan Probe, allow advanced users to enter information in a summary form rather than through the intelligent questionnaire. The nature of on-screen forms and reports will change due to changing technology. They will incorporate more graphic and hypertext features as these technologies mature.

4.2.4. *Interpretation of Scanned Documents.* An intriguing method of acquiring information from printed documents is used in the Passenger Revenue Accounting system developed by Arthur Andersen & Company for Northwest Airlines. The system scans tickets and uses an intelligent character recognition system to interpret the scanned images. Manual entry of information would not be economical because the system is expected to audit between 50,000 and 60,000 tickets per night. A single clerk can scan 17 tickets per second. Application of this technology will speed up the auditing of many kinds of printed documents.

4.2.5. *Printed Questionnaires and Reports.* Both personal financial planning systems in use at the major international accounting firms, AAFINPLAN and Personal Financial Analysis, rely primarily on printed questionnaires for data gathering and on printed reports for presentation of the analysis done by the expert system. Since most of the information needed by personal financial planning systems must be acquired from individuals and the results of the system must be reported to individuals at remote locations, it is unlikely that the printed reports will be replaced by another form of communication in the near future.

4.3. FILE TRANSFER

Expert systems that read files created by other software, and write files for use by other software, are becoming common. Applications create text files that can be edited in a word processor and included in audit workpapers. Some systems, like KPMG Peat Marwick's PEAT/1040 and Price Waterhouse's RIC-Checklist, read files created by spreadsheets and prepare files for transfer back to spreadsheets. File transfer between the in-house applications of a firm and the outside vendor software used by a firm is now the minimum standard of communication. Systems that transfer files directly to and from client software will be developed in the future.

File transfer will continue to be a common method of transferring information. Most of the expert systems used at public accounting firms run on PCs. The systems are now limited by the power of the target hardware. Using file transfer as a method of communication with other software allows multiple kinds of software to be used without a multitasking environment. Until public accounting firms-upgrade their delivery platform to a multi-tasking environment, file transfer will be the predominant form of communication among different programs. Many of the firms have yet to commit the resources to provide each professional on their staff with a computer. It is, therefore, unlikely that these firms will be willing to make the investment necessary to upgrade to a multi-tasking environment in the near term.

4.4. INTERACTIVE COMMUNICATION
WITH OTHER SOFTWARE

4.4.1. *Other In-House and Vendor Software.* Expert systems modules are now embedded in other in-house software applications.

As multi-tasking environments become more common, expert systems will begin communicating interactively with other expert systems as well as traditional in-house and outside vendor software. Extensive research is being conducted to determine the best ways to accomplish this communication. Current research in the area of group decision support (Howorka, Moeur, & Goul, 1991) will have a great deal of impact in the future.

4.4.2. *Client Systems.* Work has begun on expert systems for continuous audit of on-line systems (Vasarhelyi & Halper, 1988). In addition to performing tests of controls, these expert systems will compare current transaction profiles with historical profiles, analyze the type and frequency of data accesses by user, and identify and attempt to explain the causes of unusual variances. Work in the area of fraud detection (Lecot, 1989) has begun. Demons have been proposed (O'Leary, 1991) as a methodology for continuous review of transactions. Internal auditing will soon become a continuous real-time activity. The effects on external auditing will be longer term.

4.4.3. *CD-ROMs.* Integration of expert systems and CD-ROMs is beginning. Deloitte & Touche's Internal Control Expert includes a CD-ROM containing the firm's audit standards and the relevant, generally accepted audit standards. As both CD-ROMs and expert systems become more common, more systems will integrate these technologies. This integration is a very promising area of development.

4.4.4. *On-Line Databases.* Coopers & Lybrand's Risk Advisor uses telecommunications to acquire information about other companies in a client's industry from on-line databases. As the use of on-line databases becomes more common, so will their integration into expert systems.

4.5. ANALYSIS

4.5.1. *Artificial Neural Networks.* KPMG Peat Marwick's Bank Failure Prediction system uses an artificial neural network for data analysis. Some research (Hansen & Messier, 1991) has been conducted to determine the extent to which artificial neural networks can address accounting problems that have been analyzed by other methods. A major difficulty encountered in applying this technology to accounting problems is that neural networks do not explain how decisions are reached. More research is needed in this area to determine whether artificial neural networks will be appropriate for accounting applications.

We are now in the middle of the second coming of neural networks. Neural networks date back to the early 1950s when they were used for research on how the brain works. In the late 1960s, when research revealed that single layer neural networks could not recognize certain kinds of patterns, this area was largely abandoned. The development of parallel computers again sparked interest in neural networks. Neural networks now use multiple layers to overcome the problems encountered with single layers and are an active research area.

5. The Changing Environment and Professional Development

The use of expert systems in accounting is still in its infancy. As expert systems become more prevalent in the accounting profession, shifts in the structure of accounting firms will occur. The change in structure of public accounting firms will be driven by changing population demographics. The availability of expert systems technology to accomplish tasks, tasks that may previously have required human skills, will assist firms as they respond to a scarcity of workers expected to result from changing demographics. With proportionately fewer young people entering the work force, many of the tasks traditionally performed by relatively low-cost, entry-level workers as part of their training process will have to be accomplished more efficiently in other ways. Expert systems provide an effective way of coping with changing population demographics.

When the nature of the apprenticeship process of learning a profession changes, the formal training process must also change. As more of the tasks done by entry level accountants become expert-system assisted, care must be taken to assure that the process of learning the profession is not impaired. Some evidence indicates using an expert system can enhance the performance of those new at a particular accounting task (Boer & Livnat, 1990). However, other evidence indicates that using an expert system may actually impair the learning process (Murphy, 1989; Murphy & Phillips, 1991). Firms must carefully consider the impact of using new technology on the development of skills and expertise of accountants.

REFERENCES

Behan, J., & K. Lecot, "Overview of financial applications of expert systems." *Proceedings: Western Conference on Expert Systems*, WESTEX-87, June 1987, pp. 223-229.

Bell, T.B., G.S. Ribar, and J. Verchio, "Neural nets vs. Logistic regression: A comparison of each model's ability to predict commercial bank failures.," Paper presented at The Second International Symposium on Expert Systems in Business, Finance, and Accounting, Peat Marwick, 1989.

Bickerstaff, M., "Expert systems for the auditor," paper presented at the NIVRA Conference., September 1988.

Black, R.L., T.W. Carroll, and S.K. Rex, "Expert systems: A new tool to enhance a tax practice," *The Tax Advisor,* 21(1), 1990, pp. 3-17.

Boer, G.B., and J. Livnat, "Using expert systems to teach complex accounting issues," *Issues in Accounting Education,* 5(1), 1990, pp. 108-119.

Brown, C.E., "Accounting expert systems: A comprehensive annotated bibliography," *Expert Systems Review for Business and Accounting,* II.(1 & 2), 1990, pp. 23-129.

———, "Tax expert systems in industry and accounting." *Expert Systems Review for Business and Accounting,* 1989, pp. 9-16.

———, R. Black, S. Buehler, and T. Rogers, "Artificial intelligence: application in taxation," *Expert Systems Review for Business and Accounting,* 1(4), 1990, pp. 3-10.

———, and D. Murphy, "The use of auditing expert systems in public accounting," *The Journal of Information Systems,* 5(1), 1990.

———, N.L. Nielson, and M.E. Phillips, "Expert systems for personal financial planning," *Journal of Financial Planning,* 3(3), 1990, pp. 137-143.

———, and M.E. Phillips, "Expert systems for management accountants," *Management Accounting,* LXXI (7), 1990, pp. 18-23.

———, and ———, "CD ROM: Information at Your Fingertips," *Journal of Accountancy,* 168(6), 1989, pp. 120-126.

———, and I.K. Streit, "A survey of tax expert systems," *Expert Systems Review for Business and Accounting,* 1(2), 1988, pp. 6-12.

Coopers & Lybrand, *AShell: Expert systems for the auditing process.* Coopers & Lybrand, 1988a.

——— & ———, *Insurance ExperTAX: A tax planning tool for insurance companies.* Coopers & Lybrand, 1988b.

Gleeson, J.F.J., and M.L.J. West, "CLINTE: Coopers & Lybrand international tax expert system," In D.S. Moralee (Ed.), *Research and Development in Expert Systems IV,* Cambridge: Cambridge University Press, 1988, pp. 18-31.

Graham, L.E., J. Damens, and G. Van Ness, "Developing risk advisor: an expert system for risk identification," unpublished working paper, Coopers & Lybrand, 1990.

Hansen, J.V., and W.F. Messier, "Artificial neural networks: Foundations and application to a decision problem," *Expert Systems with Applications.,* in press.

Harmon, P., "Expert systems and the big eight accounting firms," *Expert Systems Strategies.* 4(11), 1-2, 1988.

Howorka, G., L. Moeur, ansd K.M. Goul, "The design of co-audit: A 'shell' system to support research on the next generation of audit technology," *Expert Systems with Applications*, in press.

KPMG Peat Marwick, *Loan probe: The expert system for loan loss evaluation.*, KPMG Peat Marwick, 1987a.

———, *Loan probe user's manual*, KPMG Peat Marwick, 1987b.

———, *Projection and expert analysis tools/1040 users manual.* Montvale, KPMG Peat Marwick,, 1988.

Lecot, K., "Expert database systems: Applications and case studies," Paper presented at the *Second International Symposium on Expert Systems in Business, Finance, and Accounting*, October-November 1989.

McKell, L.J., J.W. Jenkins, and R. Farr, "The structure and implementation of an expert system for personal financial planning," unpublished manuscript, Brigham Young University, 1988.

Messier, W.F., and J.V. Hansen, "Expert systems in auditing: The state of the art," *Auditing: A Journal of Practice and Theory*, 7(1), 1987, pp. 94-105.

Murphy, D.S., "An empirical investigation of the effect of expert system use on the development of expertise in auditing," unpublished doctoral dissertation, Washington State University, 1989.

———, and C.E. Brown, "The use of advanced information technology in audit planning," *Expert System Review for Business and Accounting*, in press.

———, and M.E. Phillips, "The effects of expert system use on entry-level accounting expertise: an experiment," *Expert Systems With Applications*, in press.

Nielson, N.L., and C.E. Brown, "Applications of expert systems in insurance regulation," *Journal of Insurance Regulation*, 8(1), 1989, pp. 22-35.

O'Leary, D.E., "Artificial intelligence and expert systems in accounting databases: Survey and extensions," *Expert Systems with Applications*, in press.

———, and P.R. Watkins, "Review of expert systems in auditing," *Expert Systems Review for Business and Accounting*, II(1 & 2), 1989, pp. 3-22.

Phillips, M.E., C.E. Brown, and N.L. Nielson, "Personal financial planning with expert systems: An expanding employee benefit," *Management Accounting*, LXXII(3), 1990, pp. 29-33.

Ribar, G.S., "Development of an audit expert system," *Expert systems review for business and accounting*, 1(3), 1988a, pp. 3-8.

———, "Expert systems validation: A case study. *Expert Systems Review for Business and Accounting*. 1(3), 1988a, pp. 26-28.

————, "Expert systems technology at Peat Marwick main," *Expert Systems Review for Business and Accounting,* 1(1), 1987, pp. 1-5.

Schatz, H., R. Strahs, and L. Campbell, "ExperTAX: The issue of long-term maintenance," *Proceedings of the Third International Conference on Expert Systems,* Oxford: Learned Information, 1987, pp. 291-300.

Shpilberg, D., and L.E. Graham, "Developing ExperTAX: An expert system for corporate tax accrual and planning," *Auditing: A Journal of Practice & Theory,* 6(1), 1986, pp. 75-94.

————, ————, and H. Schatz, "ExperTAX: An expert system for corporate tax planning," *Expert Systems,* 3(3), 1986, pp. 136-150.

Susskind, R., and C. Tindall, "Ernst & Whinney's VAT expert system, *Proceedings of IV International Conference on Expert Systems,* Oxford: Learned Information, 1988.

Vasarhelyi, M.A., and F.B. Halper, "The continuous audit of online systems," paper presented at AAA National Meetings, 1988.

Willingham, I.J., and G.S. Ribar, "Development of an expert audit system for loan loss evaluation," *Auditor Productivity in the Year 2000: Proceedings of the 1987 Arthur Young Professors' Roundtable,* Council of Arthur Young Professors, 1988, pp. 171-186.

The Continuous Audit
of Online Systems

MIKLOS A. VASARHELYI AND FERN B. HALPER

Introduction

This paper develops the concept and explores key issues in an alternate audit approach called the Continuous Process Audit Methodology (CPAM). The paper focuses on an implementation of this methodology, the Continuous Process Audit System (CPAS), developed at AT&T Bell Laboratories for the AT&T internal audit organization. Features of the methodology may also be applicable to external audit functions.

The paper is divided into three sections. In the remainder of the Introduction, changes in management information systems (MIS) that affect traditional auditing are discussed. In the second section, CPAM and CPAS are described and contrasted with the traditional audit approach. The audit implications related to the introduction of a CPAS like technology also are examined. The last section discusses some of the knowledge issues involved in the implementation of a CPAS application and suggests paths for future work.

TECHNOLOGY AND THE AUDITOR

Traditional auditing (both internal and external) has changed considerably in recent years, primarily as a result of changes in the data processing environment [Roussey, 1986; Elliott, 1986; Vasarhelyi and Lin, 1988; Bailey *et al.*, 1989]. These changes have created major chal-

TABLE 1
The Evolution of Auditing from a Data Processing Perspective

Phase	Period	Data Processing Functions	Applications	Audit Problem
1	1945–55	Input (I) Output (O) Processing (P)	Scientific & military applications (*e.g.*, Manhattan Project)	Data transcription Repetitive processing
2	1955–65	I,O,P Storage (S)	Magnetic tapes Natural applications	Data not visually readable Data that may be changed without traces
3	1965–75	I,O,P,S Communication (C)	Time-sharing systems Disk storage Expanded operations support	Access to data without physical access
4	1975–85	I,O,P,S,C Databases (D)	Integrated databases Decision Support Systems (decision aids) Across-area applications	Different physical and logical data layouts New complexity layer (DBMS) Decisions impounded into software
5	1986–91	I,O,P,S,C,D Workstations (W)	Networks Decision support systems (non-expert) Mass optical storage	Data distributed among sites Large quantities of data Distributed processing entities Paperless data sources Interconnected systems
6	1991–on	I,O,P,S,C,D,W Decisions (De)	Decision support systems (expert)	Stochastic decisions impounded into MIS

lenges in performing the verification and attestation functions.[1] These changes and the resulting technical challenges created for auditors are summarized in Table 1.

For example, the introduction of technology precluded auditors from directly reading data from its source (magnetic tape) and, unlike paper and indelible ink, this source could be modified without leaving a trace (phases 1 and 2 in Table 1); the advent of time sharing and data communications has allowed continuous access to data from many locations (phase 3) creating access exposures; database systems have added more complexity to auditing due to the lack of obvious mapping between the physical and logical organization of data (phase 4).

Auditors dealt with these changes, for example, by (1) tailoring computer programs to do traditional audit functions such as footing, cross tabulations, and confirmations; (2) developing generalized audit software to access information on data files; (3) requiring many security steps to limit logical access in multilocation data processing environments; and (4) developing specialized audit computers and/or front-end-software to face the challenge of database oriented systems.

However, MIS continue to advance in design and technology. Corporate MIS, and particularly financial systems, are evolving towards decentralization, distribution, online posting, continuous (or at least daily) closing of the books, and paperlessness [Vasarhelyi and Yang, 1988]. These changes are causing additional challenges for auditors and provide opportunities for further evolution in audit tooling and methodology. The current systems environment and new audit challenges in this environment are described in the next section.

CURRENT ENVIRONMENT FOR LARGE APPLICATIONS

Many large applications today typically use one type of Database Management System (DBMS) (e.g., IBM's, IMS) spread among several databases that relate to different modules of a system. Data may be kept in several copies of the database with identical logical structure and may be processed at the same location and/or in many different locations. These systems typically can support both online and batch data processing and are linked to a large set of related feeders acting in asynchronous patterns feeding transactions and receiving adjustments and responses from the main system. Additionally, the main system can be the information base for downstream systems supporting management decisions and operations.

This system may store a related family of databases including the master database, a transaction database, a pending transaction database, a control database, and an administrative database. The DBMS typically will have its own software for resource accounting and restart and recovery facilities, a query language, a communication interface, a data dictionary, and a large number of utility packages. In many corporations, system software consists of different systems with a large majority of the systems still operating in mainframe computers, programmed in traditional programming languages, and interfacing primarily with mainframe based databases. System hardware is a mix of different technologies with bridges among different standard environments, including microcomputers acting as feeders and analysis stations, large mainframes, a large number of telecommunication interfaces, medium size system buffers, and large data storage devices.

The corporate system is generally developed application by application, often at different sites. Copies of system modules may be distributed to different data processing sites, and version control plays a very important role in the consistent processing of an application. Application data typically come from both the operating entities (branches) and from headquarters. Data can be transmitted in a burst mode (accumulated by or for batch processing) or in an intensive flow (where data are entered when a transaction is measured and not accumulated for transmission) for online or close to online processing [Fox and Zappert, 1985]. Perhaps most importantly, many of these systems are real-time systems, meaning that they receive and process transactions continuously.

Auditing these systems requires both the audit of the system itself and the examination and reconciliation of the interfaces between systems. These interfaces and the error correction and overhead allocation loops pose additional problems to system audits. Table 2 displays some of the characteristics of database systems and two audit techniques (labeled level 1 and level 2) that can be used to evaluate and measure these systems.

Audit work on these systems originally was constrained by strong dependence on auditee system staff (for the extraction of data from

TABLE 2
Database Systems and their Audit

System Characteristic	Audit (level 1)	Audit (level 2)
Database structure	Documentation	Data dictionary query
Database size	User query	Auditor query
Transaction flows	Examine levels	Capture sample transactions
Duplicates	Sorting and listing	Logical analysis and indexes
Field analysis	Paper oriented	Software based
Security issues	Physical	Access hierarchies
Restart and recovery	Plan analysis	Direct access
Database interfaces	Reconciliation	Reconciliation and transaction follow-through

databases) and typically entailed reviewing the manual processes around the large application system. In traditional system audits, these procedures were labeled as "auditing around the computer." These procedures are labeled as "level 1" in Table 2 and are characterized by examination of documentation, requests for user query of the database, examination of application summary data, sorting and listing of records by the user (not the auditor), a strong emphasis on paper, physical evaluation of security issues, plan analysis for the evaluation of restart and recovery, and manual reconciliation of data to evaluate application interfaces. Level 2 tasks, listed in Table 2, would use the computer to perform database audits as well as eliminate the intermediation by the user or systems people(auditees) in the audit of database systems.[2] This hands-on approach utilizes queries to the data dictionary, involves direct use of the system by the auditor, and relies on transaction evidence gathered by the auditor using the same database technology. The level 2 approach reduces the risk of fraudulent (selective) data extraction by the auditee and allows the audit to be conducted more efficiently if the auditor is well versed in database management. Furthermore, audit effectiveness is increased because the auditor has greater flexibility in the search for evidence and it is not obvious to the auditee what data are being queried by the auditor resulting in improved deterrence fraud). Differences in desired audit approach and the resultant technological tooling necessary for performing level 2 tasks led to the development of some of the concepts used for continuous process auditing.

Continuous Process Auditing

There are some key problems in auditing large database systems that traditional auditing (level 1) cannot fully solve. For example, given that traditional audits are performed only once a year, audit data may be gathered long after economic events are recorded. This often is too late to prevent economic loss by the audited entity. Traditionally, the attestation function has not been relevant in the prevention/detection of loss on a timely basis. However, internal auditors have increasingly been asked to assume a much more proactive role in loss prevention. Another problem is that auditors typically receive only a "snapshot" of a system via several days of data supplied by the audit. Unless these data coincide with some sort of problem in the system, the data may not be a good indication of system integrity. Evaluating the controls over real-time systems requires evaluating the controls at many points in time, which is virtually impossible after the fact, even if a detailed paper transaction trail exists. Surprise audits seldom are effective in this kind of environment and compliance is difficult to measure because major and obtrusive preparation is necessary in the "around the computer" audit of systems.

In continuous process auditing, data flowing through the system are monitored and analyzed continuously (*e.g.*, daily) using a set of auditor defined rules. Exceptions to these rules will trigger alarms which are intended to call the auditor's attention to any deterioration or anomalies in the system . Continuous process auditing amounts to an analytical review technique since constantly analyzing a system allows the auditor to improve the focus and scope of the audit. Furthermore, continuous process auditing can be considered as a meta form of control and can be used in monitoring control (compliance) either directly, by looking for electronic signatures, or indirectly by scanning for the occurrence of certain patterns or specific events.[3]

Ultimately, if a system is monitored over time using a set of auditor heuristics, the audit can rely mainly on exception reporting and the auditor is called in only when exceptions arise.[4] Impounding the auditor function into the system means that tests which would normally be performed once a year are repeated daily.

This methodology (CPAM) will change the nature of evidence, the timing and types of procedures, and the allocation of effort involved in audit work. The auditor will place an increased level of reliance on the evaluation of flow data (while accounting operations are being performed) instead of evidence from level data (*e.g.*, level of inventory, receivables) and from related activities (*e.g.*, internal audit's preparedness reviews). Audit work will be focused on audit by exception with the system gathering exceptions on a continuous basis.

The continuous process audit scenario entails major changes in software, hardware, the control environment, management behavior, and auditor behavior, and its implementation requires a careful and progressive approach. The next subsection discusses some of the key concepts in the actual implementation of the approach, using a prototype software system.

KEY CONCEPTS

The placement of software probes into large operational systems for monitoring purposes may imply an obtrusive intrusion on the system and can result in performance deterioration. The installation of these monitoring devices must be planned to coincide with natural life cycle changes of major software systems. Some interim measures should be implemented to prepare for full-fledged online monitoring. The approach adopted at AT&T, with the current CPAS prototype, consists of a data provisioning module that feeds an independent and external advanced decision support system.

Data provisioning can be accomplished by three different, though not necessarily mutually exclusive methods: (1) data extraction from "standard" (existing) application reports, using pattern matching techniques; (2) data extraction from the file that feeds the application report; and (3) recording of direct monitoring data. The approach actually used in CPAS entails first a measurement phase without intrusion and minor system overhead, evolving in the future to a monitoring phase where intrusion is necessary but the audit capability is substantially expanded.[5]

Measurement

Copies of key management reports are issued and transported through a data network to an independent audit work station at a central location.[6] These reports are stored in raw form and data are extracted from these reports and placed in a database. The fields in the database map with a symbolic algebraic representation of the system that is used to define the analysis. The database is tied to a workstation, and analysis is performed at the workstation using the information obtained from the database. The basic elements of this analysis process are described later in the paper.

Monitoring

In the monitoring phase, audit modules will be impounded into the auditee system. This will allow the auditor to continuously monitor the system and provide sufficient control and monitoring points for management to be able to retrace any transactions. In current systems, individual transactions are aggregated into account balances and complemented by successive allocations of overhead. These processes create difficulties in balancing and tracing transactions.

The AT&T CPAS prototype uses "the measurement" strategy of data provisioning. This is illustrated in Figure 1. The auditor logs into CPAS and selects the system to be audited. The front end of CPAS allows the auditor to look at copies of actual reports used as the source of data for the analysis. From here the auditor can move into the actual analysis portion of CPAS. In CPAS, the system being audited

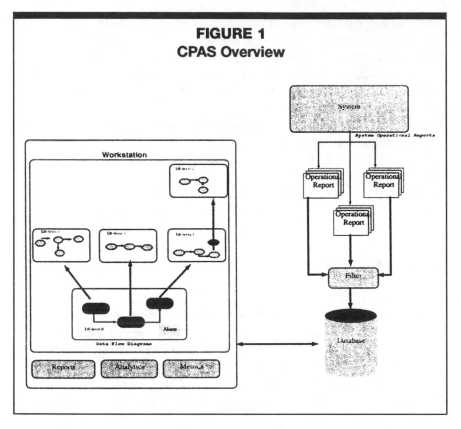

FIGURE 1
CPAS Overview

is represented as flowcharts on the workstation monitor. A high level view of the system (labeled DF level 0 in Figure 1) is linked hierarchically to other flowcharts presenting more detail about the system modules being audited. This tree oriented view of the world which allows the user to drill deeper into the details of a graphical representation is conceptually similar to the Hypertext approach [Gessner, 1990].[7] The analysis is structured along these flowcharts leading the auditor to think hierarchically.

Analysis

The auditor's work is broken down into two phases: first, the startup stage where he/she works with developers, users, and others to create a view of the system, and second, the use stage when he/she actually uses the system for actual operational audit purposes. The auditor's (internal or external) role in this context is not very different from its traditional function.

At the setup stage, the auditor acts as an internal control identifier, representer, and evaluator using existing documentation and human knowledge to create the system screens (similar to flowcharts) and to provide feedback to the designers/management. Here, audit tests, such as files to be footed and extended or reconciliations to be performed, as well as processes to be verified, are identified. Unlike the traditional audit process, the CPAS approach here requires the "soft coding" of these processes for continuous repetition. Furthermore, at this stage, the CPAS database is designed and, unlike in the traditional process, standards are specified and alarm conditions designed.

In the use stage, the system is monitored for alarm conditions and these alarm conditions are investigated when they arise and the symptoms and diagnostics identified and impounded into the CPAS knowledge base. The current baseline version of CPAS provides auditors with some alarms for imbalance conditions, the ability to record and display time series data on key variables, and a series of graphs that present event decomposition.

This logical view of the system can be associated with diagnostic analytics that count the number of exceptions and/or alarms current in the system. Detailed information about each main module is available at lower levels through a drill down procedure. This information is presented primarily as metrics, analytics, and alarms.

Metrics

Metrics are direct measurements of the system, drawn directly from reports. These metrics are compared to system standards. If a standard is exceeded, an alarm appears on the screen. For example, in the audit of a billing system, the number of bills to be issued is extracted from a user report. The number of bills not issued due to a high severity error in the data, detected by the normal data processing edits, is captured, as well as the total dollar amount of bills issued. These three numbers are metrics that relate to the overall billing process.

Analytics

Analytics are defined as functional (natural flow), logical (key interaction), and empirical (*e.g.,* it has been observed that . . .) relationships among metrics. Specific analytics related to a particular system module can be derived from the auditor, management, user experience, or historical data from the system. Each analytic may have a minimum of three dimensions: (1) its algebraic structure; (2) the relationships and contingencies that determine its numerical value at different times and situations; and (3) rules-of-thumb or optimal rules on the magnitude and nature of variance that may be deemed as "real variance," potentially triggering an alarm. For example, a billing analytic would state that dollars billed should be equal to invoice amounts received, minus values of failed edits, plus (or minus) the dollars billed that were not issued due to quality control factors. The threshold number of expected invoices for that particular day or week (allowing for seasonality) must be established to determine whether an alarm should be fired.

Alarms

An alarm is an attention directing action triggered, for example, when the value of a metric exceeds a standard. Actual experience with these issues indicates that several levels of alarms are desirable: (1) minor (type 1) alarms dealing with the functioning of the auditing system; (2) low-level operational (type 2) alarms to call exceptions to the attention of operating management; (3) higher level (type 3) alarms to call exceptions to the attention of the auditor and trigger "exception audits;" and (4) high level (type 4) alarms to warn auditors and top management of serious crisis.

For example, a type 1 alarm may be triggered if two sets of data are produced by the audited system, for the same module, for the same day, and it is unclear from the information given which data to load into the database. Of course, cycle and rerun information should be clearly passed along with the data, but sometimes this will not be as clean as expected. A type 1 alarm might also be triggered if the reports change format and data extraction procedures need to be modified. These type 1 alarms will need to be acted upon immediately, usually with a call to the system administrator or system management organization.

A type 2 alarm might be triggered if data pertaining to the same process are inconsistent. For example, data from many different reports might be used to perform an intramodule reconciliation. The data must come from different jobs in order for the reconciliation to be meaningful. A well designed CPAS application will try to gather data from different jobs and compute the same reconciliation in more than one way. If the value for the same variable (for the same run, etc.) is inconsistent between reports, this indicates a problem either with the system or the system reports and should be investigated immediately to determine how severe it is.

A type 3 alarm might be triggered if an error or suspense file is getting too large, or if some other threshold is exceeded. These exceptions are cause for concern and should be investigated because they may pose a danger to the company if not corrected.

A type 4 alarm is the most severe. For example, if, at the time of billing, many customers can not be accounted for, or if all customers were billed the same amount, regardless of how much they used a particular service, or if it appears that duplicate paychecks were sent to employees, the system should be shut down and promptly corrected.

The data and experience needed to understand the phenomena being measured to the level of specification of alarm standards are probably not available in most organizations. Experience with a CPAS like system aids in their development.

SOFTWARE IMPLEMENTATION

Figure 2 was prepared using CPAS and has the look and feel of any CPAS application.[8] It shows a high level view of a hypothetical billing system. This billing system processes transactions from multiple locations, bills customers around the country, and performs multiple bill pulls a month(i.e., not all customers are billed on the same day). The hierarchy window on the left in the figure indicates what part of the billing system is represented by the flowchart. In this example, the flowchart represents the base node of the billing system hierarchy, i.e., an overview of the system. The auditor can use the hierarchy window to move to any flowchart in CPAS by simply selecting the desired node.

As can be seen in Figure 2, the billing system consists of six major modules. Billing data first enters the Process Transaction module where high level edits are performed. Any errors from this process are sent to the Error Processing module. Corrected errors are sent back through the front-end of the system. Transactions that successfully pass through the front-end are sent to the Billing module where customer accounts are extracted, amounts due are calculated, and the bills are produced. Errors from this process are sent to the Error Processing module. Billing information is sent to the Journals function where payment and treatment information is processed and the customer database is updated. The system also contains a module that deals with any questions a customer may have about his/her account and a module that processes new orders for service. The date displayed in the figure indicates the date that the analysis uses as the base date.[9] In the example presented here, the base date (4/1/90) is also assumed to be the current date.

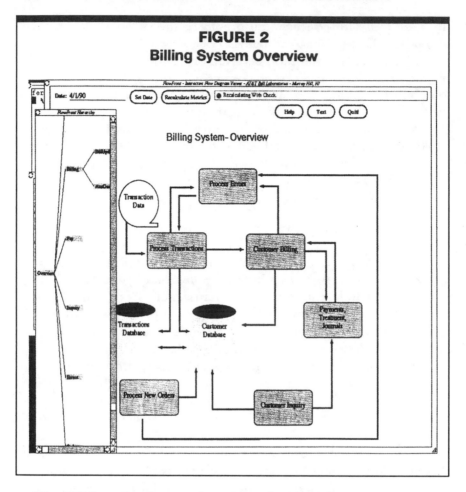

FIGURE 2
Billing System Overview

The CPAS application may be testing that the following controls are in place: (1) completeness and accuracy of input; (2) completeness and accuracy of update; (3) timeliness of data arriving to the system and timeliness of system processing; (4) maintenance of data in the database; (5) accuracy of computer programs; and (6) reasonableness of the data. For example, the auditor might have defined tests (and had them built into the CPAS application) to answer the following questions:

- Were all transactions sent to the biller received? Can all of the transactions be accounted for? Were all of the transactions loaded into the Process Transactions module? Were they loaded correctly?

- How many transactions were in error? Has the error threshold been exceeded? How long does it take errored transactions to reenter the system?

- Were all transactions posted to the database correctly? Were all the transactions initiated, executed, and recorded only once? Can all of the transactions that entered the system be accounted for (*i.e.*, either on the database or in an error file, or rejected back to the source)? How accurate are the data that were loaded to the database (*i.e.*, does the sum of the dollars on the database match what was to be posted to the database)? Are all databases synchronized?

- Were the bills calculated properly? How reasonable are the amounts billed? Were all customers who were supposed to be billed actually billed?

The alarm report displayed in Figure 3 states that there are three alarm conditions outstanding in the system on 4/1/90. Two of these are type 3 alarms, and one is a type 4 alarm. The report also shows the module where the error occurred, the value that caused the error, the standard that the value was compared against, and the average value of the error (computed for a 30 day period). The most severe alarm is, of course, the type 4 alarm. Here, ten accounts that should have been billed were not billed. This indicates a breakdown in the system and should be dealt with immediately.

The two type 3 alarms indicate that a threshold was exceeded. In this case, 2,000 transactions out of 10,000 transactions processed on 4/1/90 were in error and sent to the Error Processing module. The alarm report indicates that the standard was 850 errors per processing day. The large amount of errors also resulted in triggering the second type 3 alarm, because the dollar value associated with these errors caused the dollar value of the error file to exceed the threshold (here $200,000). The auditor should investigate this to find out the cause for the large number of errors. The auditor also should follow up to determine whether these errors are being corrected. If the errors are not being corrected in a timely manner, it may indicate that the system cannot deal with certain kinds of data or that there is a staffing problem at the error investigation unit. Additionally, the auditor (if he/she is not familiar with the history of the size of the error file) may want to change the base date to investigate whether this has been a problem in the past.

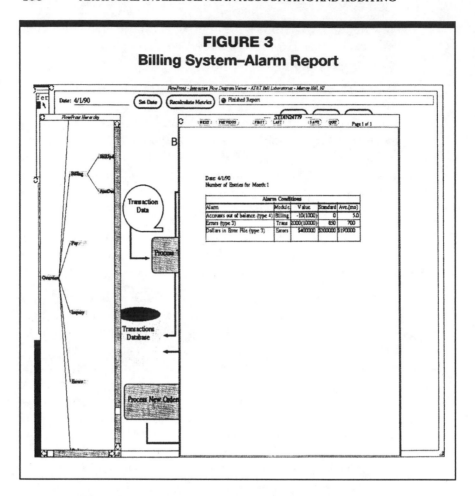

FIGURE 3
Billing System–Alarm Report

The auditor may wish to look at the Customer Billing module in more detail to gather more information about the out-of-balance condition before alerting management. The auditor would select the Billing node in the hierarchy window. A new flowchart representing the Customer Billing module would appear on the workstation monitor. This is illustrated in Figure 4. Here, the metrics, indicated as boxes next to the flowchart, show the flow of accounts through the Customer Billing module on 4/1/90.[10] The alarm (found on the lower left of the figure) indicates that there were ten accounts lost in the process, but more importantly, it illustrates that the loss occurred between the Format Bill module and the Print Bill module.

The auditor may wish to look at the history of the reconciliation. Figure 5 is a two level time series showing the number of accounts lost

FIGURE 4
Billing System–Customer Billing Module

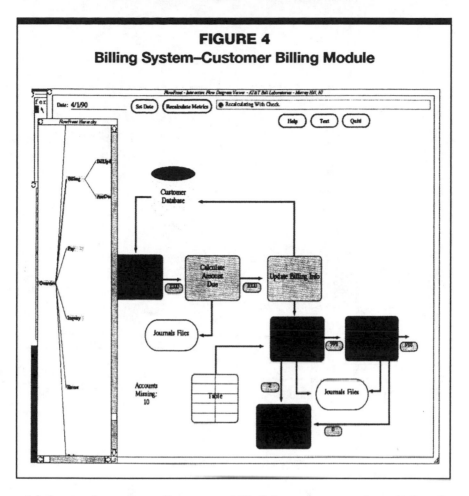

and the total number of accounts billed for a three week period ending 4/1/90.

The graph indicates that the out-of-balance condition occurred once at the beginning of the period and again on 4/1/90. The condition appeared to have been corrected at the beginning of the period, since the reconciliation did not fail again until the current day's processing. The auditor should reset the date to 3/13/90 and check the metrics to determine if the reconciliation failed for the same reason that it did on 4/1/90. This could indicate inadequacy of controls or poor compliance with internal controls. More detailed analytics and metrics relating to the actual billing process and the interface between this module and other modules in the system are found at different levels. This information, taken together, presents an integrated diag-

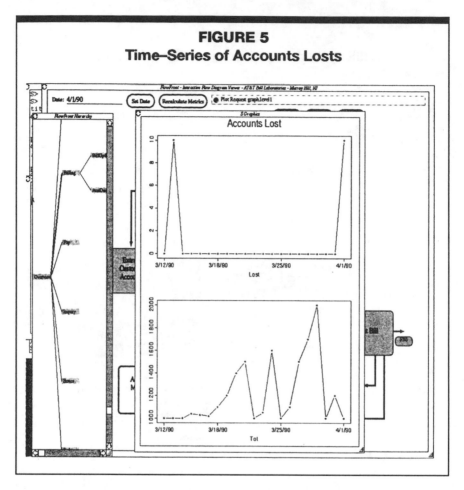

FIGURE 5
Time–Series of Accounts Losts

nostic view of the system being audited.[11]

Complementing the actual hands-on audit work is an auditor platform, accessible at any level, which can include a series of different functions. This platform should ultimately contain at least a statistical package, a graphics package, a spreadsheet package (including a filter to the database), a report generator, and a text editor. These tools can be used for *ad hoc* analysis or be linked to the "wired in" procedures in CPAS. An even richer technological environment may incorporate specific audit document preparation tools that use high technology hardware to read and interpret printed materials [Kahan *et al.*, 1986], and large amounts of information can be stored and accessed directly using optical disk (WORM) technology.[12]

Discussion

The set of analytics and heuristics used in CPAS will ultimately include a wide variety of algorithms ranging from flow based rules to expert algorithms developed using techniques in knowledge engineering.[13] These algorithms will be used both in the auditor platform, as analytical supplements, as well as impounded into software probes in the monitoring stage. Audit knowledge is needed to supplement the simple comprehension of the system being audited and to deal with the very complex stage of data gathering, analysis, and knowledge organization [Buchanan and Shortliffe, 1984] necessary for programming the auditing probes.

The CPAS prototype was tested on two very large financial systems and is currently being applied to a third. The first application of the CPAS technology was an evolving system whose features changed rapidly. The idea was to put a prototype in place that contained basic analytics and then work with the auditors, as they used CPAS, to build more expertise into the system. It was found that only a few heuristics really existed, perhaps because of the nature of tools available to the auditor or because of the lack of longevity of auditors on the job. With the use of CPAS, auditors started to suggest heuristics that previously required cumbersome or not economically feasible audit procedures (*e.g.*, time series tracking of discrepancies in a particular reconciliation). Another explanation for the limited number of heuristics identified is that the problem domain in question tended to be one with "diffuse knowledge" [Halper *et al.*, 1989], where a large set of sources of knowledge were necessary and where knowledge ultimately was captured from a much wider set of experts than originally conceived.

The two early experiences served to print out tools needed and auditors' reactions. A long-term effort in conjunction with the system standards organization would be of great use in providing the base for establishing a company wide continuous audit methodology. Substantive research is needed to determine the best approaches to operationalize and standardize the methodology in internal and external audit contexts.

The issue of startup cost to impound the system description into the CPAS platform and the maintenance of the knowledge base became very important. However, the process of knowledge acquisition and recording used under CPAS is not unlike the phases of internal control evaluation and documentation for workpapers. The level of auditor comprehension of the system tends to be deeper under

CPAM than in the traditional audit if the auditor (not a system analyst) performs knowledge capture.[14]

In the two original applications, the CPAS approach required a higher audit startup cost than the traditional audit, but the level of audit examination was also deeper and more reliable. The CPAS approach is substantially different from the traditional one and requires balancing of audit evidence and timing of the audit process. Auditors currently are used to budgeting for a particular audit and perform it as an intense effort. CPAM requires long-term monitoring and reaction to emerging evidence, something that, with limited experience, is difficult to manage. Given this, the issue of resistance to change may arise. This can be handled by the issuance of an audit manual that describes how to audit with CPAS and extensive training and technical support for the auditors.

Ideally, management also has its own version of CPAS, so they are aware when major problems occur in their system. Auditors could browse their own version of CPAS (with independent analytics) on a periodic basis and follow up on any alarm conditions to see what management has done about them.

Future work on CPAS will focus on increasing the quality of auditor work by integrating the auditor platform with the auditor workstation, increasing the use of monitoring probes, improving the quality of the auditor heuristics, and impounding more expertise into the system.

The introduction of real-time systems will require that the auditor be able to attest to the system of internal accounting controls at different points in time. Continuous process auditing can effectively help the auditor to evaluate these controls, but will require substantive changes in the nature of evidence, the types of procedures, the timing, and the allocation of effort in audit work.

ENDNOTES

The authors thank the two anonymous reviewers for their constructive comments, the editor for his thorough review of the manuscript, and Stanley Halper (Audit Committee Support Network) for his insightful comments We also thank the participants of research seminars at Columbia University, Rutgers University, the University of Kansas, the University of Nebraska, and Boston University and the attendees of the EDPAA, IIA, and AICPA professional meetings for their comments and suggestions. We are particularly indebted to Sam Parker, Chris

Calabrese, TsyhWen Pao, John Snively, Andrew Sherman, Kazuo Ezawa, Ed Raefski, David Pollak, Ron Fritz, Joe Riley, and David Lillian for their work on the prototype system.

1.   Both external and internal audits have attestation objectives. The external auditor must attest to the validity of financial statements. The internal auditor provides the primary appraisal function of company operations, including the controls over the company EDP systems. After testing and evaluation, the internal auditor can attest to the system of internal accounting controls [Halper *et al.*, 1985].

2.   At level 1, the auditor (internal or external) must obtain data through the services of a database user who has access to the DBMS. Such intermediation has been proven to be dangerous in several cases (*e.g.*, equity funding).

3.   The accounting literature has suggested other forms for supplementing traditional control techniques by creating a formal methodology of internal control representation and analysis [Bailey *et al.*, 1985: Bailey *et al.*, 1986] or by using the entity-relationship approach [McCarthy 1979, 1982] to represent accounting events.

4.   Many different types of auditor heuristics can be, "wired" into the CPAS system. The examples below are representative, but generic in nature.
     * If there is an increase in telephone traffic of 20 percent over a period, then expect an increase of similar size in billing 20 days from that day. Investigate if there is more than five percent variance.
     * If total number of errors dropped by edits is larger than two percent of the transactions processed, then investigate error type breakdown.
     * If there is a sudden large drop (in a day) of the size of the retained error file, then an error correction audit is necessary.

5.   It is envisaged that, in the monitoring phase, intrusion and system overhead may be limited by utilizing database backup and recovery traces as the main source of transaction data, dumping a copy of these traces onto a local workstation, loading the workstation with some expert software, and having it as a local interchange device.

6.   Large application systems have many user reports generated for the operational purposes of different organizational entities. For

example, marketing has sales reports that report total sales activity and also breakdown activity by region; production has inventory reports to gauge production needs; finance has payments and receivables reports for their cash flow administration purposes. Most likely, these existing reports will contain all information necessary for continuous auditing purposes.

7. The Hypertext approach is not new, being traceable to the 1960s work of Ted Nelson. It currently is quite popular due to its implementation in personal computers its affinity to object oriented thinking, and many implementations in both commercial and public domains.

8. The CPAS software was implemented under a NeWS windowing system and on a SUN workstation. The entire software was constructed using standard UNIX tools with a minimum of low-level programming. A commercially available relational database was used in the delivery device. The concept, however, can be extended and can be implemented piece by piece using standard PC tools. Conceivably, the methodology can be implemented in many different ways, from a pure PC implementation to a full-fledged distributed computing solution with the "audit computer" as the self contained destination of monitoring measurement data.

9. In order to be able to focus on a discrete period and obtain the desired level of detail, the auditor chooses base date to which all figures will relate. For example, if the auditor identifies a major drop in the outstanding errors file on March 18 (today being June 15), he/she will choose, say March 30, as a base date and perform weekly data analyses for that base date.

10. At this, or any level of the system, the auditor can choose to look at alternate metric dimensions (*e.g.* transactions, records), if appropriate. Additionally, if multiple copies of the software exist in different locations, the auditor can choose the level of aggregation he or she is interested in (*e.g.*, data from the specific data center, from a specific branch, or for the entire entity). These metrics are used to perform a reconciliation and different modules would have different metrics associated with them.

11. "Text," explaining the flowcharts and "Help," explaining how to use the system, are available at each level. The auditor can print out screens, reports, or graphs at any time for writing his/her audit reports.

12. Many firms (*e.g.*, Imnet Corporation and Teletrak Advanced Technologies Systems Inc.) are developing document image tech-

nology to access large optical data storage devices.

13. Expert systems techniques have been examined by several auditing researchers [see Kelly *et al.*, as well as implemented on a limited basis dealing with certain tax (tax accruals) and financial accounting issues (*e.g.*, bank loan portfolio estimation) in practice[Messier and Hansen, 1987; Vasarhelyi, 1988].

14. In the long range, much of this work can be linked to the use of CASE type tools where the knowledge is captured at design and could be easily transported to, if not directly used, the platform.

REFERENCES

Bailey, A. D., G. L. Duke, G. E. Gerlach, C. E. Ko, R. D. Meservy, and A. B. Whinston, "TICOM and the Analysis of Internal Controls," *The Accounting Review*, April 1985, pp. 186-201.

———, R. D. Meservy, and P. E. Johnson, "Internal Control Evaluation: A Computational Model of the Review Process," *Auditing: A Journal of Practice & Theory*, Autumn 1986, pp. 44-74.

———, K. Hackenbrack, P. De, and J. Dillard, "Artificial Intelligence, Cognitive Science and Computational Modeling in Auditing Research: A Research Approach, " *Journal of Information Systems*, Spring 1987, pp. 20-40.

———, L. E. Graham, and J. V. Hansen, "Technological Development and EDP," in Abdel-Khalik, A. R. and I. Solomon, eds., *Research Opportunities in Auditing: The Second Decade*, American Accounting Association: Auditing Section, Sarasota, Florida, 1989.

Biggs, S. F., and T. J. Mock, "An Investigation of Auditor Decision Processes in the Evaluation of Internal Controls and Audit Scope Decisions," *Journal of Accounting Research*, Spring 1983, pp. 234-55.

Buchanan, B. G., and E. H. Shortliffe, *Rule Based Expert Systems*, Addison Wesley, 1984.

Elliott, R. K., "Auditing in the 1990s: Implications for Education and Research," *California Management Review*, Summer 1986, pp. 89-97.

Fox, C., and F. Zappert, "Information Systems Evolution in the Near Future," AT&T Bell Laboratories, Private Communication, December 1985.

Gessner, R., "Building A Hypertext System," "Dr. Dobb's Journal (June 1990), pp. 22-33.

Halper, F. B., J. P. Snively, and M. A. Vasarhelyi, "CPAS-Knowledge Engineering and Representation," *Second International Symposium on Expert Systems in Business, Finance. and Accounting,* Newport Beach, Ca., November 1989.

Halper, S. D., G. C. Davis, P. J. O'Neil-Dunne, and P. R. Pfau, *Handbook of EDP Auditing,* Warren, Gorham and Lamont, 1985.

Hayes-Roth, B., *Implications of Human Pattern Processing for the Design of Artificial Knowledge Systems,* Academic Press, 1978.

Kahan, S., T. Pavlidis, and H. S. Baird, "On the Recognition of Printed Characters of any Font Size," AT&T Bell Laboratories, Private Communication, January 1986 .

Kelly, K., G. Ribar, and J. Willingham, "Interim Report on the Development of an Expert System for the Auditor's Loan Loss Evaluation," in M. A. Vasarhelyi, ed., *Artificial Intelligence in Accounting and Auditing,* Markus Wiener Publishing, 1988).

McCarthy, W. E., "An Entity-relationship View of Accounting Models," *The Accounting Review,* October 1979, pp. 667-86.

———, "The REA Accounting Model: A Generalized Framework for Accounting Systems in a Shared Data Environment," *The Accounting Review,* July 1982, pp. 554-78.

Messier, W. F., Jr., and J. V. Hansen, "Expert Systems in Auditing," *Auditing: A Journal of Practice & Theory,* Autumn 1987, pp. 94-105.

Roussey, R., "The CPA in the Information Age: Today and Tomorrow," *Journal of Accountancy,* October 1986, pp. 94-107.

Schank, R. G., and R. P. Abelson, *Scrips Plans and Understanding,* Lawrance Erlbaum Associates Publishers, 1977.

Shaw, A. N., and H. A. Simon, "Elements of a Theory of Human Problem Solving," *Psychology Review,* Vol. 65, No. 3, 1958, pp. 151-66.

Shimura M., and F. H. George, "Rule Oriented Methods in Problem Solving," *Artificial Intelligence,* Vol. 4, 1973, pp. 203-23.

Simon. H., "The Structure of Ill Structured Problems," *Artificial Intelligence,* Vol. 4, 1973, pp. 181-201.

———, "Information Processing Models of Cognition," *Annual Review Psychology,* Vol. 30, 1979, pp. 363-96.

Vasarhelyi, M. A., "Expert Systems in Accounting and Auditing," in M. A. Vasarhelyi, ed., *Artificial Intelligence in Accounting and Auditing,* Markus Wiener Publishing, 1988.

———, and W. T. Lin. *Advanced Auditing,* Addison Wesley, 1988.

———, and D. C. Yang, "Technological Change and Management Information Systems," *Proceedings of the Twenty First Annual Hawaii International Conference on System Sciences,* Hawaii 1988, pp. 191-97.

The Continuous Process Audit System: A UNIX-Based Auditing Tool

MIKLOS A. VASARHELYI, FERN B. HALPER,
AND KAZUO J. EZAWA

Preface

This paper examines the Continuous Process Auditing System (CPAS), a UNIX-based auditing tool developed at AT&T Bell Laboratories for the Internal Audit organization. The system is an implementation of a Continuous Process Audit Methodology (CPAM) and is designed to deal with the problems of auditing large paperless database systems.

CPAS was built using the UNIX operating system and the NeWS windowing system. It was constructed using standard UNIX* platform tools and enriched by a commercial relational database. This application illustrates that the UNIX system is a rich and effective environment for advanced applications that integrate mainframes and workstations, VMS, DOS and UNIX.

The authors wish to thank the participants of research seminars at several universities and the attendees of the EDPAA, IIA, and AICPA professional meetings for their comments and suggestions. We would also like to thank Mr. Stanley Halper, of the Audit Committee Support Network, for his insightful comments.

1. Introduction

Since the introduction of computers in business, the auditor's role has changed, along with the complexity of tasks they need to perform.

These changes have created major challenges in performing the auditing and attestation function. For example, 1) the advent of time-sharing and data communications has allowed continuous access to data from many locations, creating access exposures; and 2) database systems have added more complexity due to the lack of obvious mapping between the physical and logical organization of data. Today, many large application systems consist of multiple modules, often with multiple copies of databases, at many locations. The "snapshot" audit, that uses only a few days of data from the system being audited, is not effective in these real time systems because evaluating the controls over these systems requires evaluating the controls at many points in time, which is virtually impossible after the fact, even if a detailed paper trail exists, using this method.

Auditors have developed specialized audit software to deal with traditional audit functions, and have begun to use advanced technologies in support of auditing. For example, Cash et al. examines techniques that can be used to audit Accounting Information Systems. Other examples of these technologies are the use of advanced workstations and decision support systems that incorporate analytic tools and expertise to be used on top of the corporate information system. This paper describes the Continuous Process Audit System (**CPAS**), a UNIX-Based system that monitors large complex systems from an audit perspective. The purpose of CPAS is to provide auditors with an integrated diagnostic view of a system. CPAS works by gathering and collating diagnostic data produced from different parts of a system and presenting key checkpoints and analytics in a workstation environment. The purpose of the analytics is to ensure the financial integrity of the system and call auditors' attention to any anomalies. CPAS is an audit application of a general monitoring methodology developed by AT&T Bell Laboratories for the AT&T Internal Audit Organization. The methodology is supported by a set of tools, also developed at Bell Laboratories. This paper focuses on the system aspects of CPAS, and in particular, the UNIX-Based features of this implementation. For a more detailed view of the motivation and theory behind CPAS see Vasarhelyi and Halper (1991).

The paper is divided into six sections. In the next section, we provide an overview of CPAS. Section 3 provides an overview of the methodology. Sections 4 and 5 describe how CPAS was implemented. The Discussion (section 6) touches briefly on audit issues surrounding the use and development of CPAS, our evaluation of UNIX for the task of building the CPAS system, and some ideas for future work.

2. Overview of Approach

In Continuous Process Auditing, data flowing through a system are monitored and analyzed continuously (i.e. daily) using a set of auditor defined rules. System alarms and reports call the auditor's attention to any deterioration or anomalies in the system. Continuous Process Auditing, then, is really an analytical review technique since constantly analyzing a system allows the auditor to improve the focus and scope of the audit. Furthermore, it is also often related to controls as it can be considered as a meta form of control (audit by exception) and can also be used in monitoring control (compliance) either directly, by looking for electronic signature, or indirectly by scanning for the occurrence of certain events.

Ultimately, if a system is monitored over time using a set of ever-improving auditor heuristics, the audit can rely purely on exception reporting. Impounding auditor knowledge into the system means that tests that would normally be performed once a year are repeated with each cycle performed or at planned checkpoints.

The adoption of a Continuous Process Audit Methodology (CPAM) will change the nature of evidence, timing, procedures and effort involved in audit work.

- *Evidence:* The auditor will place an increased level of reliance on the evaluation of flow data (while accounting operations are being performed) instead of evidence from related activities (e.g., preparedness audits).

- *Timing:* Audit work would be focused on *audit by exception* with the system gathering knowledge exceptions on a continuous basis.

- *Procedures:* Traditional auditing involves the examination of archival data, substantially after the event and emphasizes paper-based evidence. Continuous Process Auditing involves the examination of archival and immediate data, close-to-the-event and use of magnetic recorded data.

- *Effort:* Continuous Process Auditing is expected to decrease the amount of procedural effort while focusing on a continuous review of application and audit processes.

3. Conceptual View of Methodology

Conceptually, the monitoring system consists of three levels: a data provisioning level, a knowledge level, and a presentation level (Figure 1). The data provisioning level provides the raw data for the analysis. Data can be extracted from operational reports that are produced by the system or through direct data access. The extracted data are stored in a data repository (i.e., a database) and/or stored in raw form.[1] Certain data also need to be stored in the knowledge base. This includes information about the structure of the system being monitored and analytic definitions. The analysis of the data is performed using various tools and the output is sent to a presentation level.

The main elements of the methodology include:

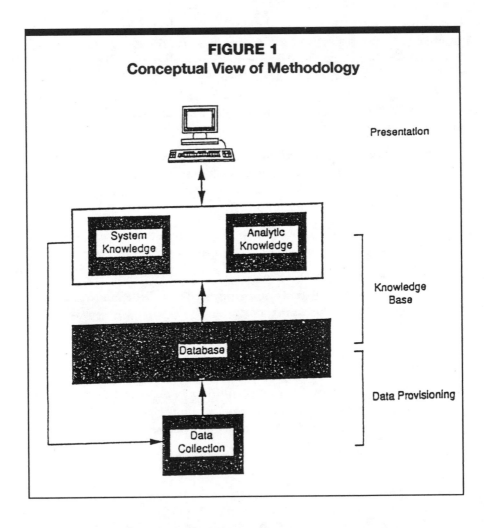

FIGURE 1
Conceptual View of Methodology

- *metrics and analytics:* metrics are direct measurements of a system. These may include things like number of errors, number of transactions input, etc. Analytics are defined as either functional, logical, or empirical relationships among metrics. These measurements can be compared against system standards and alarms (see below) "fired" if a standard is exceeded.

- *standards:* level measures determining expected metric and analytic status at a particular point in time.

- *alarms:* attention directing action, triggered by the values of metrics and analytics. Alarms may be hierarchical in nature; i.e., some alarms may just flag an event for inspection, while others may call management attention to serious problems in the system.

4. Software Implementation

Figure 2 was prepared using the CPAS tool kit and has the look-and-feel of any CPAS application. It shows a high-level view of a theoretical billing system. The hierarchy window on the left in the figure indicates what part of the billing system is represented by the flowchart. In this example, the flowchart represents the base node of the billing system hierarchy, i.e., an overview of the system. This node is called "Overview" in the hierarchy window. Other nodes in the hierarchy window correspond to flowcharts that represent a more detailed view of the system being audited. The auditor can use the hierarchy window to move to any flowchart in CPAS by simply selecting the desired node.

Information relating to 4/1/91 is shown in the figure. An alarm report illustrates any outstanding alarm conditions in the system. For example, on 4/1/91, there were two outstanding alarm conditions, an out of balance condition, and an error threshold was exceeded. The report details where the alarm conditions occurred, the actual value of the analytic, an average value for the alarm, and the standard the analytic was compared to. A time series plot shows how many times in the last three weeks the out of balance condition occurred (here, twice). More detailed analytics and metrics relating to the actual billing process and the interface between this module and other modules in the system are found at different levels. This information, taken together, presents an integrated diagnostic view of the system being audited.

FIGURE 2

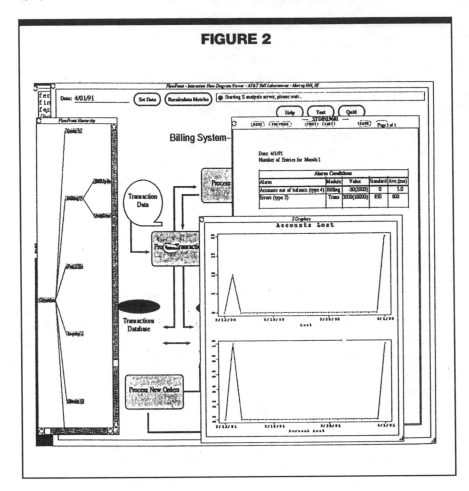

"Text," explaining the flowcharts, and "Help," explaining how to use the system, are available at each level. The auditor can print out screens, reports, or graphs at any time for writing his/her audit reports.

Complementing the actual hands-on audit work is an auditor plat-form, accessible at any level, which can include a series of different functions. This platform should ultimately contain at least a statistical package, a graphics package, a spreadsheet package (including a filter to the database), a report generator, and a text editor. These tools can be used for ad hoc analysis or be linked to the "wired-in" procedures in CPAS. An even richer technological environment may incorporate specific audit document preparation tools that use high technology hardware to read and interpret printed materials and large amounts of information can be stored and accessed directly using optical disk (WORM) technology.[2]

5. Systems Related Issues

The CPAM concept required flexible-modular design and a high degree of flexibility in order to test the concept and prototype the system. Mainframe-based development was deemed too intrusive and too costly. Consequently a workstation based approach with UNIX-type transitivity and pixel-oriented graphics was chosen.

The CPAS software was implemented under the NeWS windowing system and on a SUN workstation. The NeWS system, at that point (1987), possessed the best set of "widgets" and development tools. It used Post Script as its imaging language and could use a screen, a file, as well as a laser printer as an output medium.

The entire software was constructed using standard UNIX tools with a minimum of low-level programming. Application data were generated in IBM mainframes in the form of standard user reports. These standard system reports were analyzed by a "knowledge engineer" and specific fields chosen for collection. Job Control Language (JCL) specs were included in the application control procedures to specify that a particular copy of a report needed to be sent to a particular distribution node. This JCL specification was the only (and minimal) intrusion in the application.

Once the report was sent to the receiving destination it was placed in an electronic storage bin. A connected UNIX gateway would run periodic (say every 10 minutes) "DAEMONS or CRONS"[3] and capture (snurf) these reports, transform them into mail messages and *mail* (a standard UNIX function) them to the CPAS workstation. Under certain conditions *uucp* (UNIX to UNIX Communication Protocol) was used to transfer the report file to the CPAS workstation. These reports, upon arrival at CPAS, were identified and scanned for the desired data. For example, a report named A121 would be identified as A121.awk,[4] a program scanning routine would be activated, and extracted data placed in a relational database. A commercially available relational database (INGRES) was used as a storage device, separating the data gathering portion of the system from its data analysis and delivery device.

The graphic interface design device was called "Flow-Edit" and is not unlike many graphic design devices now: available both in the UNIX and the DOS (e.g. Harvard Graphics) worlds. This tool was used to construct the flowcharts, link the flowcharts hierarchically, and to define different metrics and alarms.

Specific metrics boxes contained data represented to be moving along a flow or contained in a level. These metrics were the result of direct *sql* queries to the relational database. The graphs contained in the windows representing analytics were drawn by a statistical package called *S*. This package was developed for "exploratory data analysis" and contains valuable graphical features. Both the tables and text were generated using UNIX's text editing, formatting and WYSIWIG features enriched by the power of PostScript display on to the screens.[5]

This concept, however, can be extended and implemented piece by piece using standard PC tools. Conceivably, the methodology can be implemented in many different ways, from a pure PC implementation to a full-fledged distributed computing solution with the "audit computer" as the self-contained destination of monitoring/measurement data.

6. Discussion

6.1 Auditing Issues

The CPAS prototype was tested on two very large financial systems. The first application of the CPAS technology was an evolving system whose features changed rapidly. The idea was to put a prototype in place that contained basic analytics and then work with the auditor, as they used CPAS, to build more expertise into the system. The issue of start-up cost to impound the system description into the CPAS platform and the maintenance of the knowledge base became very important. However, the process of knowledge acquisition and recording used under CPAS is not unlike the phases of internal control evaluation and documentation for workpapers that an auditor has to perform. The level of auditor comprehension of the system tends to be deeper under this approach if the auditor (not a system analyst) is to perform knowledge capture.[6]

The CPAS approach probably requires a higher audit start-up cost than the traditional audit but the level of audit examination is also consequently deeper and more reliable. The CPAS approach is substantially different from the traditional one and requires balancing of audit evidence and timing of the audit process. Given this, the issue of resistance to change may arise. This can be handled by the issuance of an audit manual that describes how to audit with CPAS and extensive training and technical support of the auditors in the engagement.

6.2 System Issues

UNIX provided a useful and flexible platform for the implementation of the concept allowing the utilization of a wide set of generic tools for a rapid development of the prototype. It also worked well in a hybrid environment interfacing with a Mainframe-based application. The testing of the prototype indicates its ability to rapidly converge to a full-scale implementation.

The CPAS methodology was developed with special focus on internal auditing but may be extended to external auditing work even for smaller application software (if templates can be developed). CPAS is really a specific instance of the application of a large system monitoring and management technology into an audit domain.

6.3 Future Work

Future work will focus on increasing the quality of auditor work by integrating the auditor platform with the auditor workstation, increasing the use of monitoring probes, improving the quality of the auditor heuristics, and impounding more expertise into the system.

Furthermore, future work will expand the decision support features of the prototype as well as some of its intelligence. The main features of such an expansion would include:

- Incorporating AI techniques such as evidence propagation on the belief net.

- Incorporate design analysis methodology based on influence diagrams and probabilistic estimation.

- Incorporate pattern recognition technology to evaluate time series trends.

ENDNOTES

1. Of course, software can be placed directly in the stream of transactions, and monitor the system directly, for any audit concerns.
2. Software companies, such as Teltrak Advanced Technology Systems Inc., have developed software systems that control access

to optional disk storage devices.

3. These are UNIX-based procedures that self-activate if a particular set of circumstances occurs (DAEMON) or at regular time intervals (CRONS).

4. Both *sed* and *awk* are pattern scanning languages designed for the identification of specific sequences in text.

5. The guest-editor's editorial discusses these tools earlier in this issue.

6. In the long range much of this work can be linked to the use of CASE type tools where the knowledge is captured at design and could be easily transported, if not directly used, to the platform.

*UNIX is a Registered Trademark of Unix Systems Laboratories.

REFERENCES

Ajo, A.V., B.W. Kernigan, and P.J. Weinberger, *The AWK Programming Language*, Addison-Wesley, 1988.

Alter, S., *Decision Support Systems: Current Practice and Continuing Challenges*, Addison-Wesley, 1988.

Bailey, A., L.E. Graham, and J.V. Hansen, "Technological Development and EDP" in Abdel-Khalik, A.R. and I. Solomon, "Research Opportunities in Auditing: The Second Decade," Sarasota Florida: 1989.

Becker, R.A. and J.M. Chambers, *S: An Interactive Environment for Data Analysis and Graphics*, Wardsworth, 1988.

Cash, J.L., A.D. Bailey, Jr., and A.B.Whinston, "A Survey of Techniques for Auditing EDP-Based Accounting Information Systems," *The Accounting Review*, October 1977, pp. 813-32.

Daroca, F.P. and W.W. Holder, "The Use of Analytical Procedures in Review and Audit Engagements," *Auditing: A Journal of Practice and Theory*, Spring 1985, pp. 80-92.

Date, C.J., *A Guide to Ingres*, Addison-Wesley.

Elliott, R.K., "Auditing in the 1990s: Implications for Education and Research," *California Management Review*, Summer 1986, pp. 98-97.

Ezawa, K.J., "Efficient Evaluation of Influence Diagrams," Ph.D. Thesis, Dept. of Engineering-Economic Systems, Stanford University, Palo Alto, CA., 1986.

Fukunaga, K., *Statistical Pattern Recognition*, Academic Press., 1990.

Howard, R., "Decision Analysis: Practice and Promise," *Management Science,* June 1988.

Kahan, S.T., T. Pavlidis, and H.S. Baird, "On the Recognition of Printed Characters of any Font Size, Private Communication, AT& T Bell Laboratories, January 1986.

Kernigan, B.W. and R. Pike, *The UNIX Programming Environment,* Prentice-Hall, 1984.

Roussy, R., "The CPA in the Information Age: Today and Tomorrow," *Journal of Accountancy,* October 1986, pp. 94-107.

Schachter, R.D., "Evaluating Influence Diagrams," Operations Research, 1986.

————, "Evidence Absorption and Propagation through Evidence Reversals," Uncertainty in Artificial Intelligence 5, North-Holland, 1990, pp. 173-190.

Vasarhelyi, M.A. and W.T. Lin, *Advanced Auditing,* Addison-Wesley, 1988.

Inducing Rules for Expert System Development: An Example Using Default and Bankruptcy Data

WILLIAM F. MESSIER, JR. AND JAMES V. HANSEN

1. Introduction

There has been considerable interest in recent years in the development of expert systems for various problem domains, including many business applications. In particular reviews (Messier and Hansen 1987; Michaelsen and Messier 1987) indicate that expert systems technology has been applied to a number of accounting problems. Some examples include: EDP-XPERT-a system for assisting Computer Audit Specialists in assessing the reliability of computer controls (Hansen and Messier 1986a,b); AUDITPLANNER-a system for establishing materiality levels for auditors (Steinbart 1987); and TAXADVISOR-a system for solving problems concerning income and transfer tax planning for individuals (Michaelsen 1984).

Knowledge representation in these systems is usually based on a production system architecture composed of many condition-action (production) rules. Support for representing knowledge in such a rulebased fashion can be found in the problem solving (Newell and Simon 1972) and psychology (Anderson 1983; Holland, Holyoak, Nisbet and Thagard 1986) literature. Additionally, many of the successful expert systems in areas outside business have relied on a production systems architecture (e.g., Buchanan and Shortliffe 1984).

One of the major bottlenecks with the expert system development process is the acquisition of the expert's knowledge about the problem (e.g., Barr and Feigenbaum 1982 Duda and Shortliffe 1983). Typically, the expert's knowledge is elicited through questionnaires, interviews, protocol analyses, or some combination thereof. These direct knowledge acquisition methods can be very time-and-effort consuming (Michalski and Chilausky 1980; Clifford, Jarke and Vassilou 1983). For example, Currim, Meyer and Le (1986) argue that the use of production systems in modeling consumer behavior has been limited because the decision rules have to be derived from transcriptions of protocols. Because of the tediousness of this process, they assert that applications have been limited to small samples of experts. Additionally, in auditing contexts (and possibly other problem domains), it has been found difficult to identify detailed production rules from experts protocols (Biggs, Messier and Hansen 1987; Meservy, Bailey and Johnson 1986).

One reason for the considerable time and effort, and sometimes limited success, associated with direct knowledge acquisition methods is that experts often have difficulty explaining their decision processes[1] (Michalski and Chilausky 1980; Bobrow, Mittal and Stefik 1986). These observations have motivated interest in studying alternative methods of knowledge acquisition such as induction (Holland et al. 1986). The use of inductive methods is motivated by the hypothesis that an expert's decision processes can be inferred by studying the decisions s/he makes when presented with a set of representative instances from the problem domain of interest. The appeal of this approach is that the expert is typically more confident exercising his/her expertise than explaining it. Moreover, the time requirements to develop production systems can sometimes be reduced using an induction methodology (Michalski and Chilausky 1980; Biggs et al. 1987).

Currim et al. (1986) assert that induction methods can be evaluated on three dimensions:

1. *Structural Validity:* the ability of inductive approaches to recover the true form of the expert's decisionmaking model;

2. *Diagnostic Validity:* the ability of inductive approaches to infer the relative importance of different attributes (variables) in influencing the final decision; and

3. *Predictive Validity:* the ability of inductive approaches to predict decisions made in other contexts or in holdout samples.

The results reported in this paper address only the second and third issues. Research by Michalski and Chilausky (1980) and Currim, et al. (1986) found that induction performed quite well in terms of structural validity. For example, Currim et al. (1986) found in a simulation study that induction methods were effective in recovering the underlying structure of the decision model.

In this paper, we report the results of a study whose objective was to assess the relative performance of production systems developed by inductive methods, when compared to discriminant analysis models, individual judgments, and group judgments. Our approach uses data from two previous studies on loan default and bankruptcy prediction. Production systems are developed using the same sets of variables used in each of the benchmark studies. The relative performance of the production systems is measured in two ways: (1) by comparing the attributes selected by the induction approach with those selected by discriminant analysis, individual judgments, and group judgments (diagnostic validity) and (2) by comparing the percentage of correct classifications yielded by the production system to that of discriminant analysis, individual judgments, and group judgments (predictive validity).

In §2, we describe the induction methodology. §3 demonstrates an application of the methodology to predicting loan default and bankruptcy. Some concluding comments are offered in §4.

2. Induction

Inductive inference is the process of going from specific observations about objects and an initial inductive hypothesis to an inductive assertion that accounts for the observations (Michalski 1983). In other words, inductive methods attempt to discover regularities (rules) by analyzing a series of instances or examples related to a particular problem. Instances (real or hypothesized) can be provided by an expert or obtained from archival data. After relevant attributes have been identified and their values determined for each instance, an induction algorithm is used to derive production rules.

While the application of this methodology seems to have potential, the extent to which such inductively-derived production systems can significantly contribute to expert systems development is still relatively unknown and in need of research. In the next subsection, we briefly discuss the two principal classes of induction algorithms. This is followed by a description of the inductive learning algorithm used in this study.

2.1. INDUCTION ALGORITHMS

Cohen and Feigenbaum (1982) propose a bifurcation of approaches to inductive rule formulation. The first approach is *data-driven:* a set of instances drives the search for rules. The second approach is *model-driven:* an a priori model guides the search for plausible rules.

With data-driven methods, such as the one used in this study, a set of instances is scanned, and the algorithm seeks the most parsimonious production system which defines those instances. Rules may be modified as new instances are added. These methods are thought to offer a flexible approach to production system development where there are few priors concerning feasible decisionmaking structures (Smith, Clark and Cotton 1984). With model-driven methods, rules are established a priori and are then tested against a set of instances. Consider the set of loan instances depicted in Table 1. Suppose that we had a rule suggested by the relevant literature such as this:

> IF the Earnings Trend is Positive and the Current Ratio Trend
> is Up and the Type of Product is Consumer Goods
> THEN there will be no loan default
> ELSE there will be loan default.

The model-driven approach would scan the list of instances for matches and mismatches in classification. Example 5 is the only instance whose values match the IF conditions of the rule, and the classification is as predicted. All other examples satisfy the ELSE condition.

TABLE 1
An Example Set of Loan Outcomes and Selected Attributes

Example No.	Loan Disposition	Earnings Trend– Past Five Years	Current Ratio Trend– Past Five Years	Type of Product
1	Default	Negative	Up	Service
2	Default	Stable	Down	Service
3	No Default	Stable	Up	Consumer Goods
4	Default	Negative	Up	Consumer Goods
5	No Default	Positive	Up	Consumer Goods
6	No Default	Positive	Up	Service
7	No Default	Stable	Up	Service
8	No Default	Positive	Down	Service
9	Default	Stable	Down	Consumer Goods
10	Default	Negative	Down	Service

However, Examples 3, 6, 7, and 8 are misclassified. Whether this rule should be accepted, rejected, or modified would have to be determined from guidelines provided by the analyst.

Each approach and its implementation algorithms have advantages and disadvantages. Model-driven approaches can be effective in problem domains where extensive prior knowledge exists regarding feasible decision rules. That is, the analyst must specify the decision rules *and* related heuristics for search. Problem domains not satisfying these requirements may be better served by data-driven approaches. While most data-driven methods require that the entire set of examples be searched each time a new example is added, this limitation is compensated for by the fact that they can derive a single, best-fitting set of rules.

2.2. THE CONCEPT LEARNING ALGORITHM

For this study, we selected a data-driven method attributable to Quinlan (1979, 1983).This method is a descendant of the Concept Learning System (CLS) developed by Hunt, Marin and Stone (1966). The object of the algorithm is to take objects of a known class (e.g., firms defaulting on loans and firms not defaulting on loans) which are described in terms of a fixed collection of attributes (e.g., earnings trend, current-ratio trend, and type of product) and generate a production system over these attributes which correctly classifies all the given objects.

We use the example presented in Table 1 for illustration. The first column indicates the class attribute, Loan Disposition. The remaining column names identify the diagnostic attributes to be used in arriving at a classification decision. Each row of the table represents one instance. The first instance represents a loan default when the earnings trend was negative, the current-ratio trend was up, and the product provided was a service.

The CLS algorithm proceeds by choosing an attribute, A, with permissible values, $a_1, a_2, \ldots, a_n$. For example, in Table 1 Earnings Trend is an attribute with permissible values a_1 = Negative, a_2 = Positive, and a_3 = Stable. Each member of the set of examples (C) will have one of these values (a_i) for A. This allows C to be sorted into subsets, $c_1, c_2, \ldots, c_n$, where c_1, contains those examples in C with value a_1 of A, c_2 contains those examples in C with value a_2 of A, and so forth. The result is a set of n examples which need to be related to their class.

Suppose that Earnings Trend is the attribute selected. Figure 1 shows the sorting of the set of 10 instances *(C)* into c_1 (those instances having Earnings Trend value, Negative), c_2 (those instances having value, Positive), and c_3 (those instances having value, Stable). Observe that for c_1 the value of the class attribute is always Default, and that for c_2 the value of the class attribute is always No Default. Thus, for c_1 and c_2 no further analysis is necessary. That part of the production system would read as follows:

> IF Earnings Trend is Negative
> > THEN there will be loan default
>
> ELSE IF Earnings Trend is Positive
> > THEN there will be no loan default

Since there is inconsistency in the class attribute values associated with c_3 further iterations of the process described above are required. Figure 2 depicts the resulting split on the attribute Current-Ratio Trend. Since the subsets of the new partition exhibit only a single value for the class attribute, the inductive process is complete. The production system would be completed by adding the following condition:

> ELSE IF Earnings Trend is Stable
> > THEN IF Current-Ratio Trend is Up
> > > THEN there will be no loan default
> >
> > ELSE IF Current-Ratio Trend is Down
> > > THEN there will be loan default.

This rule-forming procedure will always work provided that there are not two objects belonging to different classes but having identical values for each diagnostic attribute. In such cases, the set of diagnostic attributes are insufficient for the classification task.

We have said nothing yet about how to choose which attribute to test at each step. Indeed, one may inquire whether the order of choice makes any difference. A simple approach would be to arbitrarily iterate through all diagnostic attributes; however, induction methods can be more appealing in terms of the time and effort involved if the final production system is minimal. Minimal is used here in the sense that the procedures consider first those attributes about which there is the least uncertainty concerning their association with a particular class value.

CLS's selection process assumes that the complexity of the decision tree reflects the amount of information conveyed by the conditional probabilities linking the questions and decisions. Moreover, the link-

FIGURE 1

**Initial Split on Example Set from Table 1
Using attribute "Earnings Trend"**

		Loan Disposition	Current Ratio Trend	Type of Product	Example No.
	Negative	Default	Up	Service	1
		Default	Up	Consumer Goods	4
		Default	Down	Service	10
Earning Trend	Positive	No Default	Up	Consumer Goods	5
		No Default	Up	Service	6
		No Default	Down	Service	
	Stable	Default	Down	Service	2
		No Default	Up	Consumer Goods	3
		No Default	Up	Service	7
		Default	Down	Consumer Goods	9

ages between one question and another, or between a question and a class decision are all binary (yes or no). Therefore, the probabilities underlying potential answers to any one question are complementary. Information theory provides a convenient method of computing the conditional probabilities associated with the quality of yes/no choices. At any stage, the attribute selected is that attribute yielding the least entropy. That is, the next attribute selected is that which has the least uncertainty associated with its occurrence with class values. The discussion which follows details the method.

If an object can be classified into n different sets, $c_i, \ldots, c_n$ and the probability of an object being in class c_i is $p(c_i)$, then the entropy (measure of uncertainty) of classification $E(C)$ is

$$E(C) = -\sum_{i=1}^{n} p(c_i) \log p(c_i), \quad (\text{where } \log = \log_2).$$

The attribute chosen is the one whose classification yields the smallest entropy.

In Table 2, we split our set of examples (Table 1) on the attribute Current Ratio Trend (CRT). The entropy of each subtable $E(C|a_j)$ is given by:

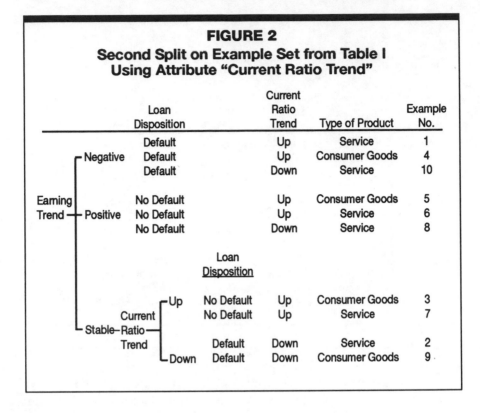

FIGURE 2
Second Split on Example Set from Table I
Using Attribute "Current Ratio Trend"

		Loan Disposition	Current Ratio Trend	Type of Product	Example No.
	Negative	Default	Up	Service	1
		Default	Up	Consumer Goods	4
		Default	Down	Service	10
Earning Trend	Positive	No Default	Up	Consumer Goods	5
		No Default	Up	Service	6
		No Default	Down	Service	8

		Loan Disposition	Current Ratio Trend	Type of Product	Example No.
	Up	No Default	Up	Consumer Goods	3
Stable–Current Ratio Trend		No Default	Up	Service	7
	Down	Default	Down	Service	2
		Default	Down	Consumer Goods	9

$$E(C|\mathrm{CRT}) = -\sum_{i=1}^{n} p(c_i|a_j) \log p(c_i|a_j)$$

where n is the number of subsets, c_i. For the data in Table 2, we have
$$E(C|\mathrm{CRT=Up}) = -p(\text{No Default}|\mathrm{CRT=Up})*\log p(\text{No Default}|\mathrm{CRT=Up})$$
$$+(-p)(\text{Default}|\mathrm{CRT=Up})*\log p(\text{Default}|\mathrm{CRT=Up})$$
$$= -\tfrac{2}{3}\log(\tfrac{2}{3})-\tfrac{1}{3}\log(\tfrac{1}{3}) = 0.92.$$

Similarly, $E(C|\mathrm{CRT = Down}) = 0.81$.

In order to find the entropy of the entire table after the split, $E(C|A)$ is computed:

$$E(C|A) = \sum_{j=1}^{M} p(a_j)\, E(A|a_j),$$

where M is the number of values for attribute A. For our example, we have:

$$E(C|\text{CRT}) = \sum_{j=1}^{2} p(a_j)\, E(\text{CRT}|a_j)$$

$$= ({}^3\!/_5 * 0.92) + ({}^2\!/_5 * 0.81)$$

$$= 0.876.$$

We complete the same computations for the other attributes, deriving the following:

$$E(C|ET) = 0.4, \quad E(C|TP) = 1.0.$$

Observing that $E(C|ET)$ yields the smallest entropy, Earnings Trend is the attribute selected for the first split as suggested in Figure 1.

In the case of integer-valued attributes we not only have to calculate the value of the entropy measure but we also have to compute the value on which to split the attribute. With an integer-valued attribute a binary split is performed by partitioning the integer range about a threshold value, chosen as follows. Assume there are N attribute vectors $V_1, \ldots, V_N$ and that we are interested in attribute A. Assume further that the V_i, are ordered in increasing value of A. For each i, $1 < i < N$, V_i can be split into 2 subsets, $\{V_1, \ldots, V_i\}$ and $\{V_{i+1}, \ldots, V_n\}$. These subsets define a value for the smallest entropy measure. We chose the minimum such value as the value of the evaluation function for A. If this value occurs for subsets $\{V_1, \ldots, V_j\}$ and $\{V_{j+1}, \ldots, V_n\}$, then the attribute for an A value is split midway between the values at V_j and V_{j+1}.

TABLE 2
A Split of the Example Set Based on Current Ratio Trend

Current Ratio Trend	Loan Disposition	Example No
Up	Default	1
Up	No Default	3
Up	Default	4
Up	No Default	5
Up	No Default	6
Up	No Default	7
Down	Default	2
Down	No Default	8
Down	Default	9
Down	Default	10

3. Application

To test the applicability of inductive inference, we obtained the data from a loan default study conducted by Abdel-khalik and El-Sheshai (1980) and a bankruptcy study by Libby, Trotman and Zimmer (1987). The study of loan default and bankruptcy provides a useful topical area since there is a substantial body of research which includes the use of (1) mathematical models and (2) human decision makers. See Zavgren (1983) for a review of this literature. Thus, by using these two studies we can compare the inductive inference methodology against discriminant analysis, individual judgments, and group judgments.

3.1. THE ABDEL-KHALIK AND EL-SHESHAI (A/E) STUDY

3.1.1. *Background.* In the A/E study, an experimental sample of 16 defaulted firms were identified and matched against a control sample of 16 nondefaulted firms.[2] Additionally, 14 defaulted firms were identified for use as a validation sample.[3] Eighteen financial ratios and trends were compiled on these firms. A discriminant analysis model developed from the control and experimental samples correctly classified 90.6% of the combined samples. Similarly, a discriminant model developed from the control and validation samples correctly classified 100% of the combined samples. The model developed from the control and validation samples was also able to correctly classify 57% of the experimental (default) firms. Twenty-eight commercial lending officers also participated in the study. They were required to judge which of the control and experimental firms would default based on the small number of financial ratios they selected. The benchmarks developed from this data and the correct classification rates (in parentheses) were: average human prediction (62.5%), "model of man" (predictions based on a linear model developed from human judgments) (62.5%), human environmental model (a mathematical model based on information selected by humans) (67.5%), and most frequently acquired cues (a discriminant model based on the four cues most frequently acquired by the humans) (75%). In addition, the use of Beaver's (1966) ratios (a discriminant model using cash flow/total debt, net income/total assets, and total debt/total assets) on the control and experimental sample produced a correct classification rate of 72%. Finally, two simple rules of thumb (current ratio ≤2.0 and total debt/equity ≤1.0) were found to correctly classify 84% and 72% of the control and experimental sample.

3.1.2. *Method and Results* Our approach was to use the same set of 18 financial indicators (attribute values) for the firms in the CLS algorithm in order to determine how effective the resulting rules would be as compared to the various benchmarks in the A/E study. All data analyses were performed using the EXPERTEASE software package (Human Edge Software Corporation 1983).[4]

Using the 18 financial ratios and trends from the control and experimental samples, the production system shown in Figure 3 was generated. In Figure 4, the production system is converted to a decision tree. Note that this production system only includes five pieces of financial information. Comparing this to the variables that were significant in the discriminant analysis (see Table 3), we find that only the net income/total assets ratio is common to both models. This set of rules correctly classifies 100% of the control and experimental samples. This result is not surprising since the data-driven method used here continues to derive rules until all examples are correctly classified.

What is surprising, however, is that these results were achieved with a relatively small and simple production system. Basically, default is predicted if the current ratio is less than 1.912 and/or the long-term debt to net worth ratio is greater than 0.486. The production system in Figure 3 was used to predict default in the validation sample. Fourteen of the 16 (87.5%) defaulted companies in the validation sample were correctly classified. A similar test was not reported by A/E.

A/E, however, did construct a discriminant model using the control and validation samples. The four significant variables in this discriminant model are shown in Table 3. The 18 financial ratios from the control and validation samples were also run on the inductive algorithm. Figures 5 and 6 show the production system and decision tree that resulted from this process. As expected, it correctly classifies all firms in the control and validation samples.[5] Note that the two attributes included in this production system are consistent with Beaver's (1966) findings for (mostly) bankrupt companies. Only the current ratio was common to both the production system and the discriminant model. Using this relatively simple production system on the experimental sample, an 87.5% (14 out of 16) correct classification rate was achieved. Table 4 summarizes the various correct classification rates from the A/E study and the induction algorithm.

TABLE 3
Significant Financial Information Used in the Abdel-khalik and El-Shesai (1980) Study

BY DISCRIMINANT ANALYSIS IN:
Experimental/Control Samples:
      Total debt/Total assets
      Trend of Long-term debt/Net Worth
      Cash Flow/Total debt
      Net income/Total assets
      Trend of Net income/Sales
      Trend of Net income/Total assets

Validation/Control Samples:
      Current Ratio
      Quick assets/Sales
      Trend of Long-term debt/Net Worth
      Net income/Sales

FIGURE 3
Production System Resulting from the Control and Experimental Samples in the Abdel-khalik and El-Shesai (1980) Study

IF the current ratio is less than 1.912
    THEN the firm will default
ELSE
    IF the ratio of long-term debt to net worth is less than 0.486 and
        IF the ratio of long-term debt to net worth is less than 0.046 and
            IF the ratio of net income to total assets is less than 0.100
                THEN the firm will default
            ELSE the firm will not default
        ELSE the firm will not default.
ELSE
    IF the ratio of working capital to sales is less than 0.222 and
        IF the ratio of net income to sales is less than 0.010
            THEN the firm will default
        ELSE the firm will not default
    ELSE the firm will default.

FIGURE 4

Decision Tree of Production System Resulting from the Control and Experimental in the Abdel-khalik and El-Shesai (1980) Study.

Current Ratio Trend < 1.912?

    Yes: --- Default

    No: Ratio of LongTerm Debt to Net Worth < 0.486?

        Yes: Ratio of LongTerm Debt to Net Worth < 0.046?

            Yes: Ratio of Net Income to Total Assets < 0.100?

                Yes: -------------------------------- Default

                No: ---------------------------- No Default

            No: ----------------------------------- No Default

        No: Ratio of Working Capital to Sales < 0.222?

            Yes: Ratio of Net Income to Sales < 0.010?

                Yes: -------------------------------- Default

                No: ---------------------------- No Default

            No: --- Default

FIGURE 5

Production System Resulting from the Control and Validation Samples in the Abdel-khalik and El-Shesai (1980) Study.

IF the current ratio is less than 1.895

    THEN the firm will default

ELSE

    IF the ratio of cash flow to total debt is less than 0.741

        THEN the firm will not default

    ELSE the firm will default.

FIGURE 6

Decision Tree of Production System Resulting from the Control and Validation Samples: Abdel-khalik and El-Shesai (1980) Study.

Current Ratio < 1.895?

    Yes: --Default

    No: Ratio of Cash Flow to Total Debt < 0.741?

        Yes: ----------------------------------- No Default

        No: --- Default

3.2. THE LIBBY, TROTMAN AND ZIMMER (LTZ) STUDY

3.2.1. *Background.* The LTZ study was concerned with examining a number of aspects of group decision making using a bankruptcy prediction task. Their sample included 39 Australian land development firms; 12 of which had failed. Five financial ratios were presented for each firm: (1) earnings to total tangible assets, (2) cash flow to total liabilities, (3) current ratio, (4) total liabilities to shareholders fund (i.e. debt to equity), and (5) retained earnings to total tangible assets. A discriminant model using these ratios correctly classified 84.1% of the firms (Libby, Trotman and Zimmer 1987).

LTZ also examined the performance of six decision schemes. These included: (1) the average individual (average across individuals), (2) actual best member (the individual in the group with highest correct classification), (3) composite group (an equal weighting of each member in the group), (4) interacting group (a decision reached through interaction by the group), (5) subjective best member (selected by the group as the most accurate individual), and (6) most influential member (the member whose opinion was followed most often by the group). The range of correct classification was from 29.6 firms or 75.9% (average individual) to 32.2 firms or 86.6% (actual best member).

3.2.2. *Method and Results.* Twenty-three firms were randomly sampled from the LTZ data set; 8 bankrupt and 15 non bankrupt. We attempted to maintain approximately the same ratio of failed to non-

---

TABLE 4
Comparison of the Results from the Discriminant Analysis from the Abdel-khalik and El-Shesai (1980) Study with the Inductive Algorithm

	PREDICTIVE OF:	
	Own Sample	Holdout
DISCRIMINANT ANALYSIS DEVELOPED FROM:		
Experimental/Control Firms	90.6	Not reported
Validation/Control Firms	100.0	57.0
PRODUCTION SYSTEMS DEVELOPED FROM:		
Experimental/Control firms	100.0	87.5
Validation/Control firms	100.0	87.5

FIGURE 7

Production System Resulting from a Sample of the Firms in the Libby, Trotman and Zimmer (1987) Study.

IF the current ratio is less than 1.533 and
    IF the ratio of earnings to total tangible assets is less than 0.092 and
        IF the ratio of retained earnings to total tangible assets is less than 0.064 and
            IF the ratio of retained earnings to total tangible assets is less than - 0.942
                THEN the business will not fail.
            ELSE the business will fail.
        ELSE the business will not fail.
    ELSE the business will not fail.
ELSE the business will not fail.

FIGURE 8

Decision Tree of Production System Resulting from a Sample of the Firms in the Libby, Trotman and Zimmer (1987) Study.

Current Ratio < 1.533?
    Yes: Ratio of earnings to total tangible assets < 0.092?
        Yes: Ratio of retained earnings to total tangible assets < 0.064?
            Yes: Ratio of retained earnings to total tangible assets <0.942?
                Yes: ------------------------------ Not Fail
                No: ------------------------------------ Fail
            No: ------------------------------------- Not Fail
        No: -- Not Fail
    No: -- Not Fail

---

failed firms as in the original sample. Figures 7 and 8 show the production system rules and decision tree that resulted. Again, the current ratio is the first attribute selected. Only two of the other four variables are included in this production system: earnings to total tangible assets and retained earnings to total tangible assets. The production system in Figure 7 correctly classifies 100% of the holdout firms (twelve bankrupt and four nonbankrupt).

4. Concluding Comments

In this study, the attribute sets induced for the production systems only partially intersect the attribute sets included in the discriminant models. However, in all cases tested, the production systems produced by the induction algorithm outperformed the discriminant models, the individuals, and the groups. This second finding, which we view as the more important, suggests that the use of the inductive inference methodology may offer some potential for expert system development. While the generalizability of our results is arguable, the instance set used may be representative of a larger class of problem domains which are characterized by interaction among diagnostic problem attributes (the analogue of independent variables). An inductive algorithm, such as the one used here, deals with those interactions directly in that a diagnostic attribute can assume different values at different locations in the production system. Results which corroborate the favorable performance of induction in deriving production rules for such problem domains have recently been reported (Parker and Copeland 1987).

This experiment benefitted from the availability of data which facilitated comparison with the results of prior studies using traditional methods of analysis. Subsequent studies should examine the performance of inductive methods in problem domains of different types and complexity. As more understanding is acquired, studies can be extended to explore the predictive ability of induced production systems on data from other time periods. Since appropriate data can be difficult to gather, an alternative procedure might be to simulate examples, then present them to the appropriate expert for decision classification. This approach could facilitate an examination of the impact on production systems of instance omission, as well as instance frequency.

Conventional wisdom is that inductive methods are limited in several ways. One limitation is that current methods are difficult to apply to very large problem domains. The availability or the range of necessary examples may be prohibitive. Whether this problem can be mitigated by partitioning the problem domain into smaller problem modules is still a research issue. A second limitation derives from the potential error introduced into a production system from omitting important instances or diagnostic attributes. Since direct acquisition of a rule can capture a more general pattern of reasoning, it is argued that direct knowledge acquisition methods carry less risk (Holsapple and

Whinston 1987). A third limitation deals with how to handle conflicting instances (i.e., two instances belonging to different classes but having similar attribute values). One solution, of course, would be to delete one or both of the examples from the data set. This may be a fruitful for future research.

While not endorsing inductive methods, Bobrow et al. (1986) maintain that one cannot just "extract" the knowledge from the expert; that one must structure it in such a way that it bears on the whole range of expected cases. They assert that a critical resource in the successful development an expert system is a good set of test cases by which to extract knowledge from the experts. It is proposed that by watching experts actually solve problems, rather than just having them describe how they do it, it is possible to understand the real process that goes on and the actual knowledge that is used.

It seems that both direct-acquisition methods and inductive methods may play a role in this process. Induction may be particularly useful in producing decision rules for small, highly-structured problem domains or modules. Confirming evidence awaits further research.[6]

Endnotes

1. There is evidence in the psychology literature (e.g. Schneider and Shiffrin 1977) that suggests that an expert's decision processes can become automatic. If this is the case, it may be difficult to elicit the expert's rules using direct knowledge acquisition methods.
2. In many domains, such as predicting bankruptcy and loan default, an expert (i.e., an auditor or loaner) make a judgment based on past experiences. Thus, from a practical perspective, a production system developed from a set of data from one time period should be tested against a set of data from a later time period. We partially accomplish this with the Abdel-khalik and El-Shesai (1980) data. The control and experimental firms were selected from the time period up and including 1975. The validation sample was selected from 1975-76 data. Thus, when we use the production systems from the control and experimental firms to predict validation sample, we test the temporal nature of the production system. Such a test was not possible with the LTZ study. We would like to thank the reviewer for pointing out this issue.
3. Abdel-khalik and El-Shesai (1980) report using 14 firms in their

validation sample. In the data provided to us, the validation sample data contained 16 firms. We were unable to determine the two companies were not included in their results. We used all 16 validation firms in our analyses.

4. All the data in both studies were scaled by equivalent factors to yield integer values for use in the algorithm. Results were reduced to original magnitudes for testing purposes.

5. Note in both Figures 3 and 5 that the current ratio is the first attribute selected. We suspect that the remaining differences between the two production systems result from the fact that the control and experimental samples were matched, while the validation sample was not as closely matched to the control sample. As a result, the algorithm would require a more detailed splitting process to classify the control and experimental firms.

6. We would like to thank Rashad Abdel-khalik, Steve Kachelmeier, Rick Tubbs, Ken Trotman, and two anonymous reviewers for their helpful comments on an earlier version of this paper. The authors would also like to thank R. Abdel-khalik, K. El-Sheshai, B. Libby, K. Trotman and I. Zimmer for allowing us to use the data from their studies.

REFERENCES

Abdel-Khalik, A, R. and K. M. Elsheshai, "Information Choice and Utilization in an Experiment on Default Prediction," J. Accounting Res., Autumn 1980, pp. 325-342.

Anderson, J. R., The Architecture of Cognition, Harvard University Press, Cambridge, MA, 1983.

Barr, A. and E. A. Feigenbaum, The Handbook of Artificial Intelligence, Vol. 11, Pinman Books, Ltd., London, 1982.

Beaver, W. H., "Financial Ratios as Predictors of Failure," J. Accounting Res., Supplement 1966, pp. 71-110.

Biggs, S. F., W. F. Messier, Jr. and J. V. Hansen, "A Descriptive Analysis of Computer Audit Specialists' Decision-Making Behavior in Advanced Computer Environments," Auditing: J. Practice and Theory, Spring 1987, pp. 1-21.

Bobrow, D. C., S. Mittal and M. J. Stefik, "Expert Systems: Perils and Promise," Comm. ACM, 29, September 1986, pp. 880-894.

Buchanan, B. G. and E. H. Shortliffe, *Rule-Based Expert Systems: The MYCIN Experiments of the Stanford Heuristic Programming Project,* Addison-Wesley, 1984.

Clifford, J., M. Jarke and Y. Vassilou, "A Short Introduction to Expert Systems," working paper, Center for Research on Information Systems, New York University, September 1983.

Cohen, P. R. and E. A. Feigenbaum, *The Handbook of Artificial Intelligence,* Vol. 111, William Kaufman, Inc., Los Altos, CA, 1982.

Currim, I. S., R. J. Meyer and N. Le, "A Concept Learning System for the Inference of Production Models of Consumer Choice," working paper, UCLA, February 1986.

Duda, R. O. and E. H. Shortliffe, "Expert Systems Research," *Science,* 15 April 1983, pp. 261-268.

Hansen, J. V, and W. F. Messier, Jr., "A Knowledge-Based, Expert System for Auditing Advanced Computer Systems," *European J. Oper. Res.,* September 1986a, pp. 371-379.

————, and ————, "A Preliminary Investigation of EDP-XPERT," *Auditing: J. Practice & Theory,* Fall I 1986b, pp. 109-123.

Holland, J. H., K. J. Holyoak, R. E. Nisbett and R. R. Thagard, *Induction: Processes of Inference, Learning and Discovery,* The MIT Press, Cambndge, MA, 1986.

Holsapple, C. and A. B. Whinston, *Business Expert Systems,* Irwin, Homewood, IL, 1987.

Human Edge Software Corporation, *EXPERT-EASE,* 1983.

Hunt, E. B., J. Marin, and P. T. Stone, *Experiments in Induction,* Academic Press, 1966.

Libby, R., K. T. Trotman and I. Zimmer, "Member Variation, Recognition of Expertise, and Group Performance," *J. Appl. Psychology,* 1987, pp. 81-87.

Meservy, R. D., A. D. Bailey Jr. and P. E. Johnson, "Internal Control Evaluation: A Computational Model of the Review Process," *Auditing: J. Practice & Theory,* Fall 1986, pp. 44-74.

Messier, W. F., Jr. and J. V. Hansen, "Expert Systems in Auditing: 'The State of the Art," *Auditing: J. Practice & Theory,* Fall 1987, pp. 94-105.

Michaelsen, R. H., "An Expert System for Tax Planning," *Expert Systems,* October 1984, pp. 149-167.

———— and W. F. Messier, Jr., "Expert Systems in Taxation," *J. Amer. Taxation Assoc.,* Spring 1987, pp. 7-21.

Michalski, R. S., "A Theory and Methodology of Inductive Learning," in *Machine Learning: An Artificial Intelligence Approach,* R. S.

Michalski, J. G. Carbonell, and T. M. Mitchell (eds.), Tioga Publishing Company, Palo Alto, CA, 1983.

———— and R. L. Chilausky, "Learning by Being Told and Learning from Example: An Experimental Comparison of the Two Methods of Knowledge Acquisition in the Context of Developing an Expert System for Soybean Diagnosis," *Internat. J. Policy Analysis and Information Systems*, 1980, pp. 125-161.

Newell, A. and H. Simon, *Human Problem Solving*, Prentice Hall, Inc., 1972.

Parker, J. E. and R. M. Copeland, "Predictive Abilities of Three Modeling Procedures: Multiple Discriminant Analysis, Multivariate Probit Analysis, and Recursive Partitioning," working paper, University of Missouri, September 1987.

Quinlan, J. R., "Learning Efficient Classification Procedures and Their Application to Chess End Games," in Machine Learning: An Artificial Intelligence Approach, R. S. Michalski, J. G. Carbonell, and T. M. Mitchell (eds.), Tioga Publishing Company, Palo Alto, CA, 1983.

————, "Discovering Rules by Induction & from Large Collections of Examples," in *Expert Systems in the Micro Electronic Age*, D. Michie (ed.), Edinburgh University Press, 1979.

Schneider, W and R. M. Shiffrin, "Controlled and Automatic Human Information Processing. I. Detection, Search, and Attention," *Psychological Rev.*, 1977, p. 166.

Smith, T. R., W. A. Clark and J. W. Cotton, Deriving and Testing Production-Systems Models of Sequential Decision-Making Behavior," *Geographical Analysis*, 1984, pp. 191-222.

Steinbart, P., "The Construction of a Rule-Based Expert System as a Method for Studying Materiality Judgements," *Accounting Rev.*, January 1987, p. 97-116.

Zavgren, C. V., "The Prediction of Corporate Failure: The State of the Art," *J. Accounting Lit.*, Spring 1983, p. 1-38.

An Object-Oriented Programming Approach To Credit Decision Making

NILS A. KANDELIN AND THOMAS W. LIN

One of the most important problems facing corporate finance managers is the granting of credit to customers. The credit granting process involves both credit analysis and credit decision. Credit analysis usually involves inspection of customers' financial statements and contacting outside credit agencies or credit references. The credit decision utilizes the results of the credit analysis process to determine the amount of credit extended, and the terms under which it is extended, to specific customers at specific times.

The purpose of this paper is to discuss a prototype object-oriented programming computational model for the credit decision making process. The model, using the Actor* object-oriented programming system, integrates both data and knowledge representation in an events-based accounting information system.

The remainder of this paper will cover the following four sections. First, we present an overview of the problem domain, the credit granting process for a corporation. This is followed by a discussion of an integrated data and knowledge based conceptual model for commercial credit decision making. Third, an objectoriented programming model is described. Finally, some concluding comments are made.

Credit Granting Process

A typical accounts-receivable (A/R) cycle, including the credit

---

*Registered trademark of the Whitewater Group, Inc.

granting process is shown in Figure 1. The two steps to the credit granting process are credit analysis and the credit decision. The credit or financial analysis step is discussed first, followed by a discussion of the credit decision and approval process.

FIGURE 1
Credit and Accounts Receivable Cycle
(Bukics and Loven, 1987, p vi)

Order		Customer		Credit/		Credit				Invoice Billing
Received	→	Request	→	Financial	→	Decision/	→	Ship	→	Accounts/Receivable
For Goods		For Credit		Analysis		Approval				

CREDIT/FINANCIAL ANALYSIS

Prior to granting credit, every potential creditor (customer) undergoes a credit or financial analysis. Credit analysis is defined by Bukics and Loven as:

> Credit analysis attempts to evaluate the risk that the customer will be bankrupt or out of business and hence, unable to pay at all. In addition, credit analysis examines the risk that the customer will pay late. (1987, p. 13)

According to Bukics and Loven, the objective of credit analysis is to determine "the customer's willingness and ability to pay, and the ability of the creditor to obtain collateral or other sources of payment" (1987, p. 33). Usually this involves inspection of the financial statements and contacting outside credit agencies or other credit references. The result is the setting of a credit limit (or credit line) for that customer.

Credit analysis involves the gathering and processing of information to answer two basic questions: the payment question and the security question. The payment question asks: "Will the customer be both able and willing to pay the debt by the due date?" (Bukics and Loven, 1987, p. 19). The security question asks: "If, on the due date, the customer does not pay, what recourse is available to the creditor, which is represented by a slot that specifies that the frame is a kind of another frame." (Bukics and Loven, 1987, p. 20)

CREDIT DECISION/APPROVAL (CREDIT CHECKING)

According to Bukics and Loven the credit decision is defined as determining ". . . the amount of credit extended, and the terms under which it is extended, to specific customers at specific times" (1987, p. 13). This is done by using the results of credit analysis, combined with the creditors' tolerance for risk for losses due to bad loans versus lost sales due to denied credit.

The credit decision or approval process occurs with every order placed. The possible actions that can result from the credit decision include no action (automatic approval of the full order), approval for part of the order, revised credit terms or even refusal of the order. Most of these decisions are based on examination of the established credit limit and the records of the orders, deliveries, and payments from the individual customer.

The credit decision must be made on a timely basis. As noted by Cole, "In the operation of a commercial credit department, speed in the processing and resulting action on orders is imperative" (1987, p. 436). Failure to act quickly on orders might sacrifice customer good-will which could result in lost sales.

Numerous institutions in both the commercial and consumer credit industry have been involved in the development of expert systems (a class of knowledge-based systems) to facilitate various aspects of the process, including commercial loan analyzers, credit approval systems, commercial account rating systems, credit applications systems, processing of administrative documents and automated teller control (Watkins 1988). The level of development activity in the credit industry is a result of many institutions identifying it as a high payoff the development of knowledge based systems.

A highly successful system in the consumer credit domain is the credit checking expert system designed for American Express. This system helps reduce the amount of bad credit authorizations (and limit the losses that result) while providing qualified customers with faster service (Olson and Cortney, 1992). While the American Express credit checking expert system is in the consumer credit domain rather than the commercial credit domain discussed in this paper, two characteristics should be noted. One is that it attempts to perform both credit analysis and the credit decision. This is necessitated by the absence of preset credit limits on American Express accounts. The second is the system is designed to aid, not replace, the human credit authorization personnel (LaPlante 1990). The potential for facilitating human interaction was explicitly included in the designs of both the conceptual and computational model.

In this application, the focus is on developing a system to support the commercial credit decision, not the credit analysis process. This was done because, in the commercial credit environment, a system to support the credit decision process would have a higher potential pay-off due to the greater volume of credit decisions that are made on an order by order basis in a commercial environment. (Borthick and West 1987, Liang 1988) In a commercial environment, the credit analysis process typically occurs on a less frequent basis. Additionally, Liang (1988) says that expert systems are best suited to problem domains where decision making is structured and involves qualitative reasoning. The credit decision process possesses these characteristics as it involves such qualtitative factors as risk tolerance. Credit analysis often utilizes more quantitative factors such as financial ratios.

The focus on the credit decision processes does not preclude the incorporation of the credit analysis process in future research with these models. This might be done by incorporating some of the capabilities of Sena and Smith's (1990) statement analyzer.

An Integration of Data and Knowledge Base Models for Credit Decision Making

To meet the primary objective of this research, a conceptual model developed by Kandelin (1990) with the integration of data and knowledge bases is used to tailor the credit decision/approval process as shown in Figure 2.

There are two types of objects (or subsystems) in Figure 2. They are data and knowledge subsystems. The data subsystem encompasses the typical transaction processing activities which involve data processing and data structures. The knowledge subsystem includes the knowledge representation and processing (such as inferencing) activities of the accounting information system. This subsystem contains the credit decision knowledge and knowledge about the decision makers' information needs. The knowledge subsystem uses the results (or outputs) of processing the data subsystem to perform or support decision making.

The links or interaction between the data and knowledge subsystems can take several forms. They include queries, query response, and scheduled reports. Most queries would be generated by the knowledge system to the data system requesting data or information

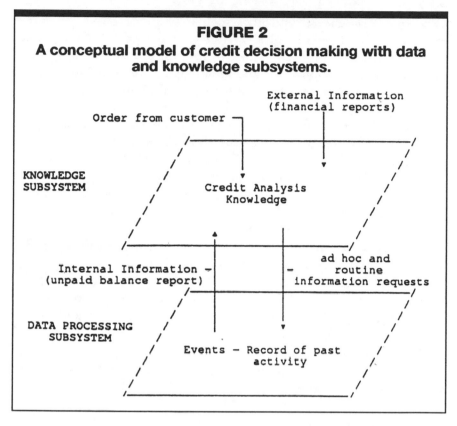

FIGURE 2
A conceptual model of credit decision making with data and knowledge subsystems.

in the form of reports. However, in some cases the data subsystem may query the knowledge system. This might occur, for example, if the data system is unable to process a certain transaction and it would query the knowledge subsystem for instructions as to how to proceed. The majority of the interactions between these two systems would be through reports that require processing activity by the data subsystem to create and act to transfer information for decision making to the knowledge system. Reports can be generated by the data system according to either a regular schedule or in response to a specific event or set of events.

The credit decision/approval process utilizes internal and external information and knowledge. The internal information comes from reports and typically involves factors that can be controlled by the organization. For a typical retail computer store, such as LTB Computer Sales Company, these include the sales transaction history items (such as average amount, number and trends), the unpaid balance (average amount and trend), and the payment history (delay between billing the receipt of payment). The external information and knowledge which involves factors that are not under the LTB Computer Sales Company's control include: industry knowledge (such as history, competition) and knowledge of general and industry specific economic conditions, and their potential impact to the creditor.

The internal information is collected and updated by the data processing subsystem in real time and the various reports are updated as the events occur. In batch processing accounting information systems, the event information is collected and the reports are generated later by referencing the historical database containing the events for a particular period of interest. Reports generated by traditional batch processing methods become outdated as soon as another event occurs and the reporting cycle must be repeated. Real-time reporting on the other hand always has a current report ready.

Figure 2 reflects the following credit decision making process. First, the commercial customer's order for computer systems is recognized by the knowledge subsystem of LTB's accounting information system. The knowledge subsystem approves or refuses the order from the customer. This activity is performed by the knowledge subsystem because until the order is approved no material is shipped and therefore no economic transaction has taken place. Only after the order is approved will the computer systems be shipped, resulting in an economic event that is processed and recorded by the data processing subsystem. If the order is refused, no economic transaction takes place and there is no impact on the data processing subsystem. After the order is received by the knowledge subsystem, the credit decision process takes place, resulting in the approval, referral or refusal of the customer order.

The conceptual model is a logical model and is not constrained by implementation details. It provides the specifications for the development of the computer based computational model. In this research, object-oriented programming techniques are used to develop the computational model.

An Object-Oriented Programming Computational Model

The credit decision process as represented in the computational model is shown in Figure 3. As a result of restricting this decision-making example to the credit decision/approval, only internal factors are explicitly considered. External factors, such as the financial condition

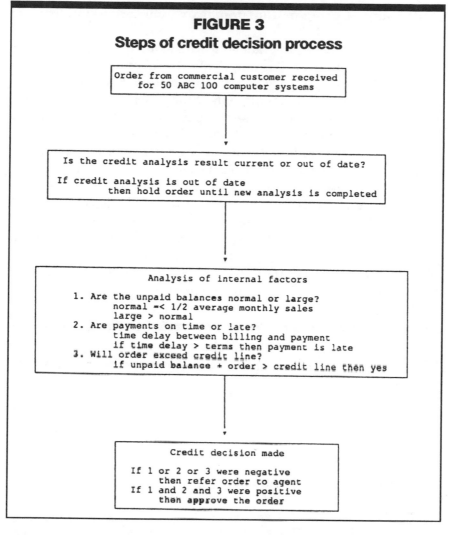

FIGURE 3
Steps of credit decision process

Order from commercial customer received
for 50 ABC 100 computer systems

Is the credit analysis result current or out of date?

If credit analysis is out of date
          then hold order until new analysis is completed

Analysis of internal factors

1. Are the unpaid balances normal or large?
     normal =< 1/2 average monthly sales
     large > normal
2. Are payments on time or late?
     time delay between billing and payment
     if time delay > terms then payment is late
3. Will order exceed credit line?
     if unpaid balance + order > credit line then yes

Credit decision made

If 1 or 2 or 3 were negative
     then refer order to agent
If 1 and 2 and 3 were positive
     then approve the order

of the buyer, industry conditions, economic forecasts would impact the decision through the credit analysis process.

A prototype computation model has been developed for the credit decision-making example application using the Actor object-oriented programming system.

Object-oriented programming belong to a unique programming paradigm (or class) of languages. It is different from the other programming paradigms, which include logic, rule-based and procedural programming. The main advantage that distinguishes the object-oriented paradigm is a superior ability to implement a larger degree of partitioning of program functionality among program elements (Tello, 1989).

The object-oriented programming paradigm encourages modular designs and code reuse (Snyder 1990). Two features that enhance modularity are encapsulation and data abstraction. Encapsulation permits interaction with a module only through its external interface. This can minimize undesired interdependencies between modules. Data abstraction defines the behavior of the object (sometimes by using other objects) without the user having to understand the implementation details. Code reuse is facilitated primarily through inheritance, which allows for properties of more general objects higher in the object hierarchy to be automatically passed on (or inherited) by the lower more specialized classes of objects. Properties that are specifically defined at lower levels take precedence over inherited properties.

The computational model for this decision making process is shown in Figure 4. The event transactions are represented as messages

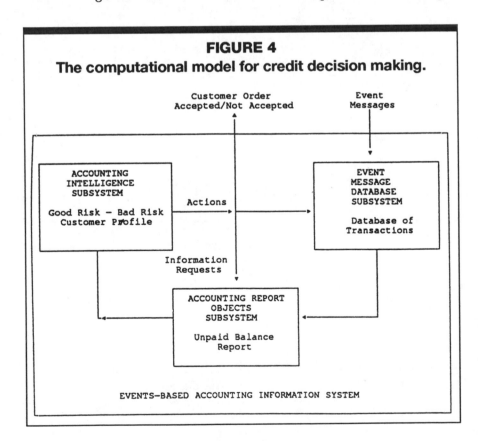

FIGURE 4
The computational model for credit decision making.

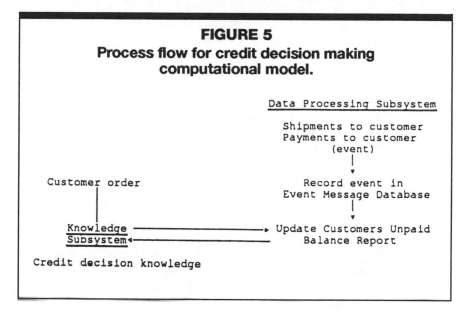

FIGURE 5
Process flow for credit decision making computational model.

and the components of the computational model are constructed as discrete objects.

The information flow of processing for the computational model is shown in Figure 5. Before any economic events occur, the LTB Computer Sales Company receives an order from the customer. This goes directly to the accounting intelligence subsystem. The credit decision is based on past activity by the customer as well as information from the credit analysis procedure. If the order is approved and shipped (or a customer payment received), an economic event message representing the transaction is generated. The event message is received by the system and recorded in the event message database. An individual company's unpaid balance report updates itself only if the economic agent identified in the event message is the customer of interest. The result of this process is that the individual customer's activity is correctly reflected in the report. The accounting intelligence subsystem contains the knowledge base used to support the credit decision.

In Figure 6, an example of an element of the REA database element (based on McCarthy's (1982) Resource-Event-Agent (REA) accounting data model) representing a payment transaction is diagrammed. The payment is from customer J. Doe to LTB Computer Sales Co. by check #140 for $423.33. The information shown in Figure 6 represents the situation where J. Doe is making a payment towards

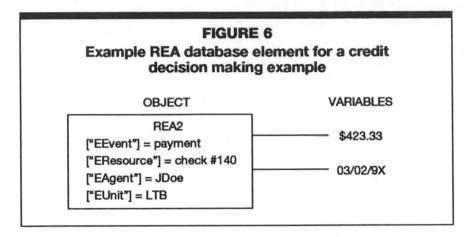

FIGURE 6
Example REA database element for a credit decision making example

OBJECT   VARIABLES

REA2
["EEvent"] = payment $423.33
["EResource"] = check #140
["EAgent"] = JDoe   03/02/9X
["EUnit"] = LTB

an outstanding balance which could be an accumulation of several orders. For other situations, such as a payment towards a specific order, additional information (such as the original order number) would be specified with the transaction, or the accounting knowledge system could assume that any unspecified payments should be applied to the oldest accounts receivable for that customer.

The unpaid balance amount for the commercial customer ordering the computer systems from LTB Computer Sales Company is maintained in real time using report object such as in Figure 7. A report object for the commercial customer showing the current unpaid balance updates itself every time a sale is made or payment is received (generating an event message in the system) from that customer. As with the other report objects, the unpaid balance report screens the event messages and updates itself only when it receives an event message pertaining to the commercial customer. If the report receives an event message where the economic agent is the commercial customer receiving a shipment of computer systems (or incurring other charges), then it will update itself accordingly by increasing the unpaid balance for that customer. If the economic agent is other than the commercial customer, the report does not update itself.

The average delay between billing and payment is calculated by searching the database and tabulating the separation in time of each "sale" transaction and its complimentary "payment" transaction.

As shown in Figure 3, four factors are considered for each customer before an order is approved. Once the values for these four factors are determined, they are compared to the knowledge frames that represent good and bad risk customers, shown in Figure 8. First, all cus-

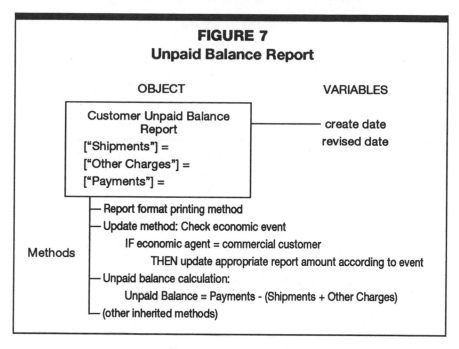

FIGURE 7
Unpaid Balance Report

OBJECT   VARIABLES

Customer Unpaid Balance
Report   — create date
["Shipments"] =   revised date
["Other Charges"] =
["Payments"] =

Methods
— Report format printing method
— Update method: Check economic event
        IF economic agent = commercial customer
            THEN update appropriate report amount according to event
— Unpaid balance calculation:
        Unpaid Balance = Payments - (Shipments + Other Charges)
— (other inherited methods)

tomers must have a known risk by having a current credit analysis on record. For a customer to be a good risk the unpaid balances must be normal, payments must be made on time, and the requested order must not exceed the credit line. The bad risk customer is described by the opposite of these criteria. If a customer's profile matches the one of a good risk customer, then the order is approved. If they more closely represent the profile of the bad risk customer then the order is not approved, but referred to a purchasing agent for review.

FIGURE 8
Frames for representation of types of customers

Frame	Slot	Value
Known Risk	credit analysis	"current"
Good Risk	AKO	Known Risk
	unpaid balance	"normal"
	payments	"on time"
	credit limit	"no"
Bad Risk	AKO	Known Risk
	unpaid balance	"large"
	payments	"late"
	credit limit	"yes"

Conclusions

This paper discussed a prototype object-oriented programming computational model for corporate credit decision making. The model is developed to integrate both data and knowledge representation and processing.

The system models use a representation scheme based on the existing research into events accounting data models and systems as well as in the integration of knowledge and data. Two models are developed: one is a conceptual model that is independent of machine implementation, the second is a computational model from which a computer prototype is developed using an objectoriented programming system.

The design of the conceptual model is not restricted by implementation details and provides the performance specifications for the development of the computational model. The computational model is constructed by mapping the conceptual model into a particular computer environment, which in this research is the object-oriented programming paradigm. The computational model demonstrates the feasibility of the conceptual model.

The computational model provides for the inclusion of useful data and knowledge for credit decision making in the AIS. It is very flexible with the ability to be adapted to meet changing user requirements. By implementing the model using object-oriented programming techniques, the design of the model is highly modular. Each of the key components can be independently modified or adapted and even new components can be added to the system without necessitating major modifications to other components or objects classes.

There are numerous report modes available in the model. The object-oriented provides many user interface capabilities, such as various reports, that can be added and modified independently from the rest of the system. Multiple report objects could process the same data to display information in different formats, if desired. The real-time nature of the system would allow the development of new types of reports in addition to the conventional accounting reports that are typically historical in nature.

Due to the different characteristics of this object-oriented computational model, systems design procedures based on the Systems Development Life Cycle (SDLC) may not be optimal. SDLC based design methodologies (used to develop many existing information systems and AISs) have been designed for systems developed using more traditional computer languages. Object-oriented languages offer the potential for improved modularity (consisting of encapsulation and data abstraction) and increased code reuse. Encapsulation permits only structure interactions between modules and reduces functionality interdependencies (Snyder 1990). Data abstraction defines the behavior of a particular object without the user (which could be another object) having to understand the implementation details. Both of these features make it possible to change certain components of an object-oriented system without affecting others, thereby blurring the traditional distinction between maintenance of existing systems an design and implementation of new systems. The ability to reuse code tends to reduce the software engineering effort need to develop a new system (Paysaye et al. 1990). However, the extreme flexibility afforded by object-oriented paradigm requires a significant conceptual design effort before coding begins. Assembly, program testing, and modification in an object-oriented environment can take a relatively short time compared to the conceptual design phase. Since accounting involvement in the system design process is desirable from an internal control perspective, perhaps other system design techniques, such as object-oriented design methodologies may be of great value. (Henderson-Sellers and Edwards 1990)

REFERENCES

Borthick, A.F. and O.D. West, "Expert Systems-A New Tool for the Professional," *Accounting Horizons,* March 1987, pp. 9-16.

Bukics, R.L. and W.T. Loven, *The Handbook of Credit and Accounts Receivable Management,* Probus, 1987.

Cole, R.H., *Consumer and Commercial Credit Management,* 7th Ed. Homewood, IL: Irwin, 1984.

Henderson-Sellers, B. and J.M. Edwards, "The Object-Oriented Systems Lifecycle," *Communications of the ACM,* September 1990, pp. 142-159.

Kandelin, N.A., "Integration of Data and Knowledge Representation in an Events Accounting Information System," Ph.D. Dissertation, Los Angeles, CA: University of Southern California, 1990.

LaPlante, A., "Bring in the Expert," *InfoWorld,* October 1, 1990, pp. 55-64.

Liang, T.P., "Expert Systems as Decision Aids," *The Journal of Information Systems,* Spring 1988, pp. 41-50.

McCarthy, W., "The REA Accounting Model: A Generalized Framework for Accounting Systems in a Share Data Environment," *The Accounting Review,* July 1982, pp. 554-577.

Olson, D.L., J.F. Courtney, Jr., *Decision Support Models and Expert Systems,* Macmillan, 1992.

Parsaye, K., M. Chignell, S. Khoshafian, H. Wong, *Intelligent Databases,* Wiley, 1989.

Sena, J.A. and L.M. Smith, "A Sample Expert System for Financial Statement Analysis," in L.M. Smith, R.H. Strawser and C.E. Wiggins (editors) *Readings and Problems in Accounting Information Systems,* Irwin, 1991.

Snyder, A., "Encapsulation and Inheritance in Object-Oriented Programming Languages," in S. Zdonik and D. Maier (editors) *Readings in Object-Oriented Database Systems,* San Mateo, CA: Morgan Kaufmann, 1990.

Tello, E., Object-Oriented Programming for Artificial Intelligence, Addison-Wesley, 1989.

Watkins, P.R., "Expert Systems For Use In Finance," in E. Turban and P.R. Watkins (editors), *Applied Expert Systems,* North-Holland, 1988.